Contents

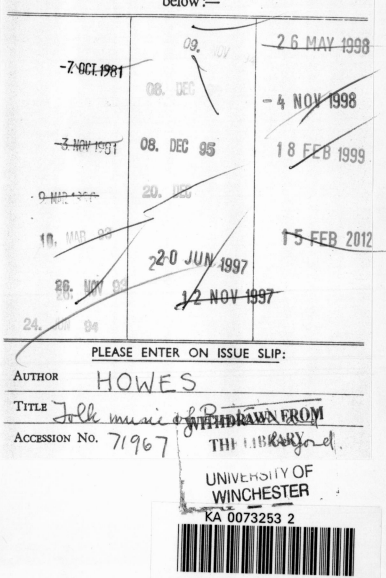

KING ALFRED'S COLLEGE
WINCHESTER

To be returned on or before the day marked
below:—

PLEASE ENTER ON ISSUE SLIP:

AUTHOR   HOWES

TITLE   Folk music of B...

ACCESSION No.   71967

Folk Music of Britain
—and Beyond

Folk Music of Britain —and Beyond

Frank Howes

Methuen & Co Ltd
11 New Fetter Lane · EC4

To my sister Marie,
who sang many of these songs

First published 1969
© *1969 by Frank Howes*
Printed in Great Britain
by The Camelot Press Ltd.,
London and Southampton

Musical Examples

Preface

In 1907 Cecil Sharp published *English Folk Song: Some Conclusions*, the first book in English about folk music as a branch of the art of music, as church music, opera and chamber music are departments of the art. And it remained for half a century the only book of substance. In 1967 Mr A. L. Lloyd published his *Folk Song in England*, which came out in time for me to learn something from it, although by then this book was far advanced. In particular I learned of the industrial songs which were to some extent the equivalents of the pre-Industrial Revolution folk-songs of the peasantry.

What I have just said is broadly but not quite literally true. Thus as far back as 1866 Carl Engel had published his *The Study of National Music*, and after Cecil Sharp's epoch-making book, a number of useful small or sectional studies appeared. The Bibliography is small enough to be given here:

Frank Kidson and Mary Neal, *English Folk Song and Dance*, Cambridge, 1915

Violet Alford, *English Folk Dances*, Black, 1923

Iolo Williams, *English Folk Song and Dance*, Longmans, 1935

Douglas Kennedy, *England's Dances: Folk Dancing To-day and Yesterday*, Bell, 1949

Douglas Kennedy, *English Folk Dancing To-day and Yesterday*, Bell, 1964

A. L. Lloyd, *The Singing Englishman*, Workers' Music Association, 1944

Reginald Nettel, *Folk Dancing*, Arco, 1962

These are the chief sources of information open to the enquirer and in their time they served a valuable purpose, but they did not, for various reasons, look at the subject as a branch of

xi

musical history – folklore yes, social history yes to some extent, description for the record certainly. Curiously enough the story is the same for the carol, which had a remarkable and contemporary revival. This too had to wait till 1958 to get its story told with adequate scholarship – by Dr Erik Routley in *The English Carol*.

In this book I have tried to take as comprehensive a view as I can of the phenomenon, folk-song, more from the point of view of a musician, than a sociologist, a field worker, an anthropologist or, though literary criticism is involved in balladry, a literary critic. I have used the comparative method proper to anthropology. Hence my title. If one is to study folk-music one had best begin with one's own. So English folk-song is the introduction to folk-song in general; I start from the British Isles, but I have not the knowledge, so huge is the sheer quantity of the material, even to attempt to be comprehensive in my comparisons, so I have excused myself and my limited choice with the phrase 'And Beyond'.

If there have been so few comprehensive studies of folk music – though they are beginning to appear in America, such for instance as Dr Bruno Nettl's *Folk and Traditional Music of the Western Continent* (1965) – this is not to ignore the vast amount of scholarship that has been applied to the subject and is available to the student in print if he knows where to look for it. Looking no further afield than our own folk-song revival we have the *Journal of the Folk-Song Society* (1898–1931) and its successor the *Journal of the English Folk Dance and Song Society* published annually. Then when the English example began to be copied in the United States and Canada the study, which meant primarily the collection and preservation of folk-songs still current in oral tradition but also secondarily publishing them with a critical apparatus of rigorous scholarship, produced a vast accumulation of knowledge and made it available for practical use and for study. I remember receiving a year or two ago two huge volumes, which I took to be another large collection from an American university press, of English and Ameri-

can ballads and songs, but which revealed itself, when the last
wrapper was removed, as a *bibliography* of such collections!
The amount of material to be studied is in fact devastating to
contemplate. This was one factor in my deciding to attempt
some sort of synoptic view, some sort of deductive generalization from the masses of facts, to try to do for this branch of music
what the early botanists decided they must do to cope with
Nature's prodigal fertility.

I realize the vanity of the attempt, but I have come to the
conclusion that it was time the subject should find an academic
home for itself. It has been a field in which individuals, usually
amateur rather than professional musicians, have done pioneer
work of the highest excellence, but if we are ever to consolidate
the study, to make it available to musicians, to musicologists
and to humane learning in general, it should be treated like any
other branch of humane learning and properly studied, which
means that its approaches should be teachable, its researches
co-ordinated. I should like to hope that if some university or
conservatoire should find a place in its curriculum for folk
music and its newly grown-up cousin, ethnomusicology, this
book might serve as an introductory text-book. But in the
meantime when there is a new and widespread interest in folk-
song, an urban revival, derived it would seem from American
gramophone records, it may serve to convey some elementary
knowledge about the subject.

My indebtedness to others will be apparent to every reader –
some specific acknowledgements are made below. Indeed I
doubt if there is a single original discovery in the entire book.
So perhaps I had better offer some justification for my hardi-
hood in writing it. If I am frankly autobiographical I shall be
providing one example of the way this elusive yet earthy thing,
folk music, captures its devotees.

The first folk-song I remember hearing was 'Matthew, Mark,
Luke and John' at the prize-giving of the Oxford High School
for Girls when I was in my teens. I liked it but found it odd, for,
being in the Phrygian mode, it sounded like none of the music

I had ever heard, for I was brought up on Mendelssohn. My father sang *Elijah* and played the *Songs without Words* and I began to play bits of *Hear my Prayer* on the organ. I also began to hear at sing-songs, socials and local amateur concerts in those pre-radio days some of Sharp's discoveries like 'O No, John' and 'Whistle, daughter whistle', and a little later folk-songs sung unaccompanied by Dorothea Webb at the University Musical Club, which sounded rather naked to my unaccustomed ear. Real acquaintance came from Walter Ford, my sister's singing teacher, who was an early member of the Folk Song Society. My sister began to sing folk-songs and I to play the piano accompaniments of them. So the start was right – first-hand acquaintance with the stuff of folk music, though I had not heard a traditional singer sing them in the traditional style. They made an immediate and quasi-biological appeal to us both and for twenty years we performed them in concert, broadcast and lecture programmes.

In 1927 when I was a junior music critic on *The Times*, my colleague, Arthur Fox-Strangways, asked me if I would take on the editorship of the *Folk Song Journal*. Lucy Broadwood, who had been its tutelary prophetess for thirty years, wanted to give up the editorship – indeed she died two years later. The Folk-Song Society, at a loss for a successor, accepted Fox-Strangways's assurance that the new young man down at *The Times* seemed to have the heart of the matter in him and at any rate knew the techniques of journalism well enough to pilot a periodical through the press, though my qualifications were questioned – rightly, by Frederick Keel, a previous editor. So I took it on with very little real knowledge of the subject. Indeed I remember saying to Dr Vaughan Williams that I relied on the Editorial Board for everything beyond proof correction. To which he replied in his downright way 'If you don't edit it, nobody will'. So I did – for nineteen years, serving at the same time on the committees of the bodies responsible for its production.

In the thirties the flow of books from American universities began. Phillips Barry's *British Ballads from Maine* was the first of these collections, which, following Sharp's discoveries in Kentucky, were made by the English faculties of universities all over the United States. Indigenous ballads like 'John Henry' and 'Frankie and Johnnie' and native folk-songs of diverse origins, Amerindian, Creole, Negro, were discovered in the process of getting such collections together. Most of these I reviewed in *The Times Literary Supplement, The Musical Times* or *Music and Letters*. In the forties I proposed, in papers read to the Royal Anthropological Society in London and the University Anthropological Society in Oxford, that the music of a human community was as proper a subject for anthropological study as cranial measurements, agricultural implements or marriage customs. Ethnomusicology, which according to Jaap Kunst, who established it in Holland, was originally the creation of two Englishmen, A. J. Ellis and A. J. Hipkins, has here and now a nucleus of scholars to keep it in cultivation. After the Second War the International Folk Music Council was founded at the instance of Dr Maud Karpeles, Sharp's heiress who continued his work, and its annual Journal has opened up comparative study. Meantime the nationalist movements, fundamentally a by-product of the romantic movement of the last century, have had a second efflorescence in Bartók and Kodály in Hungary, Janáček in Slovakia, Falla in Spain, Khachaturian in Russia and Vaughan Williams in England, all of whom in some degree fertilized their own composition with what they had absorbed from their native folk-song. As a music critic I was well placed to observe these developments. And so when the pressures of daily journalism were relaxed the internal pressures of all this varied experience of folk music have become too strong to be contained and have issued in this book, which I offer as a conspectus of its subject more than half a century on from my hearing of the 'White Paternoster'.

Acknowledgments

The majority of my musical examples are taken from copyright sources, not all of which I have been able to trace, but I thank here and now the following publishers, organizations and individuals for their permission to quote tunes, of which the sources are named in the Appendix:

First, the English music publishers, Novello & Co. (especially for Sharp's tunes), Boosey & Hawkes, J. Curwen & Sons, Stainer & Bell, Oxford University Press and B. Feldman & Co.; Cambridge University Press. Second, the following foreign publishers: Harvard University Press, University of North Carolina Press, Oslo University Press, Martinas Nijhoff and E. J. Bull of Holland, Artia of Prague and Editio Musica of Budapest. Third, organizations such as the English Folk Dance & Song Society and the Academia di Science, Letteri e Arti of Palermo – I have to thank the Palermo Academy and the Czech Foreign Trade Corporation for giving me, unasked, volumes of Sicilian and Czechoslovakian folk-songs respectively. Fourth, individuals, among them colleagues of many years' standing, Dr Maud Karpeles, Mrs Vaughan Williams, Mrs Rodney Gallop, Mr Ian Copley, Miss Mona Douglas, Mr Kenneth Stubbs, Dr Otto Anderson, Miss Peggy Seeger.

I have to thank, as it were *in absentia*, some publishers who have gone out of business or whose addresses I have been unable to discover and some organizations whose publications have been sent to me at different times for favour of possible review in *The Times*. Some of Lucy Broadwood's tunes I have been able to use by courtesy of her family and the fact that their ownership was transferred through me when I edited the *Folk-Song Journal* to the English Folk Dance & Song Society. Some of my enquiries have not been answered; some answers took the form of disclaimers. In two cases I have forgotten where I found the tunes and in some others it has seemed hopeless to search owing to deaths, removals, and to a kind of infinite regress of responsibility.

I have thanks to render of a different kind to Professor Raymond Firth and Miss Norma MacCleod, late of the London School of Economics, to Mrs Noyes, the Librarian of Cecil Sharp House, to Miss Ethel Bassin of Edinburgh, and in general to all my friends with whom I have worked for forty years in the movement for preserving our English folk music.

CHAPTER ONE

The Name and Nature of Folk-Song

When A. E. Housman gave the Leslie Stephen lecture at Cambridge in 1933 he entitled it *The Name and Nature of Poetry*, and he spent the first half of it discussing the name because he was by no means sure that the name of poetry conveyed its true nature to many people who used it. The sort of confusion he had in mind was the difference between poetry and versification and prose and what the eighteenth century called wit. In the second part of the lecture he came to talk of the nature of poetry and made the famous declaration that it was a sensation in the pit of the stomach, a pretty mixture of mockery and truth. But he had in the course of these two logical exercises – logic is concerned both by derivation of the word and in modern philosophy with the meaning of words – thrown up a good many instances of poetry and out of them revealed by induction what poetry was. Opposed to the empirical method of induction is the method of analysis: what is a folk-song?

An old song, someone says, a song of anonymous authorship someone else amplifies, known to and sung by the illiterate someone else adds. But we are not likely to arrive by sheer dissection at clear logic-proof definition without examining a great many folk-songs, and we may indeed find that they are old, anonymous and non-literate. However much the French, the Germans and the Americans may prefer the method of logical analysis the English mind generally prefers to discover the nature of anything by examining its history, its evolution: a

thing is what it is by reason of the way it got there. This historical method has been applied to folk-poetry and music and
a nice old confusion it raised: the question of origin has been a
battle-field for a couple of centuries and has thrown up the
theory of communal authorship, the denial of the possibility of
any such thing and the assertion that an individual is at the
bottom of it, the theory that so far from welling up from
underneath it came down from the educated classes, a theory of
spontaneous generation and a theory of corruption of an original
creation. The question of origin cannot be shirked. Most
writers on the subject tackle it at once.

Thus Cecil Sharp in his *English Folk-song: Some Conclusions*
deals with it in his second chapter; his first is on definition,
so that he too is after the name and nature of the thing. Bruno
Nettl in his *Folk and Traditional Music of the Western Continents*,
which was written sixty years later, deals with it on his fourth
page. In his small *An Introduction to Folk-Music in the United States*
he devotes his first chapter to definition with a survey of the
theories of origin. A. L. Lloyd in *The Singing Englishman* (1944)
duly, that is to say before very long but not so soon as Nettl,
goes into the question of origin. But folk-song of its very nature
does not lend itself to history very conveniently – it is almost
dateless and such dates as there are have to be deduced from
internal evidence. If a folk-song has got into print – and some
do, countries varying a good deal in what gets into print when
– then there is of course some documentation. William Chappell
in his *Popular Music of the Olden Time* (1859) got hold of some
folk-songs from Elizabethan times on to the eighteenth century
and relied exclusively on paper, not vocal, sources. The Scots
were active in printing their traditional songs and ballads a
century before the English. But in general folk-song is too fluid,
too evasive, too much like rivers that plunge underground and
surface unpredictably to have its history written. Also we have
to beware of that old logical fallacy of identifying origin with
nature. Things are not always what they were: they change,
and origin may not contain the essence. Actually in folk-song

the question of origin is vital, but it does not completely explain the nature of folk-song.

So let us begin with the name. 'Folk' is an old norse word that has survived in English and Scotch, but is archaic in the one and poetic in the other, though it is still used in colloquial speech in such a phrase as 'Our young folks are gone'. But it was sufficiently in current use to make it available when it was wanted in the nineteenth century as an equivalent of the German *Volk*: folk-song is a direct translation of the German *Volkslied*, which was used by Herder in 1773. Sharp found it so used in a dictionary in 1889 and the *Oxford English Dictionary* gives 1846 for the first use of 'folk-lore' (*Volkskunde*).[1] Folk-tale and folk-dance follow soon and naturally into the language. But 'folk music' had to wait. Carl Engel writing in 1866 has a footnote on his first page which reads: 'The Germans call it *Volksmusik*, a designation which is very appropriate and which I should have rendered "folk music" had this word been admissible.' The value of the word, even when it is used pejoratively in the hideous adjective 'folksy', is that it conveys a meaning distinct from the kindred words 'popular' and 'traditional'. It is, however, still liable to be mis-applied, in spite of Sharp's protest and clear distinction, to songs that achieve a currency big enough to be very generally known in a particular community, 'folk' then having its early meaning of 'the whole people' and the song having universal currency among them. Such widely known songs, however, are not folk-songs: they are popular, and may even be 'pop', which signifies the songs with a lowest common denominator of merit that will most quickly catch the favour of the thoughtless.

What folk-song means is popular by origin, not by destination. This distinction is very widely accepted, though a Belgian, M. Albert Marinus, read a paper to the conference of the International Folk Music Council in 1953 headed *Chanson*

[1] It is accepted that the word was invented by William J. Thoms and used by him in *The Athenaeum* in 1846 to signify customs and beliefs among the common people of a civilized community.

populaire – Chanson folklorique, in which he said it was hard to hold down the meaning of words to their scientific significance. But the very existence of so un-Gallic a term as 'folklorique' in French shows how useful the invention of 'folk-lore' as an English word had become. M. Marinus, while deploring the casual philology of the man who coined the word, admits its all-conquering utility: 'Le mot bien que fortement discuté gagna le continent, puis le monde'. Certainly a glance down the index of the *Journal of the International Folk Music Council* yields *la musique folklorique, le folklore musical, folclore musical Brasileiro, Folclorico Paulisto, Folclore Fluminense, la musica folklóristica in Italia, Makedonski muzicki folklor* (Yugoslav), *Česka etnographie a folkloristica v letech* (Czech), *Instrumentos musicales folklóricos de España, Norsk Folkemusikk* and *Slåtter og Folketonar*. The Germans naturally stick to *Volksmusick, Volkslied* and *Volkskunde*.

The word then, either in the form of the prefix 'folk' as we and the Germans use it or in the form 'folklore' capable of being used as an adjective as the Latin and Slav people prefer it, has found international currency and has come to stay. And however much it is misused in describing some song that sweeps a community and is then said to be a part of folk culture, it is best to insist on the retention of the word in its scientific signification, a song that somehow comes out of the people, not a song that spreads among them, still less one that is deliberately composed to catch their ears. 'It's a long way to Tipperary', the soldiers' song of the First War, had a currency and an emotional power that caused it to be described as a folk-song in the sense that it belonged to us all, us the folk. But it was not a folk-song. Its composer was known, though few people knew his name till his death was announced. He was a certain Jack Judge (1878–1938), a music-hall artist who wrote the song, words and music, in 1912, i.e. before the outbreak of war. Similarly the marching-song 'Pack up your troubles in your old kitbag' was the work of two brothers, Felix and George Powell. These were sung by soldiers and civilians alike, but 'Lilli Marlene', the chief song thrown up by the Second War, was a German product that spread across the battle lines to English troops but did not penetrate civil life very far.

Songs like these which achieve an enormous vogue, being known to the unmusical, are, because of their universality, called folk-songs, though wrongly, probably because their proper epithet 'popular' might be thought to imply that they were widely but not universally known. But these usages in spite of M. Marinus and his perfectly correct contention that language is fluid and will not stay put must be resisted. For the distinction between them is too valuable to lose by sheer care-lessless of nomenclature. R. L. Greene in his important book[2] on the English carol puts it this way: 'The phrase "popular poetry" (e.g. as in the English and Scottish popular ballads) has often been used indiscriminately to describe two kinds of composition between which the line of demarcation, sharp enough in theory, is often difficult to draw in practice. The two categories are perhaps most clearly indicated in English by the respective labels "popular by origin" and "popular by destination", the former being applied to what is called in careful German usage *Volkspoesie*, the latter to *volkstümliche Poesie*'. But *volkstümlich* adds a further complication, for applied to German lieder it means 'in a style of calculated simplicity', originally in reaction from elaborate coloratura arias. Brahms wrote both *Kunstlieder* and *volkstümliche Lieder*. We have hardly anything of the sort in the English song tradition – perhaps 'Drink to me only with thine eyes' and Vaughan Williams's 'Linden Lea'. Moreover, the line of demarcation is not so diffi-cult to draw in the case of folk-song as it is said by Professor Greene to be in the case of folk-poetry. We have a third category into which anonymous and well-known songs that are not folk-songs can be put, namely 'traditional'.

Thus the carol 'The First Nowell' has a complicated history[3]: it certainly has no ascertainable composer, has not been shaped by oral tradition and has been in print since Sandys published

[2] *The Early English Carols*, Oxford University Press, 1935.
[3] Summarized and discussed in Erik Routley's *The English Carol*, 1958.

5

it in 1833, and indeed is so repetitive that as we have it it must be a mistake. But we have it, and it is universally known: it is neither folk nor popular according to our definitions; call it then traditional. In somewhat similar fashion 'The Vicar of Bray' is classified as traditional. Chappell in *Popular Music of the Olden Time* says it occurs in *The Quaker's Opera* of 1728 and three years later in two other ballad operas, *The Grub Street Opera* and *The Welsh Opera*, where the name of the tune is given as 'Country Gardens'. Sharp collected a version of 'Country Gardens' and in *Some Conclusions* prints the two alongside for comparison. There are resemblances in outline but the differences are greater than in most variants of folk-songs. However, the resemblance was enough to strike the ear of a bricklayer at Headington, who according to a letter from William Kimber to Sharp,[4] on hearing 'Country Gardens' emerge from a piano opposite where they were working said it was 'The Vicar of Bray', which Kimber denied. But whether the same tune or not, the quasi-chemical test of the implied modulation in the middle yields positive evidence for the folk status of 'Country Gardens', negative for 'The Vicar of Bray'. It is true of course that tunes in themselves can hardly be said to modulate, since modulation is essentially a harmonic phenomenon. But simple tunes of A A B A form like 'The Vicar of Bray' and 'The Blue Bell of Scotland' do, when harmonized, gravitate to the dominant at the half-way mark, just as allemands, courants and minuets do in instrumental suites from the time of Purcell (who sometimes does and sometimes does not modulate at the double bar) onwards.

Many tunes that got into print in Elizabethan times on to the eighteenth century, of which the origin is unknown, may therefore be classed as 'traditional'. Of these 'Greensleeves'[5] is probably the most famous, and has come down to us in print and by the folk tradition in the form of the tune, rhythmically altered, to the morris jig 'Bacca Pipes'. 'Barbara Allen', the most widely distributed and widely known of all English folk-ballads, is another example of descent through three parallel

[4] Fox-Strangways's biography, p. 72.   [5] See below, chapter 7.

6

channels: it is found on broadsides as well as in oral tradition and, having got early into print, has hauled itself into litera-ture – compare it as it appears in Percy's *Reliques* with any folk-version. For 'Barbara Allen' has survived as a folk-song, and the manner of its survival as well as its protean forms are accounted for by Sharp, who formulated his definition on a remark thrown up by F. M. Boehme[6] in the course of the great controversy over the origin of ballads (of which 'Barbara Allen' is a good average example). Boehme's remark was 'First of all one man sings a song and then others sing it after him changing what they do not like', or, as he might have said, 'could not remember'. On which Sharp's gloss was 'The method of oral transmission is not merely one by which the folk-song lives; it is a process by which it grows and by which it is created.' The controversy has its own history to be told but enough of the heat has gone out of it to leave the question of origin in suspense and to recognize oral transmission as the determinant of what constitutes a folk-song. Oral transmission also accounts for the communal character of the folk-song, even of its national flavour, for in passing through many minds it takes on the character of communal authorship—many minds have in fact contributed to its creation.

The oral tradition preserves songs and ballads by the simple process of passing them on from one generation to the next by singing and remembering. As there is no writing down, no one version gets fixed and final. The song remains to some extent fluid and therefore liable to alterations, to mistakes, to corrup-tions even, but also to a process of evolution which eliminates the unfit and produces versions of tried and tested beauty satisfying to generation after generation. The song remains relatively stable in spite of the possibility of degeneration 'through the erosion of unretentive memories and inaccurate ears'. The French scholar, Jerôme Bujeaud, who collected the *chansons populaires* of western provinces of France, remarked that 'la tradition orale que l'on serait tenté de soupçonner

6 *Altdeutsches Liederbuch*, Leipzig, 1877, quoted by Sharp.

7

d'infidélité est au contraire d'une exactitude très grande et très scrupuleuse'. and he cited among examples to prove it the case of a song collected from oral tradition in 1862 traceable to a version printed at Caen in 1616. The tradition is safe with illiterate peasants, because, when all but a small upper class are uneducated, the best minds, as well as inferior minds, are illiterate, and being unlettered are forced to cultivate their memories – it is only since the Education Act of 1870 that illiteracy has become a synonym for dull and uncultivated brains. The native artistic gifts of the common people, especially before urbanization changed, and might one say vulgarized?, the habits of Englishmen, can be safely trusted to preserve their artistic inheritance. Of which the proof is that they have in fact preserved it.

The elimination of the unfit has had two uncovenanted benefits: a large proportion of the survivors are of first-class quality and little obscenity gets through. It is a happy state of affairs when the best is also the most characteristic. There are of course plenty of undistinguished tunes, notably quick patter songs in six-eight time built to carry a humorous ballad, but as far as English folk-song is concerned it was the astonishing freshness of the tunes that impressed the early collectors and made them feel like discoverers of buried treasure. Oral tradition is a refiner's fire.

With regard to obscenity Sharp, speaking out of his wide experience and from well-filled note-books, was convinced that the 'really gross and coarse in sentiment and objectionable in every way' are individual and not communal productions, that they offend against the communal sense of propriety, and when they are sung on some far-gone occasion they are sung deliberately with full intent to transgress accepted standards.[7] Stand-

[7] While I was editing the Journal of the Folk-Song Society and its successor of the English Folk Dance and Song Society (1927–45) I only had one song which I simply could not print by any however scientific editorial ethics, and that did seem to me to support Sharp's views that it was an individual deviation.

ards of what is suitable for polite ears vary from time to time, and in the early years of the revival editors and arrangers found it expedient to mollify some expressions or episodes that were thought to be too frank for the drawing-room or the public concert. There is no suggestion that folk-song avoids the facts of life, especially the facts of rural life, seduction, pregnancy, cuckoldry, maids outwitting their suitors, nor denial of the use of sexual symbolism. Every collector found poems too frank to print as they stood without causing embarrassment, though their singers saw nothing wrong in them. Alfred Williams (1877–1930), the Swindon railway worker who made a collection of poems in his locality between 1914 and 1916, *Folk Songs of the Upper Thames*, found a good many 'rough' songs, that 'were rude but not altogether bad'; mostly they were satirical; and he testified that 'the simple unspoiled rustic folks did not consider them out of place'.

Mr James Reeves opened up this discussion of what was not obscene to the folk-singer but unprintable by his publisher in his two books, *The Idiom of the People* (1958), in which he explored Cecil Sharp's manuscripts, and *The Everlasting Circle* (1960), in which he similarly examined the manuscripts of Baring Gould, Hammond and Gardiner (i.e. roughly Devon, Dorset and Hampshire texts). In all these cases he found that the texts had been expurgated for publication in the first two decades of this century, and that English folk-song, however unimpassioned its melody, was more erotic in its verse than had actually appeared from what Sharp had said. He instances 'O No, John' as a witty song that had retained its fun but lost its smirk in becoming a children's ditty. (But then are not many nursery rhymes the rubbed down stumps of ruthless rhymes, 'Ring a' roses' for instance, a song of the plague?) This rather drastic transformation was made by leaving out a single verse which dealt with tying a garter above the knee, of which *honi soit qui mal y pense* could not be pleaded. The song is one of the type of courtship by question and answer, to which 'The Keys of Heaven' and 'The Keys of Canterbury' belong. But flower symbolism for sexual activity and what Mr Reeves calls the physio-topographical kind of metaphor, though it may be slightly revolting in a silly sort of way in D'Urfey's *Pills to Purge Melancholy*, is poetic in folk-song, for, as Aristotle said, the poet is the master of metaphor and metaphor is the beginning of poetry. It has to be recognized that sexual symbolism is widely pervasive in folk-poetry, and the use of what Miss Dean-Smith well termed a lingua franca is not confined to England or to folk-song but is found in continental and mediaeval literature. Its use is at once a factor in the poetry and a mark of the folk's delicacy.

The only serious challenge to pure oral tradition as the essential distinguishing feature of folk-song comes from the Iberian Peninsula and Latin America. The street music, *fado*, the dominance of the dance and the frequency of instrumental accompaniment in Spain and Portugal, as in Latin America, where another factor, the slow fusion of several different musical traditions, Iberian, African, Amerindian, has not given time for the folk process of oral tradition to work on its raw material. Rodney Gallop described[8] some of the strands that make up the folk-music of Portugal, beginning with agricultural chants, street vendors' cries, instrumental elements from guitar and bagpipe and dance-songs – he finds not much of the florid ornament and Moorish influence that is common in Spain. A. L. Lloyd, writing thirty years later in his introduction to one of the anthologies promoted by the International Folk Music Council,[9] explains that the South American pattern did not fit the European at all points. Not only was there some polyphonic folk-song but to many of the tunes some instrumental accompaniment was an integral part of the rhythmic complex which was the chief feature of the song. By the time the International Folk Music Council held its seventh annual conference in Brazil in 1955 the question of finding a definition of folk-song that would be acceptable to a society that was not only international but interethnical had become pressing. For while in practice all

[8] Portugal, *A Book of Folk Ways*, 1936.   [9] *Folk Songs of the Americas*, 1965.

that was not identifiably art music was grist to the mill of the new organization, which aimed at promoting comparative study, it was plainly desirable to reach some agreement on what it was comparing and for the new science of ethno-musicology, for that is really what it is, to get some order into its terminology.

The definition which the Council had originally adopted was 'Folk music is music that has been submitted to the process of oral transmission. It is the product of evolution and is dependent on the circumstances of continuity, variation and selection', which had replaced the first draft, 'music that has been submitted throughout many generations to the moulding process of oral transmission', because 'throughout many generations' was inapplicable to new cultures, such as those of Latin America. The conference in plenary session finally adopted with a large measure of agreement the following comprehensive definition:

'Folk music is the product of a musical tradition that has evolved through the process of oral transmission. The factors that shape the tradition are (1) continuity, which links the present with the past; (2) variation, which springs from the creative impulse of the individual or group; and (3) selection by the community, which determines the form or forms in which the music survives.

'The term can be applied to music that has been evolved from elementary beginnings by a community uninfluenced by popular and art music and it can likewise be applied to music which has originated with an individual composer and has subsequently been absorbed into the unwritten living tradition of a community.

'The term does not cover composed popular music that has been taken over ready-made by a community and remains unchanged, for it is the re-fashioning and re-creation by the community that gives it its folk character.'

This is a satisfactory statement of the essentials of the concept folk music. Clause 2 of the first paragraph dealing with the creative impulse of an individual or a group covers the difficulty for the Boehme–Sharp definition raised by certain experiences in North America, where in negro communities spirituals seem to have been born under the emotional pressure of gospel meetings and in gangs of workmen where labour songs are sometimes evolved with or without a soloist, like the shanty-man aboard ship, by stringing together a number of melodic commonplaces to form the vehicle for a local ballad about a local event. These near-approaches to communal composition, which loosen the Boehme–Sharp conception without committing the holder to *Das Volk dichtet*, are worth examination.

The peculiar quality of the negro spiritual obtruded itself on naïve and sophisticated auditor alike. This quality is compounded of sheer striking power or impact, contagion, a sincere sentimentality that is all-conquering and an undeniably racial element. Musically considered the spirituals are only white mission hymns (which are usually contemptible as art) crossed with black rhythm out of Africa. All accounts of their origin agree that the negro is quick to respond to the telling of some story, whether of a recent event or of an episode from Scripture, that he is spontaneous in utterance (even if it is only the interjection of a Hallelujah), that he communicates his impulse to the next man who may add another phrase – for the method of communal composition is cumulative – that the atmosphere of a Gospel or a testimony meeting is electric and uninhibited. For the germ of the new tune only a snatch of the old is needed—hence the use of melodic clichés and commonplaces. Before the emancipation and for a generation after, when negroes were not educated or Europeanized, a negro community was responsive to the lead of a preacher, gang leader or acknowledged song leader. From Krehbiel and Newman White on to Alan Lomax writers on the subject admit that, given a certain stage of culture, comparable to the old illiteracy in which our own ballads were produced, given the occasion when the story of a recent event could be told or an old hymn sung, given the emotional electricity generated in such a gathering, something very like communal composition takes

place. Reed Smith in *South Carolina Ballads*[10] gives some examples which he describes at length of the generation of a
work-song or a spiritual:

'The instant flexibility of such work-songs is surprising. A
university dean was once listening to the improvisation of the
song leader of a negro road gang who were singing as they
worked in front of his house. Wishing to hear the words more
clearly, and possibly to take them down, the dean casually
strolled out and took his seat on the rock wall bordering the
road. He was thinking how intent upon their work the negroes
were and how oblivious of his presence when, without the
slightest change of expression on their part or the loss of a beat
of the rhythm, these words came floating to his ears:

> White man settin' on wall,
> White man settin' on wall,
> White man settin' on wall all day long,
> Wastin' his time, Wastin' his time.'

And of the genesis of a spiritual he writes 'There are many
instances of group authorship on record and it can still be
observed under favourable circumstances. An emotionally
charged atmosphere (as religious worship regularly charges it
among all but the most sophisticated negroes) a striking rhythmic phrase from preacher, leader, or worshipper and the thing
is done.'

One can almost hear it happening in such a spiritual as
'Nobody knows de trouble I've seen' in the simpler of its two
familiar versions [Example 1]. The 'nobody knows' of the
refrain has a syncopated formula which is repeated three times
and the very words themselves are just such a 'striking rhythmic
phrase'. The syncopated formula is completed twice with the
same cadence and once with a variant to fit the different words
('but Jesus'). Only the fourth phrase is suitably contrasted to
complete the eight-bar tune, and this phrase is made of the

[10] 1928. Chapter 3.

NOBODY KNOWS THE TROUBLE I'VE SEEN

Example 1

same four notes as the verse part that follows, which, however, is free of syncopation. 'Glory hallelujah!' and 'O yes Lord' are bits of communal utterance. The only mystery is what welds these fragments of commonplace into an infectious tune, which incidentally is pentatonic, lacking fourth and seventh.

Inasmuch as rural conditions prevailed in the United States after they had been industrialized out of existence in much of Europe, and negroes, cowboys, peasants, segregated communities such as Sharp found in the Appalachian Mountains as recently as 1917, all maintained the ways of life which had been the seed bed of folk-song in Britain, new folk-songs, or ballads half-way to becoming true folk-songs were generated. Of such 'John Henry', 'Frankie and Johnny', 'The Titanic', 'The Boll Weevil' are the examples best known outside America, but there are hundreds of songs, to be found in the collections made by the Lomaxes and other collectors which are in the stage of gaining currency. The first singer, Boehme's 'one man', a local bard, has started up a narrative ballad and what he does for a tune appears to be either to borrow a snatch of some song known to him and extend it by repetition, sequence, variation to fit his verses, or to string together a number of melodic commonplaces.

Thus in Newfoundland ballads about fishermen and lumbermen have been collected (e.g. by Mrs Elisabeth Greenleaf)[11] in which the ancestry of the tune is recognizable. An example is 'The Good Ship Jubilee' which is sung to a simple binary structure of two phrases torn from 'High Germany' [Example 2].

Example 2

In the case of another Newfoundland labour ballad 'The Badger Drive' [Example 3] the early history of the song is exceptionally well attested: the lumbermen resented the seamen getting all the songs and the resulting kudos, so the local

[11] *Ballads and Sea Songs of Newfoundland*, Greenleaf and Mansfield, Harvard, 1933.

Example 3

bard, John V. Devine, obliged with this ditty for a St Patrick's Day concert in 1915, and sang it himself to a tune obviously derived from 'Tarpaulin Jacket' with possible echoes of other sea songs. The song became popular and turned up in another collection twenty-five years later.[12]

There is a strong Celtic element in the population of Newfoundland and among Celtic people the bardic tradition is not dead: authors are credited with many of these Newfoundland songs. The likes of John Devine make up a poem about a current event and either sing it to a tune belonging to another song that happens to fit, or make up a tune from typical lilts and phrases that are common to the body of his traditional national melody, thus producing a tune which is new but not original, or original but not new.

[12] *Favourite Songs of Newfoundland*. Mills and Peacock, Toronto, 1958.

16

Dr Bruno Nettl in his small book on folk music in the US.A.[13] calls attention to the fact that the new surge of interest in folk-song since the Second War differs from that of half a century ago—and the same goes for Britain—in that it is sung by towns-people. It is now an urban phenomenon. Since the invention of the motor-car, the gramophone and the radio the character of the American community has changed, and, he says, 'the U.S. is largely an urban country' a fact which causes special prob-lems to the folk-lorist. Indeed he makes a reservation that 'American folk-music is in many ways a very different pheno-menon from its European counterpart', although in his first chapter (on definition) he had come down on the side of oral transmission as the commonly accepted criterion. In accepting it, however, he further defines it by adopting a formula proposed by Phillips Barry (author of *British Ballads from Maine*, 1929), communal re-creation. 'Oral tradition', he adds, 'might not be particularly relevant or interesting if it did not result in this essential quality' (the making of variants). But this is in effect precisely Sharp's contention: it is the process by which the folk-song grows and is created – growth being part of creation.

There is one other basic fact about the nature of folk-song. As we have it in Britain, in most of Europe, and very generally the world over, it is a form of monody. It is essentially melodic. This monodic character, however, raises technical questions, modality, pentatonicism, relation to polyphony, accompani-ments and instruments, that call for technical examination in a chapter of their own.

[13] *An Introduction to Folk Music in the United States*, Detroit, 1962.

CHAPTER TWO

Technicalities

Monody

Folk-song and plainsong are the only survivors, except perhaps Jewish cantillation, into modern Western music of the ancient monodic music of the Mediterranean civilizations. The Greeks disliked harmony when they accidentally heard it and the preoccupation of the Near East with single-line melody forced all the peoples of the eastern Mediterranean to cultivate subtlety of line for purposes of expression, whether by the differentiation of mode, or of microtones or of ornamentation. When around the first millennium AD the exciting possibilities of harmony were first glimpsed these features diminished in importance, but they remain for monophonic music. The development of polyphony through five centuries of the Middle Ages, reaching its first culminating peak in Palestrina and his fellow composers of the Golden Age of polyphony provided so many new resources that the modes and the microtones were eliminated in favour of diatonicism and the key system.

Plainsong and folk-song alone resisted the pressure of this evolution – the troubadours apparently compromising with instrumental accompaniment – 'the sole artistic protest against artistic culture that history knows'. These words of Ernest Walker occur in a passage where he is considering the aesthetics of arranging a folk-song in four-part harmony or setting it to a piano accompaniment. How is it that folk-song enthusiasts can outrage the very nature of folk-song as single-line melody by adding harmonies? Walker wrote:

It is not altogether a paradox to say that the better the work is

18

done and the more subtly expressive the supplied accompaniment, however simple, the more does the essential naïvety of the folk-song tend to disappear and the more does it become merged in the general mass of musicians' music. We obtain very beautiful polished songs for which we must needs be grateful; but we strike a blow at the root principle of the great unharmonized music – the sole artistic protest against artistic culture that history knows.

Blow or no blow, they all do it. It is true that the sound of unaccompanied melody is no longer so strange in the ear of cultivated musicians as it was a hundred years ago when they first began to be aware of their native folk-song. But everyone who has had dealings with folk-song, including the chief collectors with the most rigorous standards for the integrity of their special subject – Bartók and Kodály just as much as Cecil Sharp and Vaughan Williams – have all been willing to use folk-song, a work of art complete in itself, as the raw material for other works of art. The point about Walker's 'blow' is that plainsong, by yielding to the desire for accompanying itself with another voice, first of all as organum doubling the tune in bare fifths, led to the evolution of polyphony and so to harmony and all modern European music – such is artistic culture. But folk-song protests that it does not care about evolution or polyphony; it only cares for itself, plain monophonic melody. As a phenomenon folk-song therefore worries the historian: Walker concludes by saying that 'to the musical historian with a strong desire for strictly logical classification it is the most irritatingly elusive of all the matters with which he has to deal.' Very well, one can concur that folk-song is recalcitrant to history, evades dates and defies logic.

The aesthetics of arrangement presents a real problem to be confronted later (see below, chapter 10) but for the moment the comparison with plainsong affords further illumination of the nature of folk-song. Plainsong is international and sacred, folk-song is secular (though there are some, not very numerous, songs on sacred subjects) and national. Along with troubadour song, folk-song represents the non-clerical side of the art of music as it developed in mediaeval times. The Church was the cradle of European music through a millennium and a half: all theorizing, all text-books, the development of polyphony itself, are products of the Church. Music outside the Church did not get written down; it was simply performed, and if it survived it did so by virtue of being remembered and repeated by heart. Oral tradition in fact.

The emergence of organum out of monodic plainsong round AD 1000 is so startling a phenomenon that historians have been at a loss to account for it in face of the determined monody of the ancient world, from which our European civilization has been directly derived, and have been led to declare that all primitive music is monodic, folk-song being primitive in the sense that it shows only a small degree of organization. But the recent comparative study of folk-song, only made feasible by the invention of sound-recording, has shown that this is not a correct analysis. Curt Sachs, following, or maybe leading, a trend in musicology to pour cold water on the improbable hypothesis of a sudden development of polyphony, plumps for a universal polyphony, or at least what is know by the convenient term, heterophony:

'The deep rooted prejudice that harmony and polyphony have been a prerogative of the mediaeval and modern West does not hold water. Not one of the continents, not one of the archipelagos between them, lacks rudimentary forms of polyphony. When in musical ensembles several singers and players perform the same melody, either successively or simultaneously, they actually claim the freedom of varying in minor details. Repetition of a melody seldom agrees with its first form, nor do the voices of a chorus or the parts of an accompanied song agree with each other. Each participitant realizes the melodic idea according to personal taste and ability and to the special conditions of voices and instruments. Nobody minds the chance collisions that arise from such discrepancies, nor is anybody concerned about their consonant, or at least pregnant, character. . . . Such heterophony is certainly a rather negative form of co-operation – neither polyphonic nor harmonic and seemingly anarchic.' However, he goes on to quote a number of instances of extremely rudimentary tunes sung in parts, one in thirds and one in seconds from the Carolina Islands, a case of overlapping of parts that became a canon from Malacca and one noted by Jaap Kunst in the Malayan island of Flores, in which a canon of female voices is heard over a double drone from the men – a primitive 'Sumer is i'comen in'! (See below, Example 22.) Speaking of accompaniment in the music of the Far East, notably of Japanese flautists, Sachs further says, 'A singer's accompanist is expected to follow by an irrational particle of time, as an aide avoids riding abreast of his general.' Indian practice is the same. Nearer home there is a curious convention on Mount Athos that the priest, celebrant or singer, cannot read, so that he must have a reader to prompt him, and the liturgy goes through in canon at. a phrase distance often a quarter-tone out in pitch.[1] Long before Sachs, however, the idea that 'uncivilized nations are unacquainted with harmony' was denied by Carl Engel in his *The Study of National Music* published in 1866, showing in this as in other respects that he had a truly scientific attitude towards his subject. The progress from unison through heterophony, in which the parts wander a little from each other, to canon where they are very close behind and thence to counterpoint will be further examined later in this chapter under Polyphony.

Still, at the most primitive level music is a motif or a bit of tune endlessly repeated. Here the childhood of the race reproduces human childhood, for children adore repetition, and the simplest and most rudimentary English nursery rhyme 'Bye Baby Bunting', consists of a five-note phrase repeated in pairs over and over again. This suggests that folk-song unlike plainsong is not rhapsody but displays features of structure based on that elementary device for measuring off, and so organizing, periods in the flux of time, recapitulation.

The structure of folk-song is determined by words, which give

[1] Described by R. M. Dawkins in *The Monks of Athos* (1936).

shape to the tune and fix its length according to lines and strophes. 'Bye Baby Bunting' is classified as 'stichic' (from Greek στίχος a row or a line of verse or prose; στιχομυθία [stichomythia] is familiar to students of Greek drama as conversation in alternate lines of verse) in that its single line is repeated. In theory an even simpler structure is the single hail, call, ritual invocation, dirge, shepherd's call or jodel, of which examples are found all over Europe, but the tendency with these too is to repeat them. The next stage of temporal organization is reached when such a length of tune is balanced with a second section at once congruent and contrasting. If this is repeated we get A B A B. Thence to strophic measure with three, four or more lines to the verse. It was on this progressive plan that Dr Wiora organized his anthology of European folk-song and by it he was able to compare like of one country with like of another. This is the temporal structure of monody.

Modality

Folk-songs and folk-dance tunes, then, have indeed a temporal structure dictated by the words of the songs and the steps and figures of the dance. This horizontal structure is specified in the usual quasi-algebraical formulae of rhythm, tempo and phrase-length, such as the familiar A A B A, $(2+2)^n$ for the phrases of 'Baby Bunting', in six-eight time and so on, but tunes have also a vertical co-ordinate, tonal not temporal, that of scale, for *scala* is Latin for 'ladder'. The scale is a formula for stating in degrees (one to seven) the constituent tones of a melody which also at the same time states the relationships of the intervals formed by the tones and their relative positions. These formulae are the deductions of theorists examining the tunes *post compositionem*, not aids or instructions for composing them. Their value, like that of all formulae, is to enable generalizations to be made about an intractable number of individual instances. Of these scales one of the simplest and most widely distributed is the pentatonic, which consists of three whole-tone steps and two minor thirds to the octave. The order

22

in which these disparate steps are distributed on the ladder varies in different cultures. The most fundamental, in that it fits the harmonic series as discovered by Pythagoras, is arrived at by a sequence of rising fifths and falling fourths – the ancient Chinese had discovered this theoretical basis for it [Example 4]

Example 4

of which the features are that it is formed of whole tones and minor thirds, without semi-tones (anhemitonic) and that the 'gaps' are at the third and seventh degrees. They are not gaps of course to the singer who used the scale but only from the point of view of our more familiar heptatonic diatonic scale, but 'gaps' is the easiest way of distinguishing the various modes, or inversions, of the pentatonic scale (using inversion in the same sense as one applies it to chords and arpeggios). The form of pentatonic scale which characterizes much Scottish music, both Highland Gaelic as displayed for instance in Frances Tolmie's collection of 105 songs printed in the *Folk-Song Journal*, Vol. IV, 1911, and such a Lowland tune as that to which 'Auld Lang Syne' is sung, is differently gapped, at the fourth instead of the third [Example 5]. Different again, with its gaps at the second

Example 5

and sixth degrees, is a pentatonic scale attributed by Kodály to the Tartars of Asiatic Russia [Example 6]. Further inspection,

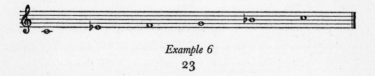

Example 6

however, reveals that Examples 5 and 6 are really modes of the pentatonic scale, formed by inverting it and regarding the lowest (and highest) notes of each position as new tonics, for a mode is just precisely the order in which the intervals, tones and thirds, or in diatonic scales semi-tones, are arranged on the ladder. The musical importance of the different modes is that they carry different expressive connotations: it makes a difference to the taste of the tune what mode it is in. There is however, another form of pentatonic scale derived from the first which contains semi-tones and two major thirds – this is called *ditonic*

Example 7

(from *ditonus* = two whole tones, i.e. a major third) [Example 7]. In Java there is an equally tempered five-note scale in use (Salendro). A refinement of terminology distinguishes a pentatonism which is based on a scale of five notes to the octave and a five-note section of a diatonic scale i.e. with the limited range of a fifth. This termed 'pentachordal'. Mr A. L. Lloyd uses this distinction, labelling the Cheshire Souling Song for instance 'trichordal' and it is used by the translators of Szabolcsi's *A History of Melody*. This is an unfortunate usage, as 'chordal' gives a wrong idea for tones, but it is based on the recognized use of 'tetrachord' for the ancient Greek four-note scale (of which two constituted the octave). It has the merit of not confusing the five-note scale of so familiar an English tune as 'The Keys of Canterbury' with a true pentatonic tune, which sounds more primitive, exotic, outlandish, call its ethos by whatever epithet seems to you most suitable. 'The Keys of Canterbury' is quite diatonic in character by comparison with a true 'gapped' pentatonic.

There is speculation whether the pentatonic scale is an evolution, by addition or transposition, from a three-note scale. Most theorists see all singing as an extension of the intonations of speech; speech when emotionally charged or ritually employed becomes rudimentary chanting; chanting expands into singing, which flowers into melody. There is greater confidence that the pentatonic scale evolved into the diatonic scale by the addition of the 'gap' notes first as decorations, then as passing notes, then as full members of the scale. In the course of this evolution enters the semi-tone, which for primitive people is not easy to sing, so that there are at least two semi-tones in the diatonic scale, major or minor. Add more semi-tones between the tones and you have the chromatic scale, which is unvocal but is mastered eventually with the help of instruments. No folk-singer would attempt what Wagner asks Wolfram to sing in *Tannhäuser* [Example 8] but he uses diatonic scales

O   pure and ten - der star——— of eve.

Example 8

freely. In the Near East he may use a scale containing two augmented seconds (=minor thirds) [Example 9] wrongly

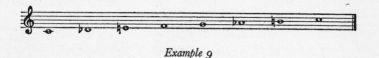

Example 9

called the Hungarian scale, for Kodály[2] denies that it is ever found in true Hungarian folk-song, though Starkie[3] testifies to its use by gypsy fiddlers (not singers) in Hungary. The chromatic semi-tone is hard to absorb. Kodály says that pentatonism does not recognize it, that though Hungarians are at home with heptatonic scales they avoid or simplify or reject as outside their tonal system the chromatic semi-tone, and

[2] *Folk Music of Hungary*, p. 67.   [3] *Raggle Taggle*, p. 76.

further quotes an instance of some Korean children in Hungarian schools who found it almost impossible to learn a diatonic semi-tone. This scale has also been called (by Bourgault Ducoudray) the Oriental scale. Near Eastern is a safer designation. It has links with classical Greek music in being constructed of two tetrachords.

In Western Europe it is the so-called Church modes that the folk-singer employs to enlarge the resources of his monody. It is tempting to speculate that our present folk melody grew in the Middle Ages when the people heard in Church Latin words sung to melodies cast in one or other of the seven available modes and that when they came to sing secular songs in the vernacular they employed the same sort of tunes. But the fact that the tunes were not of the same sort rhythmically weakens the argument for their being of the same sort modally. What seems more likely is that when you have singing without instrumental accompaniment or with the sort of linear counterpoint of a viola or wind instrument woven by way of support into the texture of a fifteenth-century motet, you will sing in the modes which lend themselves so well to polyphony, and will so produce that weaving of individual voice parts which was ultimately, viz. *circa* 1600, to give way to harmony. It was harmony that developed tonality by key and tonality by key that decided upon two modes, Aeolian and Ionian, as adequate for its purposes. It took three centuries to develop the technical and expressive possibilities latent in harmony based on key, which in its turn was based on the minor and major modes, Aeolian and Ionian, of the diatonic scale. Composers were fully occupied with these developments from the so-called monodic revolution of 1600 to the dissolution of tonality around 1900.

But monodists were not. Monody *ipso facto* is monodic—without harmony. It therefore needed the melodic resources inherent in the other modes, Dorian, Phrygian, Lydian and Mixolydian, and it therefore did not discard them. A particular mode is a particular order of arranging the tones and semi-tones within the octave and so inflecting the intervals

26

within the scale, natural, sharp or flat. For a reason that is still ultimately mysterious each mode has its particular aesthetic flavour, ethos, emotional character – hence its value to the singer. Common speech recognises this mysterious fact when it says that the minor is a more passionate mode than the major. Mediaeval theorists called the Ionian mode with its sharp third, sharp sixth and sharp seventh, i.e. our major mode, *modus lascivus*. *Lascivus* in classical Latin has the primary meaning of 'jolly', 'playful' and only secondarily 'wanton'. In mediaeval Latin it retained the meaning of 'pleasing' or 'sweet'. A major third is a sweeter interval than a minor, as the *tierce de Picardie* for a final cadence in early classical music testifies. It is the sharp seventh that is important for harmony in its function as a leading-note, but the sharp seventh too is a positive piquancy in the Ionian mode, whereas the flat sixth and seventh of the Aeolian, i.e. melodic minor, mode have a recognizably bromide effect. It is no good asking why those things should be: whatever the answer, it is involved in the psychology of perception and, while agreement on the validity of such generalizations might not be universal, it is far too general to be accounted for on any ground of convention or tradition.

Such distinctions of character somehow implicit in a scale which, to repeat, is no more than a tonal structure consisting of tones and semi-tones disposed in a certain order, go straight back to Greek thought about music. This is why the Greek names have stuck to the modes. Plato in *The Republic* actually prescribes some modes and proscribes others solely on account of their moral qualities. He is prepared to make the equivalent of such a remark in a manual of composition as 'Avoid the key of F minor as it is morally debilitating', or in a treatise on education that children must not be contaminated by anything so orgiastic as D flat major. To modern musicians this is to go too far, but even they will accept it as axiomatic that extreme chromaticism is suitable for the depiction of morbid states of mind. The Greeks attributed specific ethical characteristics to their modes because the different modes did tend to reflect states of mind and because they had not the musical resources which we more often and more powerfully employ to that end, namely harmony. The idea survived into the Middle Ages for Dowland, in his translation of the *Micrologus* of Ornithoparcus characterizes the modes thus: 'The Dorian Moode is the bestower of wisedom and causer of chastity. The Phrygian causeth wars and enflameth fury. The Eolian doth appease the tempests of the minde and when it hath appeased them lulls them asleepe. The Lydian doth sharpen the wit of the dull and doth make them that are burdened with earthly desires to desire heavenly things.'

Their music was monodic by choice, since the Greeks must occasionally have heard tones sounding together as with a drone, or on the double pipe (δίαυλος)[4] or in heterophony in a dramatic chorus, or in 'magadizing', which they thought vulgar, consisting it would seem of octaves or other concords on the large harp called μάγαδις. Harmony somehow offended against the Greek ideal of moderation, the golden mean, which we can translate as artistic economy, at any rate up to the revolution in taste after the Peloponesian War[5] and earned the same sort of aesthetic reproach as the extreme chromaticism of late nineteenth century harmony, such e.g. as Franck's, does from classically inclined musicians of our own time.

Monody then demands the use of different modes for its melodies for the sake of variety and for subtlety and force of expression. The essential intervals of each can be tabulated by the simple mnemonic of the white keys of an octave on the piano

C – C = Ionian	sharp 3, 6 and 7	
D – D = Dorian	flat 3, sharp 6, flat 7	
E – E = Phrygian	flat 2, 3, 6 and 7	

---

[4] Harrison and Rimmer deduce from later folk instruments of the same type that some kind of two-part counterpoint was playable, and therefore occasionally played on the diaulos.

[5] Described by Mrs Henderson in Vol. I of the *New Oxford History of Music*.

F – F = Lydian   sharp 3, augmented 4, sharp 7
G – G = Mixolydian   sharp 3, flat 7
A – A = Aeolian   flat 3, 6 and 7
B – B = Locrian   flat 2, 3, 5, 6, and 7 (not used probably because of its lack of a true fifth)

Or they can be transposed to the same pitch and display their differences by juxtaposition [Example 10]. But there is one

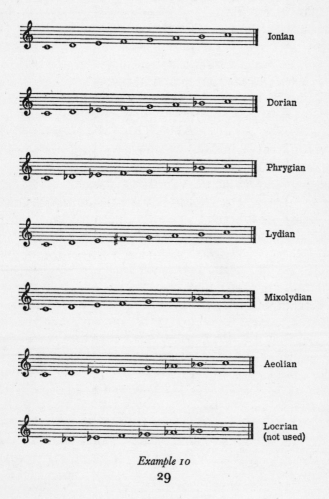

Example 10

29

logical anomaly, or historical accident about this. Since any mode is a particular disposition of tones, semi-tones and intervals, it can be used at any pitch: you can have a Dorian scale on G or B, and a folk-singer pitches his tune to suit his voice, but in modal music derived from plainsong and the polyphony derived from plainsong which employs these self-same modes, there is a tendency for Dorian music to be anchored to D as its final or tonic, e.g. Bach's Dorian Toccata and Fugue for organ, for Lydian music to be attached to F, as in Byrd's Variations on 'The Woods so Wild' or Beethoven's *Heiligedankgesang* in his A minor quartet, opus 132. There is no logic in this as any mode can be employed at any pitch, but whether it is a historical accident or whether there was some sort of pitch memory by which a composition conceived with a tonic on D carried with it the ethos of the Dorian mode and its semi-automatic adoption by the composer, these inessential associations of modes with pitches were none the less strong. They did not, however, affect the folk-singer who pitched his song where he liked, usually as high as he could manage.

In English folk-song the Phrygian and Lydian modes are of rare occurrence, 'The White Paternoster' from Devon collected by Baring Gould and 'James Macdonald' from Somerset collected by Sharp are instances. Sharp found that about two-thirds of the songs he collected were Ionian, i.e. ordinary major, that minor tunes were all in the Aeolian form, i.e. without leading notes, and that Mixolydian, i.e. major with a flat seventh and Dorian with flat third, sharp sixth and flat seventh accounted for the rest. Modality is not confined to the folk-songs of the British Isles. The French musician L. A. Bourgault-Ducoudray as far back as 1875 collected Greek folk-songs in Smyrna and Athens and prefaced his publication of them with an exposition of the modes which he endeavoured to relate to the ancient tetrachords and the ancient modes – his nomenclature differs from ours in that he has tried to go behind the names of the ecclesiastical modes to the ancient Greek modes which have proved hard to identify with modern scales. But the songs he prints are certainly modal as for instance this quasi-Aeolian lullaby [Example 11] and when he came to

Example 11

collect some French songs in Brittany he found that eight different modes were to be found in Breton song. Here is one in

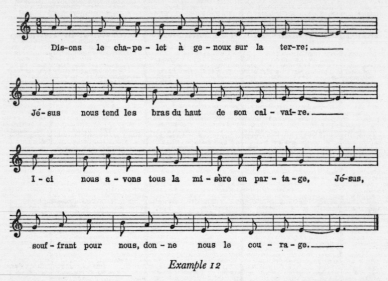

Dis-ons le cha-pe - let à ge - noux sur la ter-re;

Jé-sus nous tend les bras du haut de son cal - vai-re.

I - ci nous a - vons tous la mi - sère en par - ta - ge, Jé-sus,

souf - frant pour nous, don - ne nous le cou - ra - ge.

Example 12

the Dorian mode [Example 12]. German folk-song on the other
hand shows few signs of modality – or indeed of ornamentation,
'as good as unknown in later German folk-song' according to
Dr Ernst Meyer. Dr Meyer does, however, quote from the Erk-
Böhme collection the song 'Maikönigin' as an example of
mixolydian tonality (though it lacks the seventh degree of the
scale). Sharp observed that in Brahms's forty-nine *Deutsche
Volkslieder* eight of the tunes were in the Aeolian mode and two
in the Phrygian, improperly, as he alleged, harmonized by
Brahms so as to conceal their real modality. But in the light
of what Dr Walter Wiora, the present authority on German
folk-song, says about the approximation of German folk-song to
popular song since the eighteenth century, it looks as though in
some of the pilloried songs at any rate Brahms's reference of
them to two tonics is not so reprehensible. Dr Wiora begins his
article on German folk-song in Grove's *Dictionary* by declaring
that 'in Germany, more than in most other countries the
people's singing and music-making came under the influence of
the civic cultures of modern times. The indigenous folk-song
has been partly ousted and partly affected by organized

popular singing and art-music of a popular nature'. In short it became urbanized, as shown by 'an almost exclusive sway of the major scale' and the virtual absence of pentatonic melodies, though he insists that before the eighteenth century Dorian and Phrygian modes are to be found. Here however is a rare example of a mixolydian tune—'Maikönigin'[6] [Example 13].

Example 13

Ornamentation

Another device adopted by the folk-singer to extend his range of expression within his monodic art is ornamentation of his vocal line, which might in extreme cases become melisma. Melisma suggests another link with plainsong, a link which led one scholar, who was equally devoted to both kinds of chant, to postulate that they had a common origin in a wordless ecstatic 'jubilation', the utterance of hearts too full for words and the framing of concepts. But the Rev. George Chambers's argument, set out with great learning and citations from the Fathers of the Church in his *Folk-Song-Plainsong* (1956), begs too many questions to be acceptable. It is easier to concede that Alleluia sung melismatically is a primitive form of chant that has a validity of its own and could have come from religious impulses and on religious occasions, but folk-song seems much too firmly rooted

[6] Quoted by Ernst Meyer in *Aufsätze über Musik*, pp. 159 and 137 (1957), from Erik Boehme.

in words to permit a similar hypothesis for its origin. It is
more natural to think of such melisma as may occur in folk-song
as an extended ornament. In the folk-song of Spain and Spanish
America, which always has the sound of a strummed guitar
somewhere in the background, it is possible to encounter
something like this (from Panama) over alternate bars of tonic
and dominant [Example 14] but even in a case like this from

Example 14

Example 15

34

Sicily [Example 15] the flourish is an ornament, not a melisma with melodic value of its own. The first phrase is obviously only an elaboration of Example 16.

Example 16

It may not be possible to distinguish clearly graces from melismas, but the vocal equivalents of turns, mordents, slides, appoggiaturas, acciaccaturas are the embellishments employed by the folk-singer to decorate, to point the emphasis of, and to give free play to his immediate feelings about, his song rather than the less rhythmical melismas of plainsong. The amount of decoration varies from nation to nation and singer to singer. Thus the Hungarians with their love of embroidery, perhaps a vestigial relic of their oriental origin, are in the habit of decorating their folk melodies, at any rate of the parlando rubato type with elaborate turns, grace-notes and slides, which though less thick on the melody are not unknown in the other great type of Bartok's classification, namely tempo giusto. Thus the folk-song which Kodály took for the theme of his orchestral variations, 'The Peacock', is quoted in his biography in this

Example 17

35

form: [Example 17] though in its statement in his finale it appears as [Example 18].

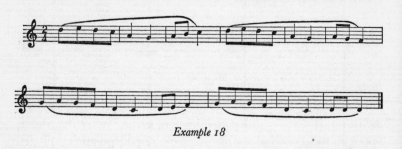

Example 18

Nothing like this is to be found in English folk-song. The English singer is content with an occasional mordent or upturning appoggiatura or changing-note figure. It is possible to compare modern traditional singers with those from whom Percy Grainger collected songs on his primitive phonograph in 1906 and the practice seems very much the same. Grainger made careful transcriptions, attempting even to reproduce dialect vowels, for the *Folk Song Journal* of his Lincolnshire collection, which included that astonishing piece of submerged history 'Six Dukes went a-fishing'. Of this song he took versions from three different singers. The first of them, George Gouldthorpe, used no ornaments – the only feature of his singing was a variation between C and C in the penultimate line of each verse. The second singer, Joseph Leaning, liked a triplet anacrusis, though for 'they' in three cases he sings a duplet; he ornaments 'fishin'' in the first line [Example A],

Example A

and puts a turn on 'raised' in 'raised him from the ground'. The third singer, Dean Robinson, whose was a simpler version, employs a slide, i.e. presumably a slow portamento, in a rising

major third and another slide down a fifth. That is all. There is
no doubt that singers do employ graces; English collectors in
the main have not attempted to record what shifted from verse
to verse and what in any case did not obscure the contour or
the main notes of the melody, except in a case like 'Bushes
and Briars' where the little turn in the last line is a constant
feature of the cadence. In recent times with the urban revival
of folk-song, in which there was not the same urgency to get
the actual words and notes down on to paper as there was half
a century earlier, more attention has been paid to styles of
performance, and ornamentation has thus come under observation; this change of orientation has coincided with the movement prompted by musicology for authentic performances of
baroque music, which has revived interest in eighteenth-
century methods of singing, and though gracing has not
recovered the amount of attention bestowed on it by Dr
Burney, it is now at least respectable for a singer in the right
context to grace the recapitulation of an *aria da capo*, so that
ornamentation is accepted as an integral part of a folk-song, but
from the nature of the case it cannot be profitably put into
music-type. It is essentially an oral phenomenon and a characteristic of the oral tradition.

Bartók, however, who probably noted more folk-tunes than
any other collector, thought that the transcriptions should be as
accurate as possible, and his opinion is not lightly to be set
aside. But an examination of his scrupulous versions makes one
wonder whether they are not only wasted labour but ultimately
self-defeating. The introduction to his book of Serbo-Croatian
songs, published in America after his death begins: 'The transcriptions of recordings of folk-music should be as true as possible.' He goes on to qualify this by reference to the inadequacy
of our staff notation and he invents a number of symbols
to indicate small deviations of pitch up to a quarter of a tone,
he abandons time-signatures in the parlando rubato songs and
systematizes his practice, which is set out in full in the introduction to his volume of Rumanian songs, published many years

later still. These Rumanian songs and instrumental tunes provide the arguments both for and against attempting to notate ornaments. It is valuable to have some of the tunes, for example this taken at random from the dance tunes [Example 19],

Example 19

which, being played on a peasant flute instead of a violin, is less rather than more highly ornamented than some of his tunes, so that one can gauge the style, but such heavy incrustations of graces are apt to conceal the melody. Moreover, since no two performances are ever alike, not even by the same player or singer, and actual variations are often quoted by Bartók himself when the tune had been repeated for him, it is actually misleading to finalise one particular rendering. The practice of our own collectors was to listen to many repetitions (as in the numerous verses of a ballad) and to get down the bony structure of the melody, the least varied notes of the tune. This gave the tune as such, a constant in the fluctuating time values, the basic notes to which the ornaments were attached by the performer. After all, performers of Schubert's songs never sing them or their several verses twice identically, so that Bartók's meticulous use of such symbols as ⌢ and ⌣ to indicate small prolongations or abbreviations of time-values is really unnecessary. But to read through his symbol-encrusted versions is to realize the extraordinary acuity of his ear and his ingenuity in pursuit of scholarly integrity, qualities that are all of a piece with the man as we know him from his compositions and his life-story.

Polyphony

Curt Sachs's words about the universality of polyphony even in quite primitive music was quoted in the section on Monody (see p. 20) and some instances were cited. None, however, from Africa which shows the phenomenon of polyrhythm as well as music from primitive Pygmies. Still more primitive is a record in my possession of a ceremony in the Pacific island of Tikopia, which was submitted as part of a thesis for a degree in social anthropology at London University. It was made from tapes taken by Professor Raymond Firth in 1951 on a return visit to the island, which he had first visited in 1928. The population is of Polynesians, who were even then living in neolithic conditions, i.e. they had no metal, though in other respects they had developed without going through the stages of the iron and bronze ages. Professor Firth has since played me some more of his recordings taken even more recently, which now show European influences, to wit more extended melodies, which even include a few chromatic semi-tones. But they still sing traditional dirges of narrow compass. The record is of a *Mako* or dance at a gathering of two villages for a dance festival. What we hear is a general hubbub of greeting and someone saying 'What shall we dance?' Then we hear a search for a tonic out of which a descending tune, consisting of F E♭ C A♭ emerges, sung by the dancers in heterophony. This is in a tetratonic scale with a gap. The tonic persists as an intermittent drone, which yields some unexpected harmonic effects of thirds and fifths. There is some sort of a break – maybe in the dancing, maybe only on the tape – and then a simple rhythm is beaten on an upturned canoe – there is nothing remotely like the complicated rhythms of African peoples, who in other respects are more primitive. Then the dance starts again with the tune a tone lower, E♭ D♭ B♭ and G♭, but there is now a lightly touched passing note on A♭ – so do tetratonic and pentatonic scales fill in their gaps, as has been suspected in theory, though the evolution of the heptatonic scale in this way has been questioned. Here, however, we have it confirmed. In addition there are some whoops and handclapping, the whoops being a kind of szforzando for expression.

This is indeed primitive music, but it is not wholly innocent of polyphony. True, the harmony is incidental, the product of a drone, but as the drone is vocal it is harmony of a sort, and the occasional 'breaks', and wrong notes for lack of breath or failure in pitch or bad shots of the heterophonic singing mark the first step away from a pure unison. We know how in our own organum, when parallel motion came in, sometimes a vocal part got stuck on a bottom note—perhaps the low note of an organ which produced first oblique motion and then contrary motion. The Tikopians, however, do not get beyond an inner pedal point or a bit of drone. But as one goes up the scale of development among different peoples the world over one finds an increasing use of rudimentary counterpoint, arising out of heterophony, until in Africa you have an extraordinary counterpoint of rhythms played out on drums and xylophones of various dimensions. Records made by Hugh Tracey[7] include a symphonic poem for fifteen drums called *Kyuma* illustrating the introduction of a maypole into Uganda. It is made up and played by the royal drummers of the ex-Kabaka's band, made up, that is to say, in a living tradition. Its elaborate polyrhythm is certainly not random drumming, but is it entitled to be called counterpoint? which implies that either the resultant pattern is foreseen, indeed intended, by the performers – as happens in academic counterpoint – or that, though not precisely contemplated, it is organized on well-defined principles so that the result is controlled, not fully foreseen on the one hand nor random on the other. This again happens in counterpoint: the writer has an idea and an intention to work it to a prospective purpose, such as a fugue, but is controlled by the degree to which he can work it – if it won't go he must do something else with it. African drumming, according to the Rev. A. M. Jones is controlled by a master pattern and by signals for changing the patterns in the course of the song. It is true polyphony and of an

[7] Music of Africa (Decca).

order that baffles Western ears, but it does not produce the effect we call harmony, i.e. the resultant of two (or more) separate tones sounding together, Browning's 'not a third sound but a star'.

This type of polyrhythm is very much an African phenomenon – rhythm is the pre-eminent element in their music whereas with us pitch-melody is apt to be the major ingredient. Indeed with us rhythm is a frame or backbone of melody, and timbre a further secondary or tertiary element. In the gamelan orchestras of Indonesia the predominant element is rhythm, as in Africa, produced by percussion instruments but with timbre a good second and tune a bad third, since the pitches have no melodic significance. Consider a more primitive case, in which a voice sings a tune against a counterpoint of rhythm: this dance-song 'kano' from the Kouyou in Africa is a primitive unison chant on C G A D descending sung by Pygmy women against three drums and a bell[8] [Example 20]. But in this next

Example 20

example from a neighbouring tribe, Babinga, there is to be something like harmony and antiphony, for there are two choruses, the women in one group singing a tune of sorts, and the men in another singing an ostinato of notes in the bass to an accompaniment of drums, all this as the accompaniment of a social dance [Example 21].

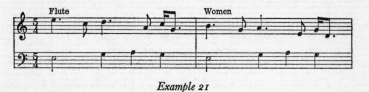

Example 21

[8] Ethnic Folkways Library. Recorded in French Equatorial Africa by André Didier.

These are examples of polyphony from a fairly primitive community. So what becomes of the notion that the most primitive music is a form of extended cry or call and that extended melody develops from that and that then inexplicably at about AD 1000 in Europe alone someone thought of parallel motion and developed that into descant, harmony and Palestrina? Historians of music confronted with what was known from classical antiquity in the Mediterranean basin, from which our civilization arose, were forced to this scheme, which ethnomusicology has now demolished. What has to be put in its place is the fact, account for it if you can, that monody was the choice of the Mediterranean peoples, the Jews, the Greeks and their successors the Byzantines and the Romans – they liked their music that way and the Greeks, at any rate until the time of Aristotle, actively disliked harmony and thought it vulgar. Islam always has disliked harmony too. But this concentration on monody is not, as was supposed, universal. On the contrary, according to Curt Sachs polyphony was universal. Bruno Nettl has a chapter in *Music in Primitive Culture* on rudimentary polyphony, in which he agrees that it is indeed universal but he begins by saying that it has attracted a disproportionate amount of attention from scholars and that this type of music comprises a relatively small part of the primitive repertory. This may well be so but I would have thought that the discovery of the fact of polyphony was sufficiently startling to warrant a good deal of scholarly attention. Nettl surveys the theories of its origin – our old, old problem – among which he describes Marius Schneider's theory of evolution by areas and stages which he plots as follows:

1 One such stage is distributed all over the world and shows 'variant heterophony'. Heterophony is a term we have already met. It is as old as Plato, who used it in *The Laws* in a description of the proper way to teach the lyre, but it is new in modern usage. It means that an essential unison is variegated by some performers making a mistake or deviating temporarily from the line, such deviations as dodging a high note, substituting a lower

or running out of breath or slipping in a quicker passing note, or doing what jazz players do in their 'breaks' from which they rejoin the tune and their colleagues. Jaap Kunst found an elaborate and less chancey form of heterophony in Java, which he described as being 'where one part performs the principal theme in its whole extent but entirely unadorned, another part strengthens certain tones of that theme at regular time intervals in a lower octave, whereas a third part elaborates it with various embellishments'. But essentially the harmony created by these chance clashes and discrepant time values is unpremeditated, though it may for that very reason be found attractive. Some such heterophony was to be heard in the Tikopia record. It is to be found in a form less random and so ordered as to lead on to part-writing in Chinese classical music.

2 Almost equally primitive is the drone, as again in the Tikopia record, but it is possible to develop a little by becoming a short ostinato, in which a short phrase is repeated while another more elaborate phrase is sung, as in an African song to the accompaniment of the sansa, or finger piano of metal tongues.

3 Parallel intervals easily occur, as they do in our own congregational singing and as happened in our Western music when it developed organum, with its 4 part S A T B singing 4ths or the same tune a 4th or 5th apart. But in folk-music, even consecutive seconds can occur, as in Yugoslav folk song.

4 Imitation, which again is fairly easy to understand given an antiphony of solo and chorus. There is a clear example quoted by both Sachs and Nettl from Samoa and a more elaborate one still from the Malayan island of Flores, already quoted [see Example 22].

In spite of Nettl's emphatic warning not to make too much fuss of this rudimentary polyphony, my view is that the ethnological discovery of polyphony has compelled us to rewrite one or two chapters in our history of early music from the Greeks to Hucbald. At a recent (1966) conference of the I.F.M.C. a paper was read on this very point and in it comparisons were made between the folk music of Georgia and early organum.

Example 22

CHAPTER THREE

Ethnology and Nationalism

These forages of folk-song into ethnomusicology make it desirable to demarcate their spheres. Historically folk-lore is a product of the nineteenth century, ethnomusicology of the twentieth. But as a matter of logic the latter (and later) includes the former, as the whole includes the part. On the other hand as a matter of semantics ethnomusicology has been by use generally confined to that music which we, with European arrogance, call primitive or exotic. (It is a solecism to speak of a product of the ancient civilization of China as primitive, so we call it exotic.) Early anthropologists and explorers in the nineteenth century wrote 'uncivilized' of such and knew what they meant and moreover were right in so far as the word 'civilization' implies an urban, civil or citizen culture. But in so far as anthropological consciences have grown more tender even the lowliest peoples are recognized as possessing a culture and it is becoming difficult to find a single word that will embrace Pygmies, Amerindians and Melanesians, unless one allows 'primitive' for it, meaning with simple culture and no reading or writing. Dr Bruno Nettl[1] tries to sort things out by defining ethnomusicology as the science that deals with the music of peoples outside Western civilization and then adds 'The ethnomusicologist ordinarily distinguishes in his work between three kinds of music: Oriental, folk and primitive.' This use of Oriental with a capital O certainly avoids the

[1] *Music in Primitive Culture.*

solecism just mentioned and allows the art to have professional practitioners, but his attempt to bring folk music into line with primitive is less satisfactory. Folk music, he says, is the music of social groups within a higher culture but which are not musically literate or professionally competent, which is true enough, but European folk music is not outside Western civilization nor even outside Western musical culture. Primitive music has no contact with any high culture as folk music certainly has. It is really better to go back to the original idea of ethnology from the Greek word ἔθνος which is usually translated 'race' but has a fundamental meaning of a community, people living together who recognize that they form some sort of a unity. *Ethnos* therefore as a prefix can apply to nations as well as pigmentation of the skin and lowly culture, and ethnomusicology will be the comparative study of the music of any homogeneous group of people.

Folk music as a study is not necessarily comparative. Indeed it begins rather as the study in depth of the music of one community, usually one's own. Comparison comes later. Indeed it is only just beginning. For not only have the materials to be assembled, of which the sheet bulk is formidable, but methods of comparison have to be devised and categories decided before a computer can be put on to look for significant resemblances – if indeed that is the deduction we are trying to arrive at. It is fair, however, to plead that 'ethnomusicology' be not restricted in meaning to the study of primitive music, even if that is where the work is most urgent and most extensive. The folk music of civilized peoples should be a part of it, as Dr Nettl asks, just as Oriental music, such as Indian music with its elaborate system of *rágas* should be. The great dividing line is between the products of a community and those of an individual composer; the communal aspect of works of musical art is what interests the ethnomusicologist, the individual compositions of the individual composer are what interest the music critic.

The nation is a modern conception but it is the main classification in the modern world, and folk music is a national phenomenon most easily studied nation by nation. The twentieth century has seen some reaction against the full acceptance of nationalism that was axiomatic in the nineteenth. The spread of ideologies across frontiers has challenged the old idea of a nation as being an entity united by law, language, custom, geography and politics, but it still does not look much like breaking down the cohesive force of national sovereignty either by a universal communism or by a union of nations or just yet by a united states of Europe. The dynamic force of nationalism in politics and culture, having exploded with unparalleled violence in two world wars, has certainly since waned and in music its liberating and fertilizing powers are no longer needed as they were in the nineteenth century. Serialism like fascism and communism has crossed frontiers, but national character still asserts itself in the arts and folk music breaks out in new places even in an educated community like our own and that of the U.S.A.

Ethnomusicology as such began as a study of instruments rather than of vocal music and is accounted – by Jaap Kunst who wrote its first text-book – about three-quarters of a century old. Kunst credits A. J. Ellis and A. J. Hipkins, two Englishmen who began measuring the tones of instruments and of scales, as its founders. *On the Musical Scales of Various Nations* and *The History of Musical Pitch* were published by Ellis, who was primarily a philologist and mathematician, in the early eighties. But a claimant with an older and, in the light of modern interest in comparative folk-melody, equal title to be the pioneer of the new study is Carl Engel, a German who came to England in 1845 and worked and published his archaeological books here. His *The Study of National Music*, already mentioned which was published in 1866, a comparative study of the most scholarly kind, cautiously sceptical, as encyclopaedic as he could make it in the conditions of the time, and complete with bibliography, is surely the first study in ethnomusicology. For he had chapters on scales, structure, relation of melodies to national character, to poetry and dance and to folklore in so far as that prescribed the occasions for music. Some of it now seems irrelevant, such as his concern with national anthems, and some of his tunes may seem in spite of his solicitude on the point dubious on the score of authenticity. But it is a splendid book, to which he had been led apparently by the study of the 'Music of the Most Ancient Nations', which became the title of a previous book. He also was interested in old instruments and became attached to the new Victoria and Albert Museum in South Kensington, where he too was associated with Hipkins. Kunst names many scholars who have continued the work, of whom Erich von Hornbostel (1877–1935) pursued both instrumental and vocal studies and investigated African music. Of him Kunst says, 'The marvellous clarity of mind and well-nigh infallible intuition with which he penetrated into the – at the time practically virgin – field of exotic musical cultures will rarely be equalled.' He was responsible for building up in Berlin an archive of sound recordings and his example was followed in Budapest by Bartók and Kodály. Which brings us back out of the primitive and the exotic into the field of European folk-song.

Of a later generation is Bruno Nettl, the son of a Czech emigrant to America, the musicologist Paul Nettl, who has written on primitive music in *Music in Primitive Culture* (1956), and on folk music in *Folk and Traditional Music of the Western Continents* (1965). A department of ethnomusicology has been established in the University of California, in Los Angeles. Marius Schneider holds a chair in the subject at Cologne. A. H. Fox-Strangways and Arnold Bake, both now dead, published studies of Indian music in England. Mr Peter Crossley-Holland, who had done field work on Thibetan folk-song, has worked at the International Institute for Comparative Music Studies and Documentation in Berlin. Field work in Africa has been done by Dr Klaus Wachsmann, Rev. A. M. Jones and Hugh Tracey. This random selection of names and facts – a more comprehensive list is to be found in Kunst's *Ethnomusicology* (1955) – indicates that the subject is now alive alike for primitive, for folk and for Oriental music and has obtained some small academic recognition. In London the Asian Music Society, of which Mr Yehudi Menuhin is President, and the English Folk Dance and Song Society do something to encourage this branch of musicology but the attitude of most English musicians is one of bored contempt of folk-song and all its works. However, there is a history of folk-song, its collective study and propagation in Great Britain which will be told in the next chapter. And the foundation of the International Folk Music Council by Dr Maud Karpeles in 1947, which publishes an annual journal, ensures that material for comparative study through the whole range of folk and exotic music is constantly forthcoming. The School of Oriental Studies, which is within the University of London, has some Polynesian recordings, was a base for the work of Dr Arnold Bake and is at the disposal of the Professor of the Chair of Social Anthropology at the London School of Economics, formerly held by Malinowski and then by Professor Raymond Firth. In Edinburgh the School of Scottish Studies pursues more consistently a more clearly defined scheme of studies. But on the whole Britain indeed seems to have been better at pioneering than at developing musicological studies. The Musical Association, which was formed for the very purpose of fostering musicological learning as long ago as 1874, was early in the field, but until Edward Dent was made Professor of Music at Cambridge the best musicological work in Britain was done by amateurs, and not until the reconstitution of the faculties of music at Oxford and Cambridge after 1946 was academic provision made for it officially, the term itself even so being avoided. Folk music first appeared in a university degree syllabus in Professor Dart's London prospectus issued in 1965.

The bibliography of Carl Engel's *An Introduction to the Study of National Music*, to give the book its full title, shows that for most countries the authorities were recent, i.e. European folk-song is found in publications of the thirties, forties and fifties of the nineteenth century, though one book on Irish bards is dated 1786 and one Russian collection was first published in

1790. It thus transpires that when the romantic movement began to blow against cosmopolitan eighteenth-century music and the various nationalist schools of composition in Europe began to revolt against the long hegemony of Italy and Austria, they could find the ammunition to their hand in this work of investigation of the national and popular musics. The nationalist movements are generally regarded as an outcome or off-shoot of the romantic movement. The old unhappy far-off things and battles long ago were the romantic subjects of the ballads which in every country enshrined the spirit of the people. So folk music became the main weapon of emancipation. There were others – in England to look no further there were the Elizabethans and Purcell – but folk-songs in the native tongue, age-old but no one knew how old, traditional ballads and dances were keys to an idiom not tied to the cadences of Mozart nor confined in the shackles of sonata form. It seems strange to think of sonata form, one of the most fertile and flexible and polymorphic creations of the human mind, as a shackle on anything, but even a superficial acquaintance with nineteenth-century symphonies outside the classical masters shows how restrictive it could be, and composers eventually saw it for themselves and wrote rhapsodies on folk-tunes instead of symphonies to get away from what was felt, for all the universality of its applicability, to be an essentially German way of thinking in sound. The rhapsodies soon showed that they were not the answer to the problem, tunes unlike themes or thematic material are not apt for development, indeed they are recalcitrant to the process, as Constant Lambert in a witty half-truth put it: there is nothing you can do with a folk-tune once you have played it except to play it again louder. The solution turned out to be to animate the old form with a new spirit, a nationally infected and inflected spirit, and it would adapt itself and accommodate a new music. This was the solution adopted by the Russians, the Czechs, the Hungarians, the Scandinavians and the English – the French never had quite the same need of emancipation, for their natural chauvinism had kept a French national music alive even at a rather lower level of achievement than that of the surrounding Germans and Italians. But the French too collected their folk-songs in the nineteenth century, looked at their troubadour legacy, published their *noëls*, and resuscitated their *brunettes*, *rondes* and *chansons populaires*, even if neither Gounod, Massenet, Saint-Saëns nor Fauré developed, nor united to form, a national school on the Russian model.

The Russians were the first in the field of endeavour to find a native music that was not smothered by the French ballet and Italian opera of St Petersburg and the German training of the Moscow conservatoire. In the corresponding literary movement inspired by the balladry of the eighteenth century it was Germany and the Scandinavian countries that nourished themselves on traditional material and so found a new romantic art – we should not have Schubert's *Erlkönig* without its discovery by Goethe. But it was the Slavonic peoples, Russian, Poles and Bohemians who first applied the fertilizer of folk music to the traditions of composition that they shared with the rest of Europe, that is to opera, symphony and chamber music. Chopin, wholly sophisticated and least folky of composers, went to the Polonaise and the Mazurka to nourish his individual genius and to procure emancipation for it – no one can say that his three sonatas are like Beethoven's thirty-two. He is hardly a Polish nationalist though – since he was so much a Frenchman and the time of nationalism had not fully come, but he is an incipient nationalist to counter-balance the belated nationalists of the twentieth century like Janáček and Khachaturian.

To Glinka (1804–57) is assigned the credit of attempting to write a Russian opera and in *A Life for the Tsar* alias *Ivan Sussanin* produced in 1836 he had a subject which allowed him, as he himself said, to contrast Russian and Polish national music. It has a Russian flavour and the second act contains Polish dances but it is still essentially an Italian opera. However, it provoked the sneer among cultivated Russian opera lovers that it was 'the music of coachmen'. Into his next opera he infused a Tartar flavour. It is not reported of him that he studied Russian folk-song but he 'recast the primitive speech of folk-song into a new and polished idiom'. The force of nationalism had begun. With Balakirev (1837–1910) the movement became more self-conscious. He met Glinka and he turned out (in 1852) a 'Grande Fantaisie sur airs nationales russes pour la pianoforte avec accompagnement d'orchestre', a forerunner of 'Islamey'. Then in 1858 he produced an overture on three Russian themes. It is to be supposed that both Glinka and Balakirev got their folk-tunes from the air they breathed, not from the books they read, although collections of Russian folk-songs had been published as early as 1782 by Trutovsky, the first collection of all, 1806 (by Ivan Prach), 1834 (by M. Stanovich), 1838 (by T. P. Sakharov). Glinka was born in a village in the Smolensk department, and Balakirev in Nijni Novgorod, where they may well have heard them currently sung, as Moussorgsky and Rimsky-Korsakof certainly did, by serfs and servants. But in any case Balakirev started to collect Circassian tunes during a holiday in the Caucasus in 1862 and went on to collect Georgian tunes, publishing an album of Russian songs in 1866.

Balakirev was the leader of the group afterwards known as the Kuchka (Cui, Borodin, Moussorgsky and Rimsky-Korsakof) to whom he communicated his enthusiasm. Nor was Tchaikovsky, who belonged not to the St Petersburg but to the Moscow school, ignorant of Russian folk-songs. After all, Beethoven had quoted some in his three Rasoumovsky quartets in 1806. Russia then was not like England in being ignorant of its own folk-song. Rimsky-Korsakof, fired with a love of peasant songs learned from his grandmother and his uncle, published a collection in 1876. The Cecil Sharp of Russia, however, was Julius Nikolaievitch Melgunov who in 1875 and 1879 published 'Russian Songs written down directly from the singing of the people, transcribed for pianoforte with text'. He evoked a system of more accurate notation and theorized on the scalic structure of the tunes (*khorovody*) which were sung in heterophony. Melgunov (1846–93) published three treatises on folk-song 'On Russian National Music' (in the *Russian Ethnological Review*), 'A Correct Method of Writing Down the Folk Songs' and 'The Rhythm of Slavonic Folksongs'.

The nationalism of the Czech composers Smetana, Dvořák and Suk had more politics than romance behind it, the contest of Slav versus Teuton. Nevertheless, folk-song played some part in giving the distinctive Czech stamp to their music. There was controversy at the time of Smetana's maturity whether the national school should be founded on folk-song or not, and though Smetana had himself in his youth composed a concert fantasia for piano on Czech folk-songs, he was against it in principle, declaring, 'By the imitation of the melody and rhythm of our folk-songs no national style will be formed, but at the most a weak imitation of the folk-songs themselves.' The weakness, however, is not in the songs but in the imitation, and two features of folk-song pervade the music both of Smetana and of Dvořák, though the two composers were quite unlike each other. These are the pattern of phrase-lengths they employ and the sharp rhythm that arises out of it. The two national dances, polka and furiant, show how its formula of two one-bar phrases followed by one two-bar phrase to balance it (or double those values) is realized in sound. The folk music of Czechoslovakia was alive in the nineteenth century, since the country was still largely rural and non-industrial – the goose-girl of the fairy tale could still be seen herding her geese from the window of the train in the present century – so that there was no question of Smetana or Dvořák having to undertake rescue operations as Balakirev, Bartók and Vaughan Williams had to, though from the sixties some collections were published. The country which is called Czechoslovakia, however, is not musically homogeneous – nor for the matter of that is Britain or Russia – but the authorities are agreed that the river Morava divides the country ethnographically into a western and an eastern region, in which the western type are more regularly constructed, while the eastern are more wayward. An example is quoted in Grove's *Dictionary* of the same song as sung in Bohemia and as sung in Moravia [Example 23], but note it is the same song and it manifests the national feature of two-bar phrases. One other generalization about Czech folk-song which

Example 23

is relevant to its influence in the music of Smetana and Dvořák is that the modern, i.e. post-Reformation, songs are largely of dance derivation.

The differences between Czech, Moravian and Slovak are recognized by their users as different dialects of the same language, as affected on the one hand by Czech contact with German, and on the other by Slovak with Hungarian during the past, but on the creation of the Czechoslovakian state in 1919 no difficulty of communication either in speech or writing existed, so that for the foreigner there is no objection to treating the folk music as a common stock. True, in published collections folk-songs may be labelled Česká, Slovenská or Moravská but their general character and structure is basically the same. Example 23 shows the identity and the extent of the difference. In general the Czech tunes are more staid than the Slovakian – as indeed appears in Example 23. But displacement of accent is to be found in Czech folk-songs as in the Furiant folk-dance – Smetana used in *The Bartered Bride* a furiant which is note for note the first part of the song 'Sedlák' – this is a rare instance of Smetana actually employing a folk-tune [Example 24]. Indeed a good many of these Czech and Slovak songs are derived from dances, so the Slovakian tunes are liable to be more erratic with pauses, Scotch snaps, triplet insertions and

'Sedlak' - Furiant

Se - dlák, se - dlák, se - dlák ě - stě je - dnou,— se - dlák;

Se - dlák, se - dlák, se - dlák vel - kej je pán

Example 24

such stimulants, but when one actually encounters a Slovakian Czardas as in 'Tancuj' one suspects Hungarian influence. Example 25 shows another common melodic device in

Tan - cuj, tan - cuj, vy - krú - caj, vy - krú - caj,

len mi pe - cku ne - zrú - caj, ne - zrú - caj;

Example 25

Czechoslovak tunes which Dvořák often used, the repetition of the first short phrase at a different pitch to form the second phrase. Here the repetition is lower but it may be at various higher intervals – compare our English tune 'Nonesuch' (q.v. below, chapter 7, Example 68). Thus in the second subject of the first movement of the G major symphony Dvořák writes

Example 26

[Example 26] which may be compared with the folk-song 'Umrem, Umrem' [Example 27]. A similar example of the

U - mrem, u - mrem, a - le ne - viem ke - dy.

Example 27

55

transposition of a phrase to make its own counterpoise can be found in the finale of the E flat string quintet (Op. 97). These features and the fondness for two one-bar phrases in succession with which to begin a tune are enough to show that Smetana and Dvořák, and indeed Janáček who came from Brno in Moravia, were imbued with their native folk music even if they never studied it or quoted it.

Dvořák, however, is remarkable in two respects. One is that he picked up not only his own Czech folk-song but could and did absorb Serbian, Polish, Gipsy, Greek and American idioms, and the other, which is possibly a consequence of this same alchemy of his mind, is that he more nearly than any other composer reconciled the claims of folk idioms with symphonic development.

While we are in this part of the world it might be worth while to look at the old controversy of how far Haydn anticipated nationalism in his use of Croatian melody. The cat was set among the pigeons by the publication in 1878–81 of 1,628 Yugoslav folk-songs in four volumes by Ferenc Kuhač who, under the influence of the all-pervasive nationalism of the time, wanted to strike another blow in the war of Slav against Teuton by claiming Haydn as a Croatian (i.e. the country between the rivers Save and Drave and the Rumanian frontier and the Adriatic, where a Serbo-Croat language is spoken). For its date Kuhač's collection is remarkable though Bartók[2] speaks slightingly of it. The book is called *South Slavonic Popular Airs* and it contains in Volume I 400 tunes and texts (in Cyrillic type) described as *chansons d'amour modernes*, in Volume II 400 more *chansons d'amour modernes* in roman script, in Volume III 400 *chansons d'amour de la période ancienne*, of which the last fifty are dances without words and in Volume IV a mixed lot of wedding songs, *chansons à boire*, ballads and blind beggars' songs. On the strength of some quite striking resemblances between some of these folk-songs and themes used by Haydn in his symphonies and quartets Kuhač claimed Haydn as a Southern

---

[2] *Serbo-Croatian Folk Songs*. Bartók and Lord, p. 26.

Slav by blood, birth and name as well as musical ancestry. Herein he claimed too much, for the Germans in the person of Ernst Schmidt hotly repudiated the claim with plenty of genealogical evidence. But the musical evidence remains as it was formulated by W. H. Hadow in his booklet of 1897.[3] Hadow had come upon Kuhač's book in the Taylorian Library at Oxford and had been so impressed that he went out to see Kuhač and got his permission to draw on his pamphlet *Joseph Haydn and the South Slavonic Folk Songs* (*Josip Haydn i Hrvatske Norodne Popievke*). Hadow accepted Kuhač whole after a thorough examination of all the evidence and his own Haydn research for his volume in the *Oxford History of Music*. The argument cannot be accepted whole, for apart from Schmidt's researches, Haydn never thought of himself as anything but an Austrian and his name is established as good German. But attempts to overthrow the musical evidence are equally vain. Better proof than mere resemblances, strong though that is, would be to examine what one must call the behaviour of the tunes, by which is meant characteristic rhythms, or intervals, or phrase lengths. Judged by this test it is clear that Haydn had got Slavonic folk-songs in his head. Thus in the last London Symphony, No. 104 in D, the finale contains an identifiable tune 'Oj Jelena' (No. 905 in Kuhač which he says was sung in Eisenstadt and is found in Croatia and Serbia). Haydn treats it as a bagpipe tune with drone [Example 28]. But the significance is in the phrase lengths (marked in Example 28 by

Example 28

[3] Reprinted and available in *Hadow's Collected Essays*, O.U.P., 1928.

square brackets): this is the familiar 1 : 1 : 2 pattern of Slavonic folk-song, as shown for instance in Example 27. Another example not previously adduced is to be found in the cello concerto at one time attributed to Kraft. The lilting tune of the finale follows a slightly different form of the same pattern of two-bar and one-bar phrases [Example 29]. This tune sounds so

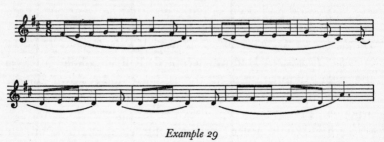

Example 29

little like Haydn that its attribution to someone else is easily understandable, especially as the themes of the two first movements show similar structures. Kuhač, it may be added, gives some example of 3–4–3-bar phrases in his Volume IV and notes that 3-bar phrases are common in Slavonic song, especially when combined with a second phrase of four bars. It is worth noting in passing that a good many of these tunes, especially if they are lively, occur in Haydn's finales. Here then we have a case where folk music has influenced a composer who, living before the cult of nationalism, had no wish to be a nationalist. We also have a case of folk-song collecting begun in that maelstrom of mixed populations in south-east Europe in the later nineteenth century. Slav *v.* Teuton is a clear issue for the ethnomusicologist.

In Hungarian folk music the ethnomusicologist has a less complicated task, though with expansions and contractions of the territory of Hungary there are some infiltrations round the frontiers. If Hungary influenced the Slovak czardas, as in Example 25 quoted above, Kodály records the spread of Czech tunes in Hungary, quoting in his book[4] a couple of examples of Hungar-

4 *Folk Music of Hungary.*

ian folk-songs derived from Czech hymns. Kodály also be-
labours the unfortunate Kuhač for claiming a Slavonic origin
for Hungarian *regös* (carols), but in general he and Bartók
took a great deal of pains to distinguish, out of their vast
experience of collecting, the stable elements in the racial whirl-
pool of south-east Europe, Slav, Teuton, Roman (Rumania),
Magyar and Turkish. Indeed 'from the outset Bartók had
been aware that without the knowledge of the music of the
neighbouring countries one could not really know Hungarian
music either', and Kodály continues 'since their collections were
next to nothing this job too devolved upon us'. The date of this
job was 1905, so that in Hungary as in England the nationalist
movement and the folk-song movement are half a century later
than the corresponding Slavonic and Scandinavian movements.
Kodály even has a chapter (*op. cit.*) on the reciprocal influence
of the Hungarians and their neighbours. If then the ethno-
musicological problems of Hungarian song are less complicated
it is because of the thorough work done by Bartók and Kodály,
who have published their findings, which are available to us in
English translations. They had one other bit of ethnological
sorting to do, to separate gypsy from true Hungarian music, a
confusion that had been given a long start by Liszt, acting with
the best will in the world, and by Brahms acting in complete
innocence. Liszt published his *The Gypsies and their Music in
Hungary* in 1859 and the rest of Europe learned what Hungarian
national music was like from Liszt's Rhapsodies, Brahms's
finales and from the songs of Ferenc Korbay, which he published in 1890. Korbay, however, repudiated gypsy origin
– 'I have not been able to hear of a single song, in any language,
of undoubted gypsy origin' – and took care to preserve in his
settings and his English translations the characteristic Hungarian rhythms, which he lists as choriambus ($-\,\cup\cup\,-$) (♪· ♩♩♪·),
antispastus ($\cup\,-\,-\,\cup$) (♩♪· ♪· ♩), and amphibrach ($\cup\,-\,\cup$)
(♩♪ ♩), though his conception of what is a folk-song would not
satisfy Kodály or us, although he is as sound as Bartók on their

origin among the peasants. Kodály, however, clears up the muddle about gypsy influence. What gypsies played – and they were often hired as minstrels at weddings and similar celebrations in town and country alike – was composed music often by upper-class amateurs – an early collector (1865) called them the 'folk-songs of the nobility' – which they then interpreted with their own gypsy style. This might include transposing them into the Near-East scale which includes two augmented seconds, which is never found in the genuine peasant song. 'They perform all music with an excess of rubato and ornaments', says Bartók, and 'their programmes, generally speaking, are adjusted to the classes for whom they happen to be catering: to the middle and upper classes they play popular art tunes or light music from western Europe, to peasants they may also play, now and then, peasant tunes.' So Brahms's finales are Hungarian but they are not made of genuine Hungarian folk-song.

It appears that there was some stirring towards national folk music in Hungary in the nineteenth century. Even Liszt at one stage, in 1838, intended to go on a collecting expedition, but the first collection dates from 1846–8, when János Erdélyi made a large collection of texts but few tunes. He managed to publish an album of twelve folk-songs with piano accompaniment or for piano alone in 1847, and there were a few more publications repeating the same couple of hundred tunes, Kodály says. But what happened in Russia and Czechoslovakia in the second half of the nineteenth century, interest in folk music and nationalism in composition, did not occur in Hungary till the first half of the twentieth century. Bartók published a selection of his songs with a good introduction and critical apparatus in an English version in 1931; Kodály in 1960 gave the full story of what he and Bartók achieved and further elaborated the special features of Hungarian song, its Asiatic origin, its classification into an old and a new style, and other points complementing Bartók's account. Bartók and Kodály then were the Hungarian equivalent of the Russian Five, leaving Dohnányi to fill the role of Tchaikovsky.

The positive features of Hungarian folk music for the ethno-musicologist, who must use the stratigraphical method of the archaeologist, are: an original pentatonism of Asiatic origin, subsequently modified to heptatonism in various modes, the rhythmic features derived from the Hungarian language which were noted by Korbay (see above) and another language-derived feature, the absence of anacrusis, which Hungarian shares with Finno-Ugric and equally characterizes Finnish folk-song; in the later new-style songs distinguished by Bartók, which may go no further back than the eighteenth century, a more regular structure, including that of the repetition of the first phrase at a distance of a fifth to constitute the second phrase (cf. 'Nonesuch') and two styles which Bartók categorized as *tempo giusto* (meaning fairly strict time) for songs perhaps derived from or borrowed for dances and *parlando rubato* for ballads, in which there is scope for *portamento*, *tenuto* and all sorts of gracing. At any rate these two Hungarian scholar-composers have left us with no problems about Hungarian music. Kodály, however, says that there is still work to be done on tracing reciprocal influences among the Carpathian and Balkan peoples.

Only one more probe is required into nineteenth-century nationalism to ascertain its connection with folk music. Scandinavia (including Finland) will serve, although it has to be noted that Tiersot (1857–1936) worked on French folk-song and published collections in the 1890s and that regional collecting in France goes back to 1862 (for Provence), and that in the Iberian peninsula, where folk-song differs from most other traditions in that some sort of accompaniment is implied, the efflorescence of Spanish composition in Albeniz, Falla and Granados was accompanied by the scholarship of Pedrell (1841–1922), at once composer and historian, who edited a *Cancioriero musical popular español*. But the date of this is 1918 and the Spanish nationalists came late in the nineteenth century and flourished in the twentieth. In the Scandinavian countries, however, perhaps under the influence of balladry, which came in with the romantic movement, folk-poetry, song and dance were cultivated much earlier. The composers who emerged with it were Kjerulf and Grieg from Norway, Berwald (perhaps) from Sweden, Sibelius, Palmgren and Kilpinen from Finland, Gade, Svensden and Nielsen from Denmark

Of these composers Grieg and Sibelius became world figures and in both discernible elements of their idiom are derived from their native folk music. In Sweden the same forces of national romanticism and the study of folk music[5] were at work, but less strongly and with no outstanding composer – Berwald was at loggerheads with the musical establishment in Sweden and is in any case a minor composer who only caught the first flush of the romantic movement (in music) but, being a descendant of a family of Swedish musicians, wrote a nationally flavoured music. Berwald's dates are 1796–1868; folk-song collecting began in 1814 and there was a group of song writers who made settings of romantic poems, which were sung by Jenny Lind. But if Sweden contributes little positive evidence to the thesis of folk music as a force in nineteenth-century composition it says nothing against it. Denmark, Norway and Finland show that the north as well as the east of Europe felt the necessity to escape from the hegemony of Germany, even if its young composers still found it necessary to go to Leipzig or Vienna for training or experience as Grieg, Sibelius, Gade, Svensden, Palmgren and Kilpinen all did.

The story is best begun with Denmark, for Svend Grundtvig, the son of the great polymath who wrote religious and secular poems for traditional tunes, made a great collection of *Danmarks gamle Folkeveiser*, which were published from 1853 onwards and established editing on a scientific principle of not 'improving' his texts but recording them as he got them. He himself collected songs in Jutland, Iceland and the Faroes. But like his contemporaries in the ballad war he was more concerned with

---

[5] This admirably comprehensive phrase is the title of a chapter in John Horton's *Scandinavian Music: A Short History* (1963), which sets out in detail what is only given here in outline.

texts than tunes, the importance of which had to await recognition for another half-century. True, in Denmark there had been collections of tunes published by C. E. F. Weyse around 1842 – this was the year before John Broadwood made his first collection of English folk-songs in the complete sense of authentic texts and tunes – but the modern study on the lines adopted in England by Cecil Sharp was the work of Evald Tang Kristensen (1843–1929), who had the help of Percy Grainger in his last collection. Kristensen published his first volume in 1871 and subsequent volumes in 1876, 1889 and 1891. Grainger, who was nothing if not scientific in his attitude to folk-song collecting, has left manuscripts of his Danish collection, in which he collaborated with Kristensen, then an old man of 85, to the British Institute of Recorded Sound and his wax cylinders to the Dansk Folkemindesamling of the Royal Library in Copenhagen.

Grundtvig is frequently mentioned by Francis James Child in his commentaries in *English and Scottish Popular Ballads*, for his task resembled Grundtvig's, who had the oldest and most copious ballad literature to conserve. Weyse's example of publishing Danish folk-melodies was followed by his pupil A. P. Berggreen in eleven volumes issued during the next thirty years. The situation was therefore ready for nationalist feelings to stir among Danish musicians. There had been Danish operas among the importations from Italy and France in the eighteenth century and the Bournonvilles, father and son, had directed the ballet. In 1841 the Royal Theatre became the home of the court orchestra, the national theatre, the ballet and the opera. The musical directors of this institution include the names of Niels Wilhelm Gade (1817–90), Johan Svensden (1840–1911) and Carl Nielsen (1865–1931). Gade's aim was to give his music a Danish tinge by grafting the idioms of folk music upon the larger forms of symphony and cantata, and he wrote the music for two acts of Bournonville's *Et Folkesagn*. But his Leipzig connections were too strong for him to carry it very far. Svensden, who was a Norwegian by birth and cosmopolitan by career, served Denmark only as conductor; his nationalism was shown in four Norwegian rhapsodies and his associations are more with Grieg. Nielsen was village-born, trained at the Copenhagen Conservatoire under Gade and became a violinist in the orchestra of the Theatre Royal, which he was later to direct, but his extraordinarily original idiom owes only its general nourishment to folk-song: 'he never ceased to regard the music of the Danish villagers as the basic nourishment of his work', says Dr Robert Simpson.[6] 'Nourishment' then is his word, as it was Gerald Finzi's of his limited ultimate debt to English folk-song. Nielsen was, however, sufficiently conscious of the connection to write some 200 songs which were deliberately simple in order that they should be current throughout the population of Denmark, not folk, in fact but popular. The picture then of the Danish situation in the nineteenth century is one of concomitance of folk and nationalist movements, not of cause or consequence.

In Norway the situation is more easily comprehensible to the foreigner and more like the Russian, Czech and Hungarian situations, in that the Norwegian flavour was easily and instantly recognized in Grieg. Nationalism was more conscious and achieved its political end in the severance from Sweden in 1905. The collection of folk music was begun about 1840 by Ludvig Mathias Lindeman. It was enthusiastically propagated by that strange character, the violinist Ole Bull (1810–80) who listened to the *slåtter* (dance airs) but was too busy as a travelling virtuoso to take up the hardanger fiddle, the peasant's instrument, but seems to have evoked the sound of it on his violin with a repertory of traditional tunes of its own. Lindeman was moved to collect folk-tunes by acquaintance with folk literature already known. Altogether he collected 1,500 tunes, many of which he arranged with piano or for choir, and being a church musician – he came to give recitals on the Albert Hall organ in 1871 – he, like a pre-incarnation of Vaughan Williams, edited the Norwegian hymnal and con-

[6] *Carl Nielsen; Symphonist*, p. 2.

tributed some sixty tunes of his own and some forty sacred parodies of folk-songs. This collection of Norwegian Mountain Melodies had a direct influence on Halfdan Kjerulf, Rikard Nordraak and Edvard Grieg. Nordraak was with Grieg in Berlin[7] when they were students and fired Grieg with enough nationalism to save him from succumbing to the powerful influence of Leipzig. Kjerulf's (1815–68) nationalism was fed by his growing interest in Norwegian folk-songs after the publication of Lindeman's first volume in 1853 and by his enthusiasm, which he shared with Nordraak, for the poetic and dramatic works of Bjornson. Grieg's songs and his 'Lyric Pieces' for piano owe something to Kjerulf's influence.

What then are the distinctive elements of Norwegian folksong that appear in Grieg and his fellow Norwegians? Modality, as elsewhere in Europe, which was submerged by major-minor tonality (i.e. the two surviving modes, Ionian and Aeolian) in professional composition but survived in folk music. Modality included the Lydian mode with its augmented fourth; the use of pedal points was suggested by the hardanger fiddle, the falling seventh, which became a Grieg fingerprint in cadences of a downward progression of upper tonic, seventh to dominant, and an alternation of duplets and triplets, as in the 'Spring Pols', of which the second section is quoted in Example 30.

Example 30

In Sweden the pattern of romantic nationalism and its affiliation with native folk music is a variation on our main theme and inasmuch as no composer of international rank has come out of Sweden, the argument from it, while conforming with the trend of the nineteenth century, is less potent. Sweden

[7] The latest book on Grieg, by Dag Schjelderup-Ebbe (1960), examines the evidence that Grieg had some feelings of guilt at his neglect of his friend during the illness that killed him while still a young man of 24 in 1866.

has its folk music, peasant music, yodelling for animals in the mountains, ballads accompanied by dancing and incorporating refrains and a later infusion of French dance tunes which percolated from town and capital to country. The French influence was the work of King Gustav III, whom we all know as the victim in Verdi's *The Masked Ball*,[8] and it had the paradoxical effect of establishing a national musical life for Sweden. The king built the opera house in Stockholm and the famous little one at Drottingholm and went on to establish in 1771 a Royal Academy of Music which became the Stockholm Conservatoire. A German arrival, Johan Gottliebe Naumann, produced some Swedish operas, of which *Gustaf Vasa* (1786) was on a Swedish subject. The symphonic composer Franz Berwald (1796–1868) had, in spite of cosmopolitan influences, an original tone of voice and he wrote Swedish opera, but his nationalism, such as it was and not appreciated by the Swedes themselves, owes nothing to folk music. It was, however, during his lifetime that the second wave of investigation of Sweden's folk heritage began – the first was two centuries earlier when Sweden was a great power and became conscious of its past and so set antiquaries to examine its tunes and songs. As with the interest in ballads in England, Denmark and Germany, the melodies tended to be neglected but in the eighteen-forties this defect was made good and collections, especially of *latår* (dance tunes), were begun by scholars, the ultimate issue of which was the publication of twenty-four volumes of them in the present century. Some composers, Hugo Alfen (b. 1872), Kurt Atterburg (b. 1887) and Oskar Lindberg (b. 1887) took some colour from their native folk music. Enough in fact to provoke a reaction in the present century, when Wilhelm Stenhammar (1871–1927) aimed rather at fertilizing his own and Swedish music in general with modern European influences, a movement that found full expression in the eclecticism of Karl Birger Blomdahl (b. 1916) which Europe encountered in his space opera, *Aniara*.

[8] At the performance of this opera at the Edinburgh Festival of 1959 by the Royal Swedish Opera a very Gallic twist was given to the production.

In Finland nationalism, all the more urgent from a tinge of ethnic feeling in the struggle for political independence, was manifested in all the arts during the nineteenth century. The composition of the national epic *Kalevala*, which was, like the *Iliad*, a conflation of legends on their national heroes in fifty runes or cantos. These legends were collected from oral tradition among the local singers who beguiled the long Northern nights with them and they were published in 1835 by Elias Lönnrot (1802–84). Their metre is familiar to the English-speaking world in that it was employed by Longfellow for *Hiawatha*. This metre finds its way into folk-tunes by way of the prevalence of two-bar phrases ending in long notes and the feature of even note-values which Bartók called in the context of Hungarian folk music *tempo giusto*. Example 31 is one of these *runosävelmä* from the *Kalevala* and its five-pulse rhythm is characteristic of the older level of Finnish folk-song.

Example 31

The eighties of last century witnessed the beginning of the struggle for national independence in musical as well as political life. The struggle was, like the similar struggle in England, directed against German predominance and yet was carried out with the help of Germans: the same may be said of Swedish influence except that neither the pro nor the contra was so powerful, since the Swedish element in Finland's population was integral with Finland as a nation. The Conservatoire was established at Helsinki by Wegelius (1846–1906) and the Philharmonic Orchestra by Kajanus (1856–1933) both in 1882. Folk-song collecting began in this decade too. The leading folk-song authority was Ilmari Krohn, who died as recently as 1960, who made a collection of some 7,000 songs between 1898 and 1933. Altogether 20,000 tunes are said to be available in either print or record. The basic characteristics of the Finno-Finnish, as distinct from the Swedo-Finnish, folk-songs are principally due to the language, which is a branch of the Uralian group. Outside Finland itself a Finno-Ugric language is spoken in Estonia and by a trans-Ural people living by the river Ob in Siberia as well as scattered communities in Russia. Finnish therefore, like Hungarian, to which it is related, is an Asiatic, non-Ayrian language, and it is hard to resist the conclusion that there is an ethnological core to the characteristics which under the pressures of the nineteenth century appeared as nationalism, even allowing for geography, religion and social organization as determinants of the modern nation state.[9] The Finns of Finland have lived in Europe for centuries squeezed by Sweden and Russia, but as the pressures of these two powers were not exercised simultaneously the nut-cracker failed to crack the nut and Finland secured its independence in 1918.

The conscious nationalism of the nineteenth century produced a composer of international status in Sibelius, who must be classed as a nationalist in spite of the denial by Cecil Gray, who wrote the first English study of the composer's music in 1931. It can indeed be argued, though never proved, that the long silence after the composition of *Tapiola* in 1925 was due to the weakening of nationalism as a source of inspiration after the attainment of independence and the emergence of some dissensions due to language, Finland still being bilingual, and internal politics. (Of course Sibelius may have felt that by then he had already said all he had to say, or like Elgar did not

[9] See my *Man, Mind and Music* for the argument.

68

altogether care for the way modern music was going, but his silence is mysterious and his previous productivity had certainly had a patriotic root.) Gray denied that there was any element of folk music in Sibelius's art worth attention, but his music is in fact pervaded by some positive characteristics of Finnish folk-song, notably absence of anacrusis, a predilection for repeated notes (as conspicuously in the oboe tune of the trio section of the Scherzo of the second symphony and in *Valse Triste*) and even time values (Bartók's *tempo giusto*). No doubt another element derived from Swedish and possibly German sources was added to the *runo* singing to produce such a song as 'Summer Evening', which is not only quoted in Grove's *Dictionary* (article Folk Song) but is to be found in both Palmgren's and Hannikainen's selections with piano accompaniments and may therefore be taken to be one of the best known [Example 32].

Ol' kau-nis ke-sä - il - ta, kun - laak-so-sa kä - ve - lin

Siell' koh - ta-sin mä ty - tön, jot' ai - na muis-te - len

Example 32

This has none of the Finno-Ugric characteristics except the simple structure and two-bar phrase lengths. Sibelius was more Swedo-Finn than Finno-Finn, and in any case the sheerly geographical quality of his music, evocative of the northern landscape in which he dwelt, was more manifest than his nationalism until the tone-poem *Finlandia*, with its political undertones,[10] declared otherwise, and subsequent analysis has shown the roots of his music in Finnish folk music. Palmgren (1878–1951) is a lesser figure, a Finnish Grieg perhaps. Kilpinen (1883–1959) was a great song-writer and in his output of more

[10] It used to be said that it was banned by the Russians.

than 600 songs he followed, according to Horton,[11] more than one tradition, the German *lied*, the Swedish strophic song and in the Finnish songs the line that ran from the *runo*. Indeed a Finnish critic[12] writes that he was equally at home with Finnish, Swedish and German texts, that he corrected any translations of alternative texts in the three languages himself, but that the nordic and archaic atmosphere was due not only to use of traditional harmony but to his preference for diatonic to chromatic writing, to his use of pentatonism and the ecclesiastical modes and to an avoidance of thirds in his harmony. Plainly there was a strong German element in his work, but equally he was a Finnish composer, who like Sibelius avoided the cleavage between Swede and Finn in his nation. Jarnfelt (1869–1958) was another Finn known abroad though he became a Swedish subject. Tanno Karila[13] gives brief biographies of no less than seventy composers with lists of their works who are not well known outside Finland, but are indicative of the vigorous musical life of a small nation, which has indeed made its mark on the world largely by its music.

These then were the principal nationalist movements in Europe which, under the influence of romanticism, stimulated research into each country's past and aroused pride, scientific interest and aesthetic pleasure in its traditional music and at the same time somehow produced a revitalized art music. Cause and effect changed places between the two, folk music and art music, but they were inter-connected. Nationalism is now no longer so powerful, probably because it is no longer historically necessary. But it persisted as a fructifying force into the present century, where its operations are to be seen in Bartók, Kodály, Janáček, Vaughan Williams and Khachaturian.

[11] *Scandinavian Music, op. cit.*, p. 151.
[12] Einari Marvia in the catalogue of Kilpinen's works (Helsinki, 1960).
[13] In a booklet issued in English by the Association of Finnish Composers.

CHAPTER FOUR

National Idioms and Instruments

National Idioms

In tracing the history of folk-musical scholarship in various countries of Europe in the last chapter, some of the national characteristics were noted in passing, such as the rhythmic features of Hungarian tunes, and some, such as the phrase structure of southern Slavonic tunes, were actually illustrated. These features of interval, mode, phrase-length, form and behaviour produce so rich a variety of musical effect and national flavour that it may be worth setting them out on a panorama of Europe. It is not, it could not be, claimed that these samples provide formulae of scientific or statistical validity for every nation in Europe. Not every nation will be represented in this brief concourse and every nation has plenty of tunes that do not show these features, but if using the comparative method one can account in musical terms for the impression one gets of national differences at an international festival it is worth a little technical analysis, whether or not it casts any psychological light on differences of national temperament. Such national differences would afford but a risky guide to political behaviour but they add riches to European life, for, as someone once said, it is better for all to be different and at amity than all alike and at enmity. And cosmopolitanism tends to be colourless. Another though similar (and equally superficial) examination of folk instruments may lead to the opposite conclusion that all Europe is one if it is compared with Africa with its drums, Asia with its partiality for strings and Indonesia with its gamelan. So let us take a quick survey of tunes and instruments. I scratched the surface of this anthropological approach to folk-song in a former book[1] and shall take the liberty of quoting some of the examples again and adding a few new ones.

Enough was said about the irregular patterns of phrase lengths as a characteristic feature of south Slavonic folk-song to save the necessity of quoting further examples. But no instance was given of the features which Finnish and Hungarian share as members of the Finno-Ugric group of languages: these were the absence of anacruses and what Bartók called *tempo giusto*, the repetition of notes of the same time value and often of pitch. This Hungarian tune collected by Bartók, which has several other Hungarian characteristics [Example 33] may be com-

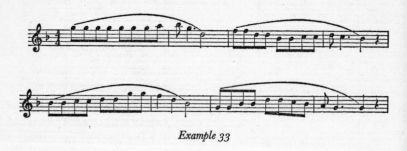

Example 33

pared for behaviour with this Finnish tune collected by Ilmari Krohn [Example 34]. The Hungarian tune exhibits the Scotch

Example 34

snap, isometric two-bar phrases, and pentatonism modified only by the passing supertonic of the last bar, all of them

[1] *Men, Mind and Music.*

features remarked by both Bartók and Kodály. The Finnish
tune is heptatonic but circular, as the accidentals and the repeat
mark show. Instances could be multiplied. Example 35 shows
not only the Scotch snap and isometric structure of Hungarian
song but the upward transposition of the first phrase to provide
the second balancing phrase.

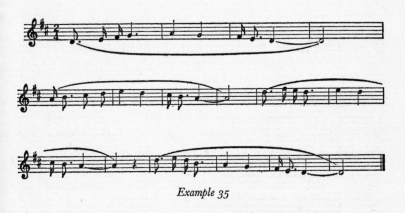

Example 35

Russian folk-song is a large subject full no doubt of differences of dialect between Ukraine and Georgia, Novgorod and
the Urals, but a Russianness familiar to most Western Europ-
eans is the use of the intervals of the falling fourth and falling
fifth at cadences and in the skeleton of the melody. The 'Volga
Boat Song' owes its character to the falling fourth, and so does
this almost equally familiar snatch of song [Example 36].

Example 36

A fine tune from Melgunov's collection shows the same feature
of cadential and built-in fourths, the Phrygian effect of the
'Volga Boat Song' being reproduced in the flat second of the

73

from Melgunov

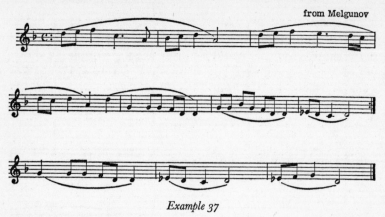

Example 37

cadence in the second part of the tune [Example 37]. For good measure two from Rimsky-Korsakof's collection may be quoted [Examples 38 and 39]: in Example 38 a falling fifth absorbs the fourth and in Example 39 rises as well as falls.

Over Fields and Over Meadows

Russian from Rimsky-Korsakov

Example 38

The Old Pear Tree

Example 39

Cadence alone may impart a national flavour as in Portuguese song, which loves to insert a triplet on the penultimate note. Hardly more than an ornament perhaps, yet very persistent and pervasive. Example 40 shows it at its simplest; Example 41 has other ornaments and obviously comes from a singer who is accustomed to gracing his songs. Example 42 is in the Phrygian mode like the Russian.

Example 40

Example 41

Our most easterly excursion on this tour of Europe is to Turkey. Its contribution is rather like the Finnish and Hungarian,

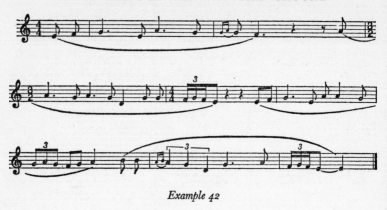

Example 42

to which languages Turkish is allied, in that its curious
rhythm must be derived from speech, in this case probably a
verse form. The nine-eight time signature does not indicate
compound time, but a simple time of four and a half to the bar,
as appears in Example 43, which is broken down in Example 44
into an alternating four-five pulse. This division also occurs in
Example 45, which is taken from an anthology edited by
Granville Bantock, who made himself into an Orientalist.
This tune also shows the Near Eastern feature of the interval
of the augmented second, which is found as far west as Yugoslavia, a relic probably of Turkish rule [Examples 43, 44, 45].

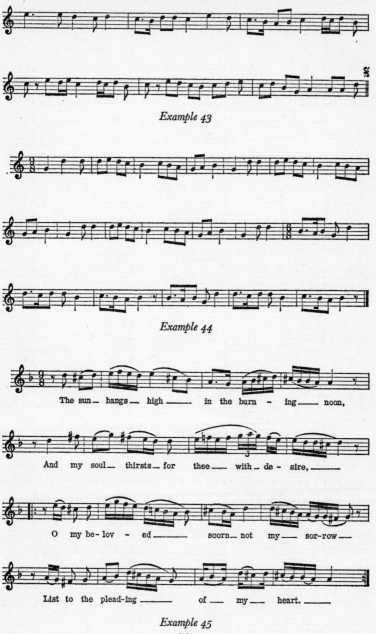

Example 43

Example 44

The sun— hangs— high —— in the burn - ing —— noon,

And my soul— thirsts— for thee—— with— de - sire, ——

O my be- lov - ed—— scorn— not my—— sor-row—

List to the plead-ing —— of — my — heart. ——

Example 45

77

A rhythmic feature noticeable in the fiddle tunes used for accompanying the Norwegian folk-dances, *Springleiker*, is the frequent introduction of triplets into bars of simple three-four time which diversify the other subvidivisions into even and dotted duplet quavers. One example, 30, has already been quoted. Example 46 is another such tune from eastern Norway, where the Hardanger fiddle is less used than in the western districts but where Dr O. M. Sandvik found plenty of players on the ordinary violin with their heads full of traditional tunes still (i.e. between 1911 and 1948).

Example 46

It is thought by so learned an expert as Dr Walter Wiora that this kind of comparative study has gone far enough and he suggests that after so much nationalism internationalism should have an innings. So he collects together in his anthology,[2] as remarked on p. 22, a number of tunes tabulated with their variants from different countries and so shown to belong to the same families. It is an impressive demonstration in support of his argument, but it does not lessen the interest of national traits appearing in national song and dance. Indeed, it provides

[2] *European Folk Song*, Arno Volk Verlag, Cologne, 1967.

further examples of the operation of whatever basic (and maybe) biological act of choice is at the bottom of these marked national preferences, as it is of national costume. Similar preferences for the instruments used by various peoples are worth a glance.

Folk Instruments

No branch of ethnomusicology has been so well studied as organology, as we must call the lore of musical instruments. Primitive sound producers such as the musical bow were observed by unmusical anthropologists; museums have been filled with specimens of idiophones, membranophones, aerophones and chordophones from the ends of the earth; interest has been fostered in Britain by the foundation of the Galpin Society, and several excellent books furnished with copious pictures have appeared since the Second War; Jaap Kunst, the Dutch pioneer in ethnomusicology, based his collection at Amsterdam on the gamelan orchestras of Indonesia; American authors have produced dictionaries of their names, and altogether there is no lack of authoritative information to be had by anyone who wants it. There is no intention therefore to skim over the surface here of what is easily available in depth elsewhere, but not all folk music is vocal and, while it is unlikely that any pattern of distribution will emerge from it, some sort of survey is required, more particularly into folk instruments.

Kodály distinguishes between home-made and manufactured instruments, 'Art-music may be played on home-made instruments', he says (questionably) 'just as folk music can be played on manufactured instruments' (undeniably). The violin, so perfect an instrument as to have undergone hardly any evolution since it was invented, is used by peasants as accompaniment for dancing in many parts of Europe. The Cobla, the dance band of Catalonia contains besides pipes which are folk, a cornet and a double bass which are not. The cornet and clarinet are used by Hungarian gypsies who use no folk instruments, unless the cimbalon, a Hungarian national instrument, is included in that category. Instruments that are used in the orchestra, in the military band and in the brass band, though often borrowed to accompany dancing, need no attention. On the other hand manufactured instruments that are popular but have no currency in polite music, like the accordion and harmonica (mouth-organ) have been adopted for folk-dancing, and clarinet and saxophone have become regular constituents of jazz bands. The guitar observes no snobbish distinctions but is used in classical, popular and folk music. It has become the instrument *par excellence* for accompanying folk-song, the reasons being the frets which secure good intonation, its portability and its strummability. Strumming is not accounted a virtuous exercise by music critics, but it has its uses; it is informal, it can be done by the singer and is quasi-improvisatory, from which it follows that it is essentially simple and not likely to lead to an over-elaboration unsuitable to a folk-song. The guitar has in a matter of thirty years superseded the piano as the folk-singer's accompaniment.

It can hardly be described as a folk instrument, though, still less as home-made, since it has a long history and requires fine craftsmanship for its construction. Even the modern electric guitar, though no doubt vulgar, is too technically elaborate to be called folk. The name is thought to be derived from the Greek *kithara* (κιθάρα) so that the guitar has a longer European history than its cousin, the lute, which was an import from the Arab world in the thirteenth century. They differ in the shape of their backs, the guitar's being flat and the lute's pear-shaped. Oddly enough, however, both instruments have flourished side by side in Spain, where the Moors were responsible for introducing the oriental lute, and the guitar has had an aristocratic tradition and a classical repertory as well as a popular tradition of music of the streets. The Spaniards and Portuguese have carried the guitar to South America, where it modifies the conception of folk-song as pure monody. In the sixteenth century an English guitar, the cittern, was popular, as proved by its fame as a barber's shop instrument for beguiling the time of waiting clients, whereas the lute was to achieve an aristo-cratic blaze of glory in the lutenist ayres of Campian and Dowland before its decline in mid-seventeenth century. More-over, besides the cittern was the gittern which, in spite of apparent probability, belonged (according to Galpin) to a different family and had a different etymology for its name, though both employed the same sort of technique. But there is the evidence of Thomas Wythorne, the first of the English madrigal composers and the first English autobiographer (1528–96), that they are different instruments, technically differentiated at least by the fact that one, the gittern, was strung with gut strings and played with a plectrum and the other, the cittern, was strung with wire and usually played with the fingers. Wythorne's words are that he went to dancing and fencing classes 'and also learned to play on the Gittern and Sittern, which two instruments were then strange in England and therefore the more desired and esteemed'. So there thus began a game protracted over the centuries of hide-and-seek between the guitar and its companions of the plucked string group, whereas in Spain, as just noted, the guitar maintained its place both as a classical and as a popular instrument – it is an essential ingredient in *flamenco*.

The present position in Britain resembles that of Spain in that, though far less extensively used, it has gained an esteem previously held only by the lute and has recovered for popular use the favour which had over the centuries passed from the cittern to the mandolin and banjo. The up-grading of the guitar as a concert instrument followed the recitals of Andrés Segovia in the twenties and has led to its cultivation by such virtuosi as Mr Julian Bream and Mr John Williams. Twenty years later it established itself in popular favour as the folk singer's instrument, kindled in some degree by the appearances in Britain of the American singer, Burl Ives, who accompanies his folk-songs on it.

But the guitar is not a national instrument, however strong its present association with the Iberian peninsula and so of

Latin America. It came into Greece thousands of years ago across the Aegean from Asia Minor and spread across Europe, modifying its shape, stringing and technique as it made its way through Italy and France to Spain. In Russia a collateral of triangular shape with three strings is the popular balalaika. Modern changes initiated in America have been an enlargement to twelve strings and electric amplification which has altered the shape of the ordinary guitar, and in Hawaii laid it on its back so that it is played as though it was a zither – this is the so-called steel guitar, because the notes are stopped by a sliding bit of steel instead of the fingers, which imparts its distinctive glissando.

The guitar is not unknown in Germany, Austria or Italy, but Austria's more characteristic folk instrument of the plucked string catetory is the zither and Italy's the mandolin which, however, being treated as a melodic instrument, could be accompanied by a guitar. The mandolin is a product of Naples derived from the mandore family, indeed it is described by Anthony Baines as 'compounded from every kind of fretted instrument, Oriental or Western, known in eighteenth-century Naples'. Its twin strings per note are played with a plectrum. The banjo's associations are with negro America, true folk instrument also of the eighteenth century – even earlier in Jamaica – of which the structural features are its circular body and vellum belly. Its inclusion in jazz bands has developed it in various ways, such as an increased number of strings and the use of a plectrum for playing it. While the guitar has had concertos with symphony orchestras composed for it and the mandolin is prescribed in the score of *Don Giovanni*, the banjo remains strictly proletarian.

Another type of plucked string instrument which at different times and in different places developed various shapes and stringing is what may be generically called a zither, which has a flat sound-box without a neck. It started as the psaltery, which came from Asia about the tenth century AD. Most of its derivatives are played flat on the knees or a table and may be plucked with plectra or hit with sticks, in which case they are called dulcimers or in Eastern Europe *cimbal*. A simple form, what Mr Baines calls a farm-house instrument, is the Alpine zither found in South Germany and Switzerland. In Russia it is the *gusli* which is used for the accompaniment of singing and in Finland it is a *kantele*. The Indian *vina* and the Japanese *koto* belong to the same genus, though of unlike appearance and sound quality. Its diffusion therefore is such that its only national significance is the particular form adopted in any particular country. In Hungary, for instance, it has been developed into an orchestral instrument, the cimbalom, whereas on the other hand a primitive form of it, the mountain dulcimer, is still used in the Cumberland Mountains of Kentucky as a folk instrument. This has only three strings, of which two are drones, and it was introduced to Europe by Jean Ritchie at an Albert Hall Festival of the English Folk Dance and Song Society on the radio and on record in the early fifties. By and large therefore in Europe and America the polymorphous zither can be classed as a true folk instrument.

In the opposite classification is the violin, which is universally used outside Asia and Africa as an accompaniment to folk-dancing. It has, however, a less sophisticated cousin in western Norway, the Hardanger fiddle, a member of the viol clan (and therefore fretted and bowed) which has four sympathetic strings and can claim to be a folk instrument, in that, as already stated, Ole Bull (1810–80), the Norwegian violinist, imitated it, though he never took the trouble to learn to play it, in his recitals, in which he specialized in national music of his own composition and extemporization. It is played still for the accompaniment of the *Halling*, the dance with the leap, though Sandvik says 'it is now becoming rare' (1967).

Another instrument of the bowed string type still in use as a folk-dance accompanist is the hurdy-gurdy, which was seen and heard in the Albert Hall in February 1968. This *vielle*, to give it its French name, was brought by dancers from the Loire region of France. It is played not with a bow but with a resined wheel turned by a handle and stopped by a finger box on which keys are mounted. It goes back a long way in European history and had a wide distribution, came down in the world as the instrument for beggars and street musicians, but it is now very much a French folk instrument, though occasionally to be found in Rumania and Hungary also.

The most primitive and universal of the chordophones is the harp, of which the musical bow is the prototype and the modern Erard concert harp with a compass of six octaves the furthest development. It has been in use since antiquity and therefore has a long history and because of its diffusion shows in spite of its basic simplicity – three pieces of wood and some strings – a good many variations in size, construction, compass and the availability of semi-tones. It has, however, a special place in folk music studies because of the tradition, still alive, of harping in the Celtic fringe of the British Isles. The Gaelic language, in its Scottish, Irish and Welsh dialects alike, demands a harp to match its peculiar lyricism and we have here a case of a preference, neither strictly speaking national nor regional, but perhaps ethnic. In Scotland the harp, i.e. *clarsach*, lost its status as a national instrument to the bagpipes and only two specimens survive,[3] so that its revival at the end of the nineteenth century had to be by means of conscious reconstructions, and in the twentieth Miss Patuffa Kennedy Fraser got the firm of Morley in London to make her one based on an Irish design. In Ireland on the other hand the tradition was strong and continuous and its effect on the collection of Irish folk-song is described below in Chapter 9. One feature of the Irish harp, which was even more a solo than an accompanying instrument, is that its strings were of brass and the traditional way of activating them was by long finger-nails, but something smaller and portable with gut strings was needed and provided by the Dublin maker, John Egan, about 1820. This type of *clarsach* is the Gaelic harp used by Celtic folk-musicians nowadays.

[3] Collinson, *The Traditional and National Music of Scotland*, p. 234.

Not, however, in Wales, where an excess of puritan non-conformity diverted the energies of the Welsh from harp playing to hymn singing, but the encouragement of *penillion*[4] singing by the Eisteddfodau revived the native form of the harp, though it changed the object of its affection to the big modern concert harp. In this small corner of the world the orchestral concert harp is thus a folk instrument.

Pipes of course are universal and are of three types, whistles, horns and reeds. Reeds are single, double, free and beating. They have been and are used by folk-musicians in innumerable shapes and forms, pitches and timbres, and since they are innumerable no attempt will be made to catalogue or describe them here, for the details of their range and construction, which is what an organologist wants to know about them, have been chronicled in many easily accessible publications. The woodwind and brass choruses of the modern symphony orchestra represent their highest development and, except perhaps the clarinet, lie right outside the province of folk music. But some of their less developed, keyless predecessors are still played by peasants. Thus shawms, the oboe's predecessors, are made in many sizes and pitches in Turkey; a huge flute of recorder type that reaches from the mouth to below the knees is mentioned (and pictured) by Kodály. Odd mixtures like the ocarina (a globular flute) and the hornpipe or pibcorn, in which a single reed is at one end and a cow-horn at the other of a six-holed pipe, were used in Mexico and Wales respectively. The variety is endless. But two types stand out in their wide distribution, the bagpipe and the flageolet of various kinds associated with a small drum. The English whittle and dub, i.e. pipe and tabor used by Morris dancers, is a very simple affair with three holes, playable by one hand; it has its equivalents in Provence, the *gaboulet*, and in the Basque country, the *txistu*, which are one-man bands. Larger pipes with more holes with a second player to manage the drum are an extension of the same tonal-rhythmic dance-band.

[4] See Chapter 9, p. 251.

85

We are familiar in Britain with two main types of bagpipes, the Highland large bagpipe which is mouth-blown and the Northumbrian small-pipe[5] which is blown by bellows operated by the right arm – the function of the bag is to provide an air reservoir to regulate the wind pressure. The number of drones has varied at different periods but is now customarily three; a double reed is mounted in a pipe called the chanter. The Irish pipe, called union or *uilleann*, is a more elaborate instrument of greater compass capable of some harmony and detached notes by stopping the end against the knee. There are according to Mr Baines, who calls it 'this most variable of wind instruments', four species of bagpipe differentiated according to their bore and reed – thus in Bohemia and Poland a single reed is used in the chanter – and at least nine kinds are still being played in Europe.

Folk music does not confine itself to the obsolete; indeed it would not be folk music if it was not always up to date as well as traditional. So now all over Europe and America the accordion in one of its forms has become the commonest instrument for the accompaniment of folk-dancing. That it has a coarse and vulgar tone does not greatly matter, since for more than half its time it will be heard out of doors and for the other half will need to assert itself against the natural din of dancers. Its bellows allow it to shape its phrasing firmly and to mark the rhythm with a squeeze. It was invented as long ago as 1822 by a German and has been increasing the number of its press-buttons, its melody and bass keys ever since, till it acquired a fractional-sized piano keyboard. It is a free-reed instrument easily portable and capable of harmonic accompaniment to its own melody. Before it achieved its modern popularity it had a predecessor, also employing free reeds, in the concertina, which was an English invention (by Charles Wheatstone) of the same period. It is a more refined instrument and had some vogue in the polite music of the miscellaneous concert or musical evening – I

[5] For further information about the Northumbrian small-pipe, see below page 176, Chapter 7.

remember accompanying solos on it on the piano when I was a boy, but it never raised itself to the class of chamber or serious music – what wonderful terminology our class-conscious art employs! The harmonica, which used to be called a mouth-organ till it rose sufficiently high socially to be played by a virtuoso like Larry Adler and have a concerto written for it by Vaughan Williams, is generically the same as the concertina, i.e. free reeds operated by puff and suck, but is a wonderfully compact six inches, and it too is a godsend to a tap-dancer or small ensemble for folk-dancing. It came from the same inventors as made accordion and concertina and the German firm of Hohner, according to Mrs Lilla Fox,[6] sold thirty-six million harmonicas in the single year 1930.

Drums are the chief but not the only instruments of per-cussion to be used by folk-musicians in the accompaniment of dances, where their value is obvious. They are of various sizes and are struck by various kinds of beater; some have two heads and some have snares and some do not. They are not tunable like the timpani of the orchestra. The tabor used with the pipe mentioned above is a simple drum of great antiquity which has persisted in the English folk tradition. It is two-headed and may have a snare and is played with a single stick. The tambourine of about the same size has only one head and is fitted with jingles but has no snares and is played with the bare hands. It too has a long but slightly more exotic history in that it came over from the Near East into Europe a second time with the janissaries or Turkish music that became fashionable in the eighteenth century. But for drums, as for tuned percussion like the xylo-phone, one must go to Africa or Indonesia to find more complex usages and more highly developed folk art. Idiophones, that is noise emitters from their own substance, Bottom's tongs and bones, the triangle used with eerie effect in the Abbots Bromley Horn Dance, were reinforced with domestic objects during the skiffle craze of the fifties and can be so invoked anywhere at any time, as petrol tins have been in the steel orchestras of Trinidad.

[6] *Instruments of Popular Music*, 1966.

It is fairly clear from this quick look at European folk instruments that their distribution does not proceed on national lines as the songs and dances do. The shape of the songs would seem to be at any rate in part determined by language, the dances rather more directly by national character, as witness the mazurka, the polka, the czardas, the saltarello, the hora, the fandango, the morris. But instruments being based on a limited number of ways of provoking sound – though Heaven knows the permutations and combinations produce variety enough in detail! – seem to go either by continents or regions. Flutes, drums and bagpipes are pan-European but differ by region; the Celtic harp belongs to West, not to Great, Britain, the Hardanger fiddle to west not east Norway. Perhaps someone will work out the anthropological significance of these facts – if they have any – but facts of folk music they are.

CHAPTER FIVE

History of the English Revival

We have looked at the folk music of Europe, but how did matters stand in Great Britain? Although folk-song collections were made in Scotland and Ireland in the eighteenth century, there was no nationalism in English musical life till the end of the nineteenth century. When the Prince of Wales summoned the meeting at St James's Palace in 1882 to launch his scheme for the foundation of a new national conservatoire, a scheme out of which the Royal College of Music was to come, he asked 'Why is it that England has no music recognized as national? (in comparison with Germany, France and Italy which he had just named). It has able composers but nothing indicative of national life or national feeling.' Francis Hueffer, music critic of *The Times* from 1878 to 1889, observed that in spite of an array of talent, Carl Rosa's operatic efforts, Barnby, Cowen 'whose Welsh and Scandinavian symphonies are as good as any by any living master' (Brahms was still alive!), and Sullivan (whose addiction to operetta he deplored), 'a genius in the proper sense of that much abused word . . . has not yet made his appearance . . . [and] in secular music at least we have not a distinctively national type of art.' Indeed, the lack of a national style was recognized by most commentators on the Victorian scene, even though the country at large was content to go on living on Handel and Mendelssohn and Mendelssohn's epigones, who were numerous and of whom Sterndale Bennett might have founded an English school had his talent not been Mendelssohnized at Leipzig and crushed to pulp by the working conditions of English musical life. The English musical renaissance did not begin till 1880 when Hubert Parry broke on the scene.[1] In the 1890s the relevance of English folk-song was realized by the publication of *English County Songs* edited by Lucy Broadwood and J. A. Fuller Maitland in 1893 and the foundation in 1898 of the Folk Song Society. England's delay, however, was not all loss, since the ethics of collecting, editing and preserving the materials of oral tradition were not realized all at once and some considerable outrages were perpetrated by Scottish and Irish editors.

There may have been more politics than romance in the Scottish literary movement arising out of the exile of the House of Stuart and the absence of a court from the Scottish capital. However it came about, polite society in Edinburgh began fairly early in the eighteenth century to take an interest in Scottish vernacular poetry, both lyrics and ballads. The movement was primarily literary, just as the interest in the great ballads awakened in Bishop Percy (1729–1811) a little later was literary and so continued right on to Francis James Child, so that it is only in the present century that it has been possible to impress upon editors not only that the tune is as important as the text, but also that the two are integrally related. It was common form to print the texts without the tunes, a few of which might be found in an appendix. Scottish editors and collectors, however, sometimes erred in the other direction by keeping the tunes and getting new verses written to them. Burns was an offender but may be forgiven for the sheer quality of the lyrics he produced on the basis of the traditional songs he swallowed.

The first of these editors to make Scottish popular song available in print was Allan Ramsay (1686–1758) who published his *Tea-Table Miscellany: A Collection of Choice Songs Scots and English* serially from 1724. This compilation contained poems by Ramsay himself, his friends and Caroline poets as

[1] See my *English Musical Renaissance*, 1966.

well as some traditional songs and ballads, e.g. 'Barbara Allen'. The poems were designed to be sung and the names of the tunes were designated but there was no music. A separate volume of music only, however, *Music for Allan Ramsay's Collection of Scots Songs*, was published very soon after the first numbers of the *Tea-Table*, and in London in 1725 *Orpheus Caledonius* appeared, the first printed song-book with words and music lawfully united. Johnson's *Scottish Musical Museum*, also a serial publication, was issued in six volumes between 1787 and 1803, which contained new poems written to pre-existing tunes, including poems by Burns. Johnson was a music engraver and was not therefore likely to overlook the claims of the airs. Sir Walter Scott, whose interest was mainly in the narrative ballads of his own Border country, included some of the tunes in his 1833 edition – the original was 1802–3 – but doubt was thrown subsequently on their antiquity. Scott in his Introduction speaks of Allan Ramsay's 'unhappy plan of writing new words to old tunes without at the same time preserving the ancient verses'. Thus do editorial consciences grow more tender! Scott was followed by Motherwell with his *Minstrelsey*[2] and Kinloch with his *Scottish Ballads* in 1827, both of whom printed tunes in appendices. Finally came William Christie's *Traditional Ballad Airs*, a folk-song collection in the modern sense, made in 1876 and 1881, not long before the English pioneers began their field work. Even Christie and his son were criticized by later workers in the same territory, viz. north-east Scotland, in that they touched up the music and sometimes developed and extended the melodies in order to popularize them by assimilating them to art songs.[3] Ramsay doctored

---

[2] In his introduction Motherwell surveys his predecessors in the field and lists no less than thirty-two altogether, going back to Chapman and Myllar in 1508 and taking in the Wedderburns' sacred parodies, *Ane compendious Booke of Godlie and Spirituall Sangis* of 1567, of which he hotly disapproves.

[3] See *Last Leaves of Traditional Ballads* by Gavin Greig, p. xliii: 'They conceived it to be necessary to arrange the music they had gathered and to develop the melodies into second strains which they had not found current among the people.'

the words to make the songs polite, Christie doctored the tunes to commend them to middle-class amateurs. The English collectors profited by the well-intentioned errors of their Scottish (and Irish) predecessors and knew better than to tamper with either tune or words; especially did they realize the sacrosanctity of the tunes and abstained from altering their modes so as to facilitate their harmonization in the ordinary major and minor modes. Some of them, notably Lucy Broadwood, began to collect Gaelic airs in the Highlands and Islands, though the work of the Kennedy Frasers is better known in connexion with Hebridean folk-song. Frances Tolmie of Skye, who contributed over a hundred airs from the Western Islands to the *Journal of the Folk-Song Society* in 1911, is the true pioneer of the native music of the Hebrides.

The history of the collection of Irish folk tunes follows very similar lines, and editorial scrupulousness was not achieved till the experience of English collectors had been thoroughly assimilated. Stanford's treatment of the Petrie collection was not altogether blameless, but Herbert Hughes who, unlike Stanford, was a collector, at last brought modern standards of editorial ethics to bear on Irish folk-song.

The chief Irish collections are those of Bunting, Petrie and Joyce. Bunting (1773–1843) had his interest drawn to native Irish music by a competition festival of harpers held in Belfast in 1792. This fired him to make a comprehensive collection, from which he published three different volumes in 1796, 1809 and 1840. The songs in the first two of these collections have been reissued in modern times by the Irish Folk Song Society, whose editor, D. J. O'Sullivan, has gone back to the original manuscripts, where the airs are unharmonized. Words and tunes were separately collected, and Bunting was content with instrumental versions obtained from harpers, so that the association of words and tunes is often problematical. Their divorce was further encouraged by the fact that Ireland was bilingual. Gaelic words were collected by Bunting's collaborator, Patrick Lynch, but he published his first volume with only the titles and without the texts. When it was desired to extend knowledge of these tunes it was found necessary to provide them with English words.

Thomas Moore (1779–1852) was first in this field, but unlike Burns, who paid regard to the originals, he recklessly wrote new verses of his own, generally of a sentimental character, even if the tune happened to be gay or polemical – thus he turned the political 'Shan Van Vocht' ('Oh, the French are on the sea') into 'Love's Young Dream'. Bunting naturally was not too pleased to find his collection raided and the traditional character of his songs thrown overboard. He regretted that 'the work of the poet (i.e. Moore) was of so paramount an interest that the proper order of song writing was inverted and instead of the words being adapted to the tunes, the tune was too often adapted to the words'. To which Moore retorted 'Had I not ventured on these very admissible liberties, many of the songs (i.e. tunes) now most known and popular would have been still sleeping with all their authentic dross about them in Mr Bunting's first volume.' 'Admissible liberties' and 'authentic dross' are good! But there is no doubt about the success of Moore's efforts both as poet and singer in spreading a knowledge of the songs.

Stanford reissued Moore's *Irish Melodies* in 1895 with 'the original airs restored'. He compared Moore's with Bunting's version and was naturally horrified when he found modal tunes tidied up with sharpened sevenths, their speeds changed and bars lopped, as, for example, in 'She is far from the land' (Example 47 a and b)[4]. His edition has, however, been criticized, as also has his editing of the great Petrie collection, on the ground, not that his principles were at fault, but that he did not carry them quite far enough in that he was not sufficiently careful to collate alternative versions from different sources.[5]

[4] Stanford attributes this 'editing' to Sir John Stevenson, a Dublin musician and Moore's musical colleague, who had a great admiration for Haydn.
[5] Frank Kidson, writing in Grove's *Dictionary* article 'Moore', says that Stanford's restorations are not always justified and later workers like D. J. O'Sullivan have pointed out instances where Moore was using versions other than Bunting's.

She is far from the land where her young he-ro sleeps, And lov-ers a-round her, sigh - ing; But cold-ly she turns from their gaze and weeps, For her heart in his grave is ly - ing.

Example 47a

She is far from the land where her young her-o sleeps, And lov-ers a-round her sigh - ing, But cold-ly she turns from their gaze and weeps, For her heart in his grave is ly - ing.

Example 47b

After Bunting's came the collection of Dr George Petrie (1789–1866). Petrie was a younger contemporary of Bunting and Moore and he spared from a busy and multifarious life enough time, energy and enthusiasm for Irish folk-song to collect a couple of thousand airs and to take part in the founding of a 'Society for the Preservation and Publication of the Melodies of Ireland', a piece of pioneer work in the scientific treatment of folk-song that anticipated the English equivalent, the Folk-Song Society, by nearly fifty years.

To his collection contributions were made by Dr P. W. Joyce who published *Ancient Irish Music* in 1872, and *Irish Peasant Songs in the English Language.* In 1906 he issued a supplementary collection, *Old Irish Folk Music and Songs.* In this book he included two features which may have been derived from English experience: he mentions copyright and he sets the words syllabically under the notes in the Anglo-Irish songs.

Incidentally it may be worth mentioning that though the songs of four nations of Britain are in general distinguishable – each has definite characteristics as well as a more pervasive general character recognisably its own – there is plenty of traffic between the countries, and England and Ireland carried on quite a lively interchange of each other's folk-song. Thus 'Dives and Lazarus' turns up in Ireland as 'The Star of the County Down'; 'The girl I left behind me' ('Brighton Camp') has been found on Dublin street broadside ballads; and in Joyce are to be found versions of 'Brennan on the Moor' and 'Searching for Lambs', which very soon after were found by Cecil Sharp in Somerset. Scotland and Ireland, however, were earlier aware of the existence, the quantity and the value of their native folk-melody than England, which remained quite surprisingly deaf to what was going on under its very ears. English people had been told that they had no folk music and they meekly accepted it in the nineteenth century, having been prepared by the Italianate tastes of Burney and the musical profession in the eighteenth, who regarded all such native products as rude. From being rude it became non-existent, and we find Thomas Moore complacently writing in the introduction to his *A Selection of Popular National Airs* (1818) 'It is Cicero, I believe, who says *natura ad modos ducimur* (We are led to harmony by nature, modos = measures) and the abundance of wild, indigenous airs which almost every country, except England, possesses, sufficiently proves the truth of his assertion.' Carl Engel writing in the sixties remarks that it is odd that there are no collections of peasant songs in England as in other countries and gently wondered whether the English rustic is so completely unvocal as this would seem to indicate and whether it would not be worth while for a musician to undertake a search in some of the more isolated districts. Engel's words – in *The Study of National Music* (p. 173) – are the *locus classicus* for this extraordinary delusion: 'Although the rural population of England appear to sing less than those of most other European countries, it may nevertheless be supposed that they also, especially in districts somewhat remote from any large towns, must still preserve songs and dance tunes of their own inherited from their forefathers.' As Cecil Sharp pointed out in *English Folk Song: Some Conclusions*, no musician had the curiosity to see whether the English countryside was as barren as was thus assumed. Even the squires and the parsons seem, most of them, to have been unaware that their villagers had other music than the hymns played by waits in church and dances in the local public houses and schoolrooms, truly traditional English music.[6]

The exceptional parson, however, has proved to be the *fons et origo* of the modern revival, which ultimately dates back to 1843, when the Rev. John Broadwood (1798–1864) of Worthing, who later became squire of Lyne in Sussex – Lyne is not a cure of souls but the home of the Broadwood family[7] – and who published in that year a small collection of true English folksongs. This historic document deserves detailed attention. Broadwood's little book of sixteen songs is hard to come by, but there is a copy in the British Museum which can be found under the author's name of Dusart, not of Broadwood, whose name nowhere appears in it. Dusart was the professional musician[8] whose aid Broadwood sought to provide simple piano accompaniments for his airs. What the researcher finds more easily is *Sussex Songs. Arranged by H. F. Birch Reynardson*,

[6] I was myself astonished to find that in my own village of Standlake in Oxfordshire a local family, aptly named Cantwell, in 1956 sang a version of 'The Nightingale' which was printed in *English Dance and Song* for February 1964, where I first encountered it.

[7] Still occupied by Capt. Evelyn Broadwood, the present head of the piano manufacturing firm.

[8] He was organist of the Chapel of Ease at Worthing where John Broadwood was living between 1841 and 1847.

which is undated but speaks in its Preface of Broadwood's collection having been made 'about fifty years ago' and of having 'been considerably added to by his niece, Miss L. E. Broadwood'. This collection contains twenty-six songs and all Dusart's harmonies have been replaced by Reynardson's. Reynardson was some connexion of the Broadwoods and the date of his revised and enlarged edition of Sussex songs was 1889.[9] Dusart's harmonies were no loss.

The original version has a remarkable title page, in which every fount of type in the office of Balls & Co., of 408 Oxford Street, who published it for private circulation, seems to have been used – roman, italic, gothic in every size. The lay-out but not the typographical extravaganza is reproduced.

OLD ENGLISH SONGS

AS NOW SUNG BY THE PEASANTRY OF THE

WEALD OF SURREY AND SUSSEX

AND COLLECTED BY ONE WHO HAS LEARNT THEM
BY HEARING THEM SUNG EVERY CHRISTMAS FROM EARLY CHILDHOOD

BY

THE COUNTRY PEOPLE

who go about to the Neighbouring Houses, Singing,
or
"Wassailing," as it is called, at that season.

The Airs are set to Music exactly as they are now sung,
to rescue them from oblivion and to afford a specimen of genuine
Old English Melody.
The Words are given in their original Rough State
with an occasional slight alteration to render the sense intelligible

HARMONIZED
FOR THE COLLECTOR IN 1843
BY

G, A. DUSART

Organist to the Chapel of Ease at Worthing

[9] The authority for this is Frank Kidson in Grove's *Dictionary*.

The Contents are as follows:

1 The Moon shines Bright.
2 A Wassail, A Wassail.
3 The Noble Lord.
4 Rosebuds in June.
5 A Sweet Country Life.
6 The Ploughboy.
7 The Privateer.
8 The Fourteenth of July.
9 Gipsy Song.
10 The Serving-Man and the Husbandman.
11 The Bailiff's Daughter of Islington.
12 The Poacher's Song.
13 In Lancashire.
14 The Damsel in the West.
15 The Woodcutters (Harvest Supper Song).
16 Lord Bateman.

The title-page is explicit that the 'airs are set to music exactly as they are now sung', and it was related in the Broadwood family that the Rev. John had an accurate ear but that he relied on Mr Dusart, the Worthing organist, to write them down, but was told 'that can't be right, sir'. 'This must be a sharp' (or natural or flat, as the case might be). There is another story[10] which makes the same point about Mr Broadwood's insistence on the modality of the tunes. According to this Mr Broadwood played the 'German flute' and when the organist cried out against a flattened seventh Mr Broadwood, who had an accurate memory and a good ear, confirmed his vocal intervals by violent blasts on the flute and replied 'Musically it may be wrong, but I *will* have it exactly as my singers sang it.'

If the songs are examined for mode it would appear that it

[10] See *Musicial Association Proceedings*, LXIV, p. 68, for Capt. Broadwood's account of Miss Lucy Broadwood's description of her uncle's collecting methods.

was not merely a case of unfamiliarity with flattened sevenths that caused the trouble. The first impression the reader gets is of minor modes with sharpened sevenths, but closer inspection shows that sixths and sevenths are both liable to inflexion. In the first five songs, all in the minor, all sharpen their leading-note in such a figure as ♩. ♪ ♩ where the crotchets are the tonic, but all flatten their seventh when it occurs in a strong position as a melodic note, especially in a descending passage. Thus No. 1 with the signature of E minor is in the Aeolian mode with an alternatively inflected seventh. No. 2, the Wassail song, purporting to be in F minor, sharpens its seventh before the tonic as above, but in the chorus climbs to E flat on a strong beat by means of a sharpened (♮) D. The tune is therefore really Dorian with an inflected seventh. No. 3 (D minor) has its sixth and seventh both inflected and modulates to the dominant major in the middle. In No. 4 (F minor) a change is made in the 1889 edition by flattening a B in a cadence figure which Broadwood prints as a natural. No. 5 (G minor) sharpens both sixth and seventh. No 7 is so queer that I print it. Its tonic is uncertain, and like No. 16, hovers between C and F [Example 48]. The

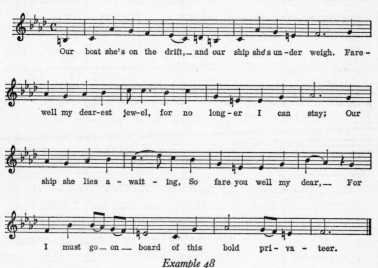

Our boat she's on the drift,— and our ship she's un-der weigh. Fare -

well my dear-est jew-el, for no long-er I can stay; Our

ship she lies a - wait - ing, So fare you well my dear,— For

I must go — on — board of this bold pri - va - teer.

Example 48

99

remaining songs are in the major mode, and one of them, No. 12, modulates to the dominant in the middle. Another, No. 13, though in C has an inflected F sharp occurring between two G's – this is probably another example of these Sussex singers' tendency to inflect their sixths and sevenths. Such inflexions and the dominant modulations were perhaps responsible for Mr Dusart's suspicions that the tunes ought to correspond even more closely to current, conventional, composers' practice.

The fact that several of the peculiarities noted above occurred in several songs at first struck me as suspicious, and I wondered whether for all his flute-blasting the parson had got his way with the organist. But on the whole I think they are peculiarities of time and place and that 'The Privateer' is a testimony to Mr Broadwood's insistence on oral transcription.

Another 'squarson' who reaped an even greater harvest some forty-five years later was the Rev. Sabine Baring-Gould, rector of Lew Trenchard in Devon, who produced in 1889 the first part of *Songs of the West*, 'Folk Songs of Devon and Cornwall collected from the mouths of the people'. Three other parts followed and all were printed in one volume in 1891. A revised edition omitted twenty-two songs subsequently thought not to be true folk-songs which were replaced to make a total of 121. This edition was made with the collaboratian of Cecil Sharp as musical editor in 1905. Behind its dedication lies some history and some biography. 'To the Memory of the late D. Radford Esq. J.P. of Mount Tavy at whose hospitable table the making of this collection was first planned, also to that of the Rev. H. Fleetwood Sheppard, M.A., my fellow-worker in this field for twelve years.'

Baring-Gould (usually pronounced Gold) wrote in his introduction to *Songs of the West*: 'One evening in 1888 I was dining with the late Mr Daniel Radford of Mount Tavy, when the conversation turned to old Devonshire songs. Some of those present knew "Widdecombe Fair", others remembered

"Arscott of Tetcott'; and all had heard many and various songs sung at Hunt-suppers, at harvest homes[11] and sheep-shearing feasts. My host turned to me and said: "It is a sad thing that our folk music should perish. I wish you would set to work and collect it – gather up the fragments that remain before all is lost." ' He undertook the task and he had for collaborator besides Fleetwood Sheppard, a Yorkshire parson, who was a good musician, the Rev. F. W. Bussell a don of Brazenose College, Oxford, who had an alto voice. It makes an incongruous picture, these three parsons going off to invade cottages seeking folk-songs, for Bussell always dressed as a dandy – I have myself a mental picture of him standing on the raft of the Brazenoze College barge which was next to that of my own college as I got into our boat for an outing in practice for the Summer Eights, a very odd sight, in a frock-coat with a flower in his button-hole. Miss Dean-Smith in the *E.F.D.S.S. Journal* (1950) remarks: 'One cannot but laugh at Baring-Gould and Bussell collecting folk-songs together – Bussell fashionable and elegant, an orchid in the button-hole, sitting on the copper while the cottage dame stoked the fire beneath, and Baring-Gould note-book and pencil in hand, following her trips between copper and wash-tub, the one taking the tune of anything she might be persuaded to sing, the other the words.' Baring-Gould relied mostly on his two collaborators for notating the tunes, but he could and did memorize them and then with the help of a piano write them down, for he was musical ('though I had not been taught fingering on any instrument'), as his hymn, words, tune and harmony, 'Now the day is over' testifies. The Rev. William Purcell, who produced a biography of Baring-Gould in 1957, in which he does full justice to this many-sided man, also notes the incongruity of the partnership 'Here was a strange trio, indeed; one of them lacked the necessary technical equipment, another had no love for the type of music to be collected, and the third lacked the opportunity to spend much

[11] Both John Broadwood and Cecil Sharp were indebted to harvest-homes for songs.

time at the task.' And he concludes with a verdict that can be endorsed 'Despite these handicaps they produced a collection of songs that is monumental in its importance and comprehensive in its range'. Furthermore it should be observed that his collection came out before Barrett's *English Folk-Songs* (1890), Frank Kidson's *Traditional Tunes* (1891), Lucy Broadwood and Fuller Maitland's *English County Songs* (1893) and Cecil Sharp's *Songs from Somerset* (1904), had launched the revival, and that, though he often bowderlized the words for understandable if subsequently deplored reasons in what he published, he deposited in Plymouth Public Library manuscripts of the words as he had taken them down and their music, for he observes 'to the antiquary everything is important, exactly as obtained, uncleansed from rust and unpolished'. Both his biographer and Mr James Reeves question whether, as far as the music is concerned, this is quite true, since in rewriting the words or composing new verses he may have clipped the tunes a little to fit.

Still there he stands, a great Victorian character who did not die till 1924 at the age of ninety, hymnologist, novelist, antiquarian, parish priest, and pioneer of the folk-song revival. The pearl of his collection is 'The Evening Prayer' or 'The White Paternoster', one of the few English tunes in the Phrygian mode [Example 49].

Another pioneer of the generation of Baring-Gould and Lucy Broadwood was Frank Kidson (1855–1926), a Leeds antiquary who collected authentic Yorkshire folk-songs among English songs from printed sources – he was in this respect a follower of Chappell, whose *Popular Music* he was engaged in indexing. For he was a bibliographer (as well as an expert on Leeds pottery) who published a book on *British Music Publishers, Printers and Engravers from Queen Elizabeth's Reign to George the Fourth's* (1900) and a book on Handel's publishers. His great index of 100,000 entries in fifty-seven volumes of English songs was never published. But he did publish in 1890 a volume of *Old English Country Dances* (tunes only) anticipating Sharp, and in the next year *Traditional Tunes*; some thirty years later there

Example 49

came out two volumes of sixty songs each from his collection with piano accompaniments by Alfred Moffatt, *A Garland of English Folk-Songs* (no date but after 1923 when he was made M.A. *honoris causa* of Leeds University) and *English Peasant Songs* (posthumous). These publications show, as also does the book he wrote in 1915 for the Cambridge University Press along with Mary Neal, *English Folk-Song and Dance*, that he appreciated the nature of the oral tradition, though Vaughan Williams in an obituary notice firmly aligns him with Chappell as distrustful of the oral tradition. Certainly Kidson was willing, as he explains in his prefaces, to supply missing texts or amend corrupt words, but he prints versions of 'The Trees so High', 'The Dark-eyed Sailor', 'The Sprig of Thyme', to take instances at random, which are certainly traditional and near relatives of the most strictly authentic versions from oral tradition. He was a foundation member of the Folk Song Society and was hailed by the scrupulous Lucy Brodwood as a true pioneer. In 1906 he contributed to the *Folk-Song Journal*, No. 9, thirty-one songs (as well as one or two folk-tales) which he had himself collected from various parts of Yorkshire, Leeds,

Knaresborough, Scarborough and Whitby, some from people not of Yorkshire origin. This selection, as he explained, he 'had gathered some ten or twelve years ago', to form a projected sequel to *Traditional Tunes*. Already in 1905 he had contributed to *F.S.J.* No. 7 a substantial article on 'The Ballad Sheet and Garland'.

Slightly earlier a small part in the revival which has been generally overlooked was played by William Alexander Barratt, a versatile musician (1834–91), organist, vicar-choral of St Paul's Cathedral, B.Mus. of Oxford (1870) and music critic of *The Morning Post*. In 1890 he brought out a volume of fifty-four songs with piano accompaniments and historical notes. In his preface he says of the songs that 'the majority were noted from the lips of singers in London streets, roadside inns, harvest homes, festivals on the occasion of sheep-shearing, at Christmastide, at ploughing matches, rural entertainments of several kinds and at the "unbinding" after choir suppers in country districts. A few are still sung, some have completely disappeared from the people by whom they were once favoured. A considerable number have not previously appeared in print. The words of some on broadsides fifty years ago have been used for collating the texts. The melodies have all been derived from singers themselves.' The flavour of the book is a little more urban, like Kidson's, than the early collections of Broadwood and Sharp.

The difference of emphasis upon oral and printed sources just noticed persisted all through the nineteenth century and was a real issue in that historical context, even if in the light of knowledge so gained the two traditions can now be regarded as complementary. Lucy Broadwood herself had no objection to making good textual lacunae from broadside versions, though of course her attitude to the modal character and the precise notation of tunes was wholly strict. But then, so was Kidson's, since he comments in his prefaces on the preservation of modal characteristics (even if Moffatt used conventional hymn-book harmony in his accompaniments).

This would be the place for discussing William Chappell's

contribution to English traditional melody. For he represents the antiquarian tradition to which both Frank Kidson and Anne Gilchrist belonged, and to which in 1966 an American scholar, Dr Claude Simpson, contributed his encyclopaedic dictionary of broadside tunes, *The British Broadside Ballad and Its Tunes*. Both Kidson and Miss Gilchrist were north-country musicians and supported the retrieving of the oral tradition by Lucy Broadwood, Cecil Sharp and Vaughan Williams. Their book-knowledge of tunes was invaluable for annotating the folk-songs which the Folk-Song Society was printing in its *Journal*. The difference between the two points of view may be illustrated from a note to 'The Sheep-shearing Song' in the first volume of Sharp's *Folk Songs from Somerset*, published in 1904, where there is a debate on which came first, the orally derived or the print-derived version. The partisans for either view are at bottom looking for an original version, which being 'original' will also be 'authentic'. Folk-song collectors soon learned to acknowledge 'variants' but there was a tendency at first to think of variants as 'corruptions of an original'. There certainly are corrupt versions caused by the 'erosion of unretentative memories and inaccurate ears' but there is also the argument, already developed in Chapter 1, that the oral tradition is not only strong but creative.

Sharp collected a song beginning 'It's a rosebud in June' with this tune:

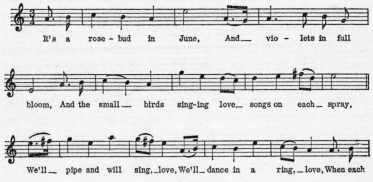

lad takes his lass all — on the green — grass, And it's
all ——————————— to plough — where the fat ox - en
graze low, And the lads and the lass- es to — sheep shear-ing go.

Example 50

This is indeed a fine Dorian melody, which he got from William King of East Harptree, Somerset, in the parlour of 'The Castle of Comfort' on Mendip in April 1904. He contributed it to the *Folk-Song Journal*, Vol. I, pp. 262–3, where it was annotated by Frank Kidson, who found a 'similar' song in print with air attached in *The Merry Musician or A Cure for the Spleen*, Vol. I (1716), and he himself possessed a version on an engraved sheet where it is called 'The Sheep-Shearing Ballad', and attributed to John Barrett. He conjectures that it was sung on the stage in a play called *The Custom of the Manor*. Kidson thinks Mr King's tune, with which he won the prize at a competitive festival at Frome in 1904, was a traditional survival of it. Sharp, however, in his note to the song contended that no eighteenth-century tune could be in the Dorian mode and that Barrett's tune, though not in fact pure Dorian, had enough Dorian traces to preclude eighteenth-century origin. Kidson mildly dissented, 'I am rather inclined to believe that the Somerset singers have got hold of Barrett's air and song and altered it. (The second verse of Barrett's 'Sheepshearing Ballad' is certainly not folk.) I must confess, however, that there is evidence equally strong for the other view, viz. that Barrett adapted an existing traditional song and melody'.

There we have the issue in a nutshell and the solutions offered, certainly with reasons given but ultimately according to the predilections and prejudices (in the strict sense) of the disputants: Kidson had his documents, Sharp his oral tradition, and it was the most natural thing in the world for each to come down in an issue so nicely balanced and lacking in decisive elements, on the side of his own axioms of scholarship.

The traditions are like branches of a river which flow into and out of each other. Sometimes their separateness can be clearly discerned, sometimes they join in a main stream. One of the tributary sources, the antiquarian, runs from William Chappell (1809–88). This remarkable man has never had his due from English historians. His great work was *Popular Music of the Olden Time* which came out in 1859, nearly twenty years after his *National English Airs* containing 245 tunes, which it superseded. In the same year (1840) the Musical Antiquarian Society, of which he was a moving spirit, began its brief career of republishing the Tudor composers and Purcell. It is amusing to discover that his missionary zeal in these two movements, which led half a century later to the modern renaissance of English music after its long eclipse and subservience to continental influences, was due to his antipathy to Dr Burney, the eighteenth-century musical historian, and his irritation with a Scottish nationalist in the employment of his firm. It is an odd if non-significant coincidence that both these founding fathers of English nationalism, Chappell and Broadwood, were members of families who manufactured – and still do – pianofortes. Burney had committed what was in Chappell's eyes the greatest of all sins of scholarship – he had neglected to verify his references and had made matters worse by misquotation; moreover, he had no ears for anything but Italian music. Hence anything that was bad enough for Burney's disparagement (such as English music of the Tudor period) was good enough for Chappell's championship. As for the tiresome Scottish nationalist, he goaded Chappell to disproving his taunts that England had no national music. He would show the conceited Scot with his boasts about his native Caledonian melody – and it must be remembered that the Scots had been active in collecting their folk music back in

the eighteenth century – how far back English melody went –
to 'Summer is icumen in' and beyond.[12]

Chappell's full title is as worthy of full quotation as Broadwood's. It is set out with less variety of type – only one line in a
Gothic fount – but still in diverse sizes

The Ballad Literature
and
Popular Music of the Olden Time:

A History of the
Ancient Songs, Ballads, and of the
Dance Tunes of England,

with

Numerous Anecdotes and Entire Ballads
also
A Short Account of the Minstrels

by

W. Chappell F.S.A.

He was not only a Fellow of the Society of Antiquaries but a
member of the Camden Society, which testifies further to his
interest in ballad literature. For the Musical Antiquarian
Society he edited its volume of Dowland's songs, and he was a
founder member of the Musical Association. He was your true
antiquarian, who wanted documentary evidence for all his
statements, and when he could not substantiate a date he said so
and presented such evidence as there was for the reader to
judge the proffered conjectures for himself. He was inclined to
regard unwritten songs as corrupt versions of printed copies and
he remarks of the airs in a selection he published with piano
accompaniments by Macfarren that 'we are rarely left to such
doubtful evidence as tradition for proof of their antiquity'. In

---

[12] He has a little dig at the Scot in discussing the consecutive fifths of the
ground bass of 'Summer is icumen in' when he says that they make a 'very
indifferent effect on a modern ear except perhaps the lover of Scottish reels!'

this same introduction (to *Old English Ditties*) he makes the surprising statement that 'secular music seems always to have been greatly in advance of sacred', and justifies it by an early appreciation of the practice of sacred parody, for he continues 'and so secular tunes were frequently appropriated as hymns' and not the other way about. *Popular Music of the Olden Time* was revised, none too happily, by H. E. Wooldridge in 1893 and later scholarship has corrected and enlarged our knowledge both of ballads and of tunes, but after a hundred years it remains a classic and has in fact just (1966) been reissued in paper-back.

Wooldridge's revision was undertaken with admirable intentions. He had acquired a copy of the 1855 subscribers' serial edition of *Popular Music of the Olden Time* – the substance of the two-volume 'public' edition of 1859 – which Chappell himself had interleaved and annotated. He was troubled by Macfarren's harmonizations of the tunes because in the course of his work for the *Oxford History of Music* he had soaked himself in the music of the Middle Ages and had come to understand its modal character. Even the key signatures in Chappell he found were anachronistic and it would seem as though this concern of scholarship in the early music (i.e. before the mid-seventeenth century) was his animating motive in undertaking the edition, for he reharmonized most of the tunes himself, and they do certainly sound more authentic than in Macfarren's settings. He also felt that the book could be lightened of much of the literary material which had been published after 1855, notably in Chappell's own edition of *The Roxburghe Ballads*. This enabled him to reduce Chappell's amiable garrulity from two volumes to one. But by now the editorial bug had bitten him, and the mild phrase in his preface 'the somewhat varied structure had grouped itself' (round the new recognition of the music's importance) is not warrant enough for the wholesale jettisoning of Chappell's introductory and connecting historical essays, nor for dividing the ballads from the dance tunes. His dispensing with the complete words of the ballads he justified on the grounds of their newly-won accessibility and his lack of space, but it spoiled the book for the musician who has not Percy or Child on his shelves, and the cloven hoof is shown in the rash remark, also in the preface, 'For while it has never at any time been seriously pretended that the ballads, considered as poetry, could be said to attain even to the lowest standard required by the art, and such interest as they may now excite remains purely antiquarian, the tunes have always been recognized as admirable.' This is a remarkable opinion for so cultivated a man as Wooldridge (1845–1917), who was Slade Professor of Fine Arts at Oxford, himself a painter and a polymath, and shows that in comparison with the scholar whose work he was revising he had a blind spot. So that while his revision is scholarly in its concern for the modes, in its preference for the earliest known versions of the tunes, in its addition of thirty-five tunes and in its incorporation of Chappell's new literary references, it is not really a substitute for the original Chappell.

The publication of *English County Songs* in 1893 is a landmark in the folk-song revival. Its compilers were Lucy Etheldred Broadwood and J. A. Fuller Maitland, who was already a Fellow of the Society of Antiquaries and since 1889 music critic of *The Times*. It is not entirely clear how either of these two musicians became interested in folk music. Lucy Broadwood, however, probably inherited it from her uncle, as Vaughan Williams says,[13] and, as she describes in connexion with one of her most remarkable finds, 'The Sussex Mummers' Carol', she came into immediate contact with it in 1880 when the Sussex Tipteerers sang it at the end of their performance of the mummers play of 'St George, the Turk and the Seven Champions of Christendom'.[14] She also at some time became aware of the broadside tradition of English ballads, which she alludes to in the introductions both of *English County Songs* and her own later collection (1908) *English Traditional Songs and Carols*. She possessed a collection of broadsides of her own which is still

[13] *Journal of the English Folk Dance and Song Society*, 1948 Jubilee number.
[14] See Example 52 below.

preserved at Lyne. Maitland – incidentally his name was not officially hyphenated – though he describes how his interest was aroused in old music and fostered by Rockstro has no more to say in his autobiography[15] of his initiation into folk-song than 'I had worked on folk-song some years before this', 'this' being his relish for 'the fragrant beauty of Byrd, Bull, Morley and their contemporaries' and the realization 'to what extent they used the truly English idioms of folk-song'. He then goes on to narrate some of the experiences he and Lucy Broadwood had on their collecting expeditions. Some of their correspondence during their collaboration has been published in an article by Miss Dean-Smith in the 1964 *Journal of the English Folk Dance and Song Society*.

Cecil Sharp (1859–1924) collected and published a greater number of English tunes than any of the pioneers, for besides the 800 odd folk-songs and ballads with innumerable variants in addition, he collected the traditional sword and morris dance tunes and then went off to America in 1916 and collected 1,612 tunes representing about 500 separate songs from no less than 281 singers. He was not the first person to tap the survivals of British song taken to North America in the seventeenth and eighteenth centuries, for he had discovered on visits undertaken for other purposes in 1914 and 1915 that a Mrs Olive Campbell had found a singing tradition still alive in the Appalachian Mountains in Carolina, Kentucky and Virginia and had already collected some seventy tunes. He wrote to her to make sure he would not be a trespasser on her territory and received an encouraging reply to come and carry on the good work. The astonishing results of his labours triggered off a movement for systematically investigating the British heritage transplanted to and preserved in North America, which was already conscious of the value of folk-art. F. J. Child's great work for the ballads was completed in the last decade of the nineteenth century. H. E. Krehbiel took up the study of negro spirituals and slave songs in the first decade of the twentieth century. After the

[15] *A Door-keeper of Music*, 1929, p. 223.

First War individual musicians like the Lomaxes, father and son, and the English departments of American universities set about getting survivals, ballads of indigenous origin, Creole and other ethnic songs of the American melting-pot into print with American zeal and thoroughness. The study flourishes there as nowhere else. Sharp caught the tide as it was beginning to flow and added impetus to it.

Sharp was a professional musician, though his musical career was unconventional. He had been to school at the most musical of English public schools, Uppingham, gone on to read mathematics at Clare College, Cambridge, and then emigrated to Australia for nine years, where he eventually became a musician and met the Rev. Charles Marson, who was to lead him to 'The Seeds of Love' in a Somerset vicarage. Back in England he conducted, composed, played the piano, taught in a preparatory school, for which he compiled a song-book and became the Principal of a Conservatoire at Hampstead. But on Boxing Day 1899 something happened which changed the course of his life: he saw the Headington (Oxford) side dance five morris dances of which the tunes were played on a concertina by William Kimber, (who lived until Boxing day 1961, still playing tunes for people to dance to). Sharp did not come back to folk-dance till after his encounter with folk-song in 1903. He published the first of five volumes of *Folk Songs from Somerset* in 1904. Two and a half years later in 1907 he published his *The Morris Book, Part I* with tunes harmonized for piano. This was precipitate and premature and he had to revise the dance notation. He had come back to morris through the Esperance Girls' Club run by an energetic social worker, Miss Mary Neal, whom Sharp had introduced to Kimber, but they soon fell out over a difference of ideal between the social and the scientific application of the dances – incidentally the morris is authentically an all-male dance and should be approached, as one member of the Bampton side once put it, 'more like parson's work'. Sharp went on to train his own dancers and teachers and ultimately in 1911 founded the English Folk Dance Society.

This in turn led him on to explore the surviving traditional country dances for mixed couples and thence to the seventeenth-century collection assembled by John Playford in *The Dancing Master*, first issued in 1651 but going through no less than seventeen editions, with additions and subtractions, between then and 1728 (the year of *The Beggar's Opera* in which some of its tunes are requisitioned). He continued to write piano accompaniments for, and to publish songs in his collections, to lecture and to consolidate his discoveries, persuading the Board of Education that English children should be fed with traditional music. In 1907 on the strength of the 1,500 songs he had by then collected he had written a book in which he sought to establish the character of folk-song as such and the nature of English folk-song in particular. This was *English Folk-Song: Some Conclusions*. It remained the only comprehensive book on the subject in existence till 1967, when Mr A. L. Lloyd published his *Folk Song in England*. The full story of his activities was told in the official biography of him written by A. H. Fox-Strangways and Maud Karpeles, his literary executor in 1933, subsequently rewritten and published by Maud Karpeles in 1967. In it a table of his collecting activities, excluding his transcriptions of Playford, is given which credits him with a total of 4,977 tunes, of which 501 were provided with accompaniments, 1,118 were published without accompaniment in the *Journal of the Folk-Song Society* and elsewhere, and 3,358 remained unpublished, being mostly alternative and inferior versions.

The greatest scholars of the movement – for by 1898 the enthusiasts had converged and combined to found the Folk-Song Society – were two ladies, Lucy Etheldred Broadwood (1858–1929) and Anne Geddes Gilchrist (1863–1954), representatives of that stalwart class of maiden aunts of independent means, to which English social and cultural life owes more than it has ever acknowledged. Both were trained musicians who had a literary background of miscellaneous book-learning, Miss Broadwood archaeological and religious, Miss Gilchrist historical and folkloristic. The wide range of their reading in these (and other) diverse fields elucidated many a problem thrown up by the text of a song, and their annotations to the *Folk-Song Journal* throughout its thirty-five issues form a compendium of recondite knowledge otherwise inaccessible.

Lucy Broadwood was the great-granddaughter of the John Broadwood who founded the firm of piano makers (originally Tschudi and Broadwood) and niece of that Rev. John Broadwood, squarson of Lyne on the Surrey-Sussex border, who had published his collection of local folk-songs in 1843. She was a country-woman familiar with rustic arts and crafts, for her father had a house on Tweedside as well as one in London which was visited by musical celebrities, Liszt among them. She recalled that her earliest musical impression was a version, worn-down to nursery scale, of the ballad of 'Lord Rendal', sung to her by her father when she was little more than two years old, 'The Wee Little Croodin' Doo' [Example 51].

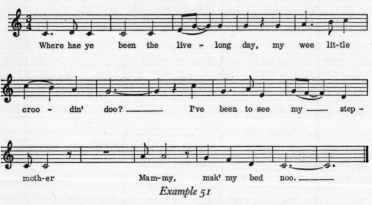

Where hae ye been the live - long day, my wee lit-tle croo - din' doo? _____ I've been to see my ____ step - moth-er Mam-my, mak' my bed noo. _____

Example 51

Henry Broadwood had got it from his mother, who was a Stewart of Perthshire – hence the Scots descent. She also recalled the brilliance of Liszt's double thirds. So here were the musical sources out of which *English County Songs* came in 1893. She was an original member of the Folk-Song Society, was on its original committee, became its secretary and editor of its *Journal* in 1904 and served it in various capacities after relinquishing those particular offices till the last years of her life, when she was its President. She contributed to the *Journal* songs which she herself collected in Sussex and Surrey (1902), in Ireland and the Highlands of Scotland. She published in 1908 a volume of *English Traditional Songs and Carols* with simple but suitable piano accompaniments of her own composition and ample annotations. These notes reveal that she had by this time acquired a knowledge of broadside sheets, from which she was able sometimes to supply verses missing from the versions she had collected from gypsies, farm labourers and their wives and others, including especially Mr Henry Burstow, a shoemaker from Horsham who had an enormous repertory. This volume contained the 'Sussex Mummers' Christmas Carol', a tune remarkable for its beauty, for its words which hark back to the sixteenth century in embracing the Nativity and the Crucifixion, and combine the characters of a hymn and of a wassailer's greeting, for its delivery by the Sussex Tipteerers at the end of their presentation of their mummer's play, for the lasting impression it made on the collector herself then just embarking on her life-work, and for its conversion into a piano solo by Percy Grainger,[16] pianist, composer and folk-song collector [Example 52].

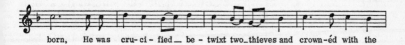

Example 52

[16] One of his 'Room-Music Tit-bits'. I used to play it as a boy and it served as one of my own initiations into folk music.

In the correspondence about folk-song, which Miss Dean-Smith edited and published,[17] her correspondents include J. A. Fuller Maitland, with whom she collaborated in *English County Songs*, Percy Grainger, Dr P. W. Joyce (the Irish collector), Frank Kidson and various persons who could supply her with local knowledge. It was Lucy Broadwood, more than any other single person, who established folk music as a branch of humane learning and made the Folk-Song Society, subsequently (1932) amalgamated with the English Folk Dance Society, a learned society, which secured for the subject the highest standards of scholarship and editorial ethics.

Anne Gilchrist, of Scottish ancestry but born and musically educated in Manchester, a life-long Lancastrian, added a knowledge of Scottish psalmody, hymn-tunes and printed sources to her first-hand experience of folk music. She joined the Folk Song Society in 1905 and for the next fifty years till her death at the age of ninety she poured out a stream of annotations for the *Folk-Song Journal* and articles for its successor *The Journal of The English Folk Song and Dance Society*. Folk-dance also was in her purview, for she contributed accounts of the Lancashire morris and the Lancashire custom of Pace-Egging. Two true stories illustrate her knowledge not only of tunes but where to put her hand on them. I myself once wanted to identify a particular tune, so I put it on a postcard and sent it to her. Back by return came the answer: the Genevan Psalter of 1625. The other tale is more involved. When King George VI was still Duke of York he founded a camp for boys at which a community action song was a feature of camp life, 'Under the spreading chestnut tree'. The Czech composer Jaromir Weinberger, wishing to pay England a compliment, wrote a set of orchestral variations on it. A colleague who was required to provide a programme note for it asked me about its origin. I did not know, nor could anyone at Cecil Sharp House enlighten me. However, when it was played over the radio and Miss Gilchrist heard it she recognised

[17] In Vol. IX, No. 5 (1964) of the *Journal of the English Folk Dance and Song Society*.

it at once and sent off to me a furious note to the effect that the tune was 'Go no more maids a-rushing', which is to be found in the Fitzwilliam Virginal Book and had survived in some transformation as a singing game. She expanded her discovery in an article in the *Musical Times* for March 1940, quoting a minor version by Byrd cited by Chappell, another one, also minor, by Farnaby called 'Tell mee Daphne', which is in the Fitzwilliam Virginal Book (No. 280), and a version of the folk-song riddle-song 'My love sent me a chicken without a bone', etc., to which 'Go no more maids a-rushing', now in the major, was attached as a chorus, which she found in an 1877 publication *Nursery Rhymes and Country Songs* by M. H. Mason, who said she got her songs by oral tradition from her grandmother.

This labyrinthine bit of scholarship not only illustrates Miss Gilchrist's unique double knowledge of tunes in her head and in her library, but also the kind of puzzles that confront students of folk-song. She was in this respect a true disciple of William Chappell, but unlike Chappell she found room for oral tradition and all its lore too. Vaughan Williams used sometimes to say of her half-teasingly that her vast knowledge made her trace resemblances and relationships between tunes that did not exist. He too had a good knowledge of tunes but of course he was more musician than scholar.

Ralph Vaughan Williams collected over 800 songs between 1903 and 1913, which have been listed with great care by Mr Michael Kennedy in his part of the official biography of the composer. He has, moreover, in an essay on the relationship of nationalism to folk music given a full account of Vaughan Williams's approach to folk-song, which was not, as is generally thought, a case of love at first sight, although he afterwards described it as a kind of recognition of something he had always known. His first song was 'Bushes and Briars' collected at Ingrave, near Brentwood in Essex on 4th December 1903, a mere three months after Sharp's collecting of 'The Seeds of Love'. Again, contrary to what we have most of us supposed, the two events were not linked, because, as Mr Kennedy says,

Vaughan Williams who knew Sharp did not speak to him about his new interest in folk-song 'because I thought he would not be interested'. However, they found themselves together on the committee of the Folk-Song Society and thereafter laboured together in the cause with the same outlook. Mr Kennedy's book-list makes it unnecessary to recapitulate the history of Vaughan Williams's involvement with folk music which was life-long, which was consciously expounded by him in lectures as far back as 1902 and reformulated in the book (also originally lectures) *National Music* of 1934, and which contributed to his idiosyncratic musical style. His prestige as a composer, after the manner of the nineteenth-century nationalists, did much to force the recognition of English folk-song upon English people, who otherwise, unlike the Scots with their own, tend to dismiss it, sometimes even with a sneer. Other of his services to it were his incomparable piano accompaniments and vocal arrangements. His accompaniments achieve the paradox that, while he believed that such harmony should be impersonal, in fact the more of Vaughan Williams there is in them the more is the essence of the tune made manifest.

Others who contributed substantially to the discovery and rescue of folk-songs in the early days of the Folk Song Society and contributed to its *Journal* were William Percy Merrick (1868–1955), who was a pioneer, since by 1900 he had sixty songs taken from a single singer, a farmer Henry Hills, who had learned them at harvest-homes, rabbit hunts and cricket matches in mid-Sussex; Mrs Ella Leather, who recognized folk-song as part of folk-lore and collected carols by phonograph in Herefordshire (some of them afterwards set by Vaughan Williams); Henry E. D. Hammond, an Oxford classic and retired shcoolmaster from Edinburgh Academy (1866–1910), who made a big haul of 600 songs in Dorset; George B. Gardiner (1852–1910), another schoolmaster from Edinburgh who scoured Hampshire for texts while the tunes were noted by three colleagues, of whom one was the composer, H. Balfour Gardiner; George Butterworth, killed in the war, who used folk-songs and the idiom of English folk-melody in his compositions; Clive Carey (1883–1968) the singer; E. J. Moeran (1894–1950), the composer, and, last but not least in the list, Maud Karpeles (b. 1885), Cecil Sharp's amanueusis and literary executor, who continued the work of collecting up to, through and beyond the First War.

The Folk-Song Journal never bore the word 'English' as part of its title, though its main work was to put English songs into the permanence of print, but it took in from time to time songs from Ireland, both Gaelic and Anglo-Irish, and Gaelic songs from Scotland. Some amount of comparative study naturally began to appear in its pages, which equally naturally turned the attention of the movement to similar movements abroad. Moreover, Cecil Sharp in the war, as already related, went off to the United States and took with him as assistant Maud Karpeles. After his death she saw that his Appalachian collection was put into print and in 1929 she went back to America, to Newfoundland this time, and collected 200 songs from the fishing community there.

These international implications of English nationalism as manifested in the revival of its folk music and dance were first fully realized by Maud Karpeles. Exchanges of teams of dancers were a feature of the post-war work of the English Folk Dance and Song Society, and in 1935 Miss Karpeles organized a great international festival of folk-dancing in London, which at a time when political tension had again begun to increase, was attended by teams from eighteen European countries. After the Second War she founded the International Folk Music Council, which had an even wider membership that included Asian and African cultures. So much was a natural corollary of half a century's interest in folk-art, for the time had come for comparative study to begin on the accumulations of actual material and of knowledge gained in acquiring it. As the world grew smaller through the development of air travel it was easier, indeed it became imperative, for all peoples to learn more about one another, and since folk-art touches the deeper springs of culture it affords at least a beginning of international understanding. Ethnomusicology has put down roots in several universities and recording of native music now goes on all over the world. In Britain this work in folk music has been undertaken by the B.B.C., by the Library of Cecil Sharp House and by the British Institute of Recorded Sound, though the study of folk music is still unorganized and is left to the initiative of individual scholars, ignored for the most part by the academic world, except in Edinburgh where the School of Scottish Studies is attached to the university.

CHAPTER SIX

Ballads

Before the discovery, rescue, preservation and revival of folk music in the nineteenth century, as described in previous chapters, there had been its literary equivalent in the discovery and publication of the English and Scottish popular ballads. The ballad is one great class of folk-song and was recognized as such even by those scholars who concentrated on the poem to the neglect of the tune. Indeed the first break-down of his huge corpus of material that any scholar or folk-song collector will make is into ballad, however hard to define, and song or lyric, no matter what difficulty of classifying border-line cases may arise. As a matter of history this great body of anonymous literature was isolated in the eighteenth century and study of it has continued ever since, sometimes with its music, more often without. In particular the problems of its origin, definition and diffusion have been endlessly debated. Balladry is indeed a large subject in itself but it is also, as is now realized, an integral part of folk-song, which can throw as much light on folk music as folk music can throw on it. No book on folk music can neglect it in spite of the attention it has already received. What then is a ballad?

In spite of the objections to beginning the study of a subject with a definition already noted in Chapter 1 and despite Quiller-Couch's warning (in the introduction to the *Oxford Book of Ballads*) that a ballad is not to be defined, it still seems wiser, in view of the extraordinary variety of meanings that the word bears, to consider the name as a preliminary to the discussion of the nature of the ballad. Musicians may think of it as a piano piece by Chopin or Brahms, or at a lower level the bad songs sung by professionals for a cash consideration and by amateurs for ease of execution in Victorian and Edwardian drawing-rooms. Literary people associate the word with tragic tales of the Scottish Border. This is the basic denotation of 'ballad', a narrative in verse about a stirring event, but it is related to ballet and ballett (the Elizabethan madrigal form).

Ballad, the word is derived from late Latin *ballare* or old French *baller* (both derivations are given and come to much the same thing), for the word does not exist in classical Latin but is borrowed from the non-classical Greek βαλλίζειν used in Sicily and Magna Graecia as a derivative from classical Greek βαλλεῖν 'to throw' in the sense of to 'throw the leg about' i.e. to jump or dance. Hence our words *ballet* for the art of dancing and *ball* for an occasion of dancing as well as something to throw. The root idea then is that a ballad is a dance-song. The *Oxford English Dictionary* quotes an instance of ballad being used as a song to accompany a dance as late as 1612. Could this have referred to 'If all the world were paper', which is the only English dance that survived to the modern revival with a text? Modern English folk-dancers have applied the rhyme

> If all the world were paper
> And all the sea were ink
> If all the trees were bread and cheese
> What should we have to drink?

to a round country dance for eight, which Sharp found in Playford's *The English Dancing Master* (1651), and it is the only English dance with vocal accompaniment outside the 'calling-on' songs of the sword dances. Its words date from 1641 and are a parody of the more inflated hyperbole of Jewish mysticism and they are sung to a very simple tune [Example 53]. The dance seems to have disappeared from the carol and the song from the accompaniment at a pretty early date in England – *circa* 1400 has been suggested. In the case of the carol, which is like the ballad in being a dance-song, the refrain of the earliest

Example 53

nativity carol *circa* 1350 – 'A child is boren amonges man' implies a round dance:

> Honnd by honnd we schulle ous take
> And joye and blisse schulle we make

But as late as 1597 Morley in *A Plaine and Easie Introduction to Practicall Musicke* says in classifying the vocal forms, madrigals, canzonets, etc., 'There is also another kind more light than this (villanelle) which they term Balletti or dances, and are songs which being sung to a ditty may likewise be danced. . . . There be also another kind of Balletts commonly called "Fa-las". The first set of this kind which I have seen was made by Gastoldi; if others have laboured in the same field I know not, but a slight kind of music it is and, as I take it, devised to be danced to voices.' Modern attempts to dance country dance to tunes with known verbal associations, e.g. 'Newcastle', usually break down on tempo – dancers want to take them too quickly for singing. Still, there are even yet in Europe some surviving dance-songs, such as have been shown by Norwegians at the winter festivals of the English Folk Dance Society at the Albert Hall. Many of Playford's tunes bear the names of ballads current in his day and many of his tunes were assigned ('to be sung to the tune of . . .') to broadsides by their printers or authors. Miss Evelyn K. Wells contributed a catalogue to the *Journal of the English Folk Dance and Song Society* for 1937–9 in which she lists all the ballads she can find against Playford's tunes. Thus for 'Cuckolds all a row' (no. 67) she finds in the various collections of broadsides (Pepys, Roxburghe, etc.) no less than nineteen ballad titles.

The question arises in parenthesis, if ballads and carols are both dance-songs, what is the distinction between them. Apart from the difference in character, which is readily perceived but less easily prescribed, the formal answer is that the carol has a burden which is repeated at the end of each verse – 'The Holly and the Ivy' shows the structure to perfection: stanzas narrating life and passion of Christ are followed, each of them, by a constant burden in which pagan and ecclesiastical elements are jumbled together without grammar, connected only with the seasonal associations. In the earliest carols presumably you stood still to deliver your narrative and then moved round, holding hands, as you sang the burden. Ballads make use of refrains but they are more often inserted like an incantation between the lines, as in the 'Twa Sisters o' Binnorie' where Scottish place-names break up the narrative – 'Bonny St Johnston stands on Tay', 'Stirling for aye'. Similarly the ballett breaks up its text with fa-las, deliberately, to lighten its rhythm whereas in the carol the burden is relegated to the end so as to secure more continuous singing and more continuous dancing. Incantation and dance are both vestigial survivals of magic ritual.

'Ballade' is the name of a verse form found in Middle English and French, which has no connexion beyond derivation and perhaps the fact of the last line of the seven-line stanzas being repeated in each stanza rather like a refrain – the envoi is not a refrain. Musicians with their reckless disregard for accuracy in nomenclature have borrowed this form of the word to indicate a romantic kind of piano piece. Chopin based one of his four *Ballades* on a Polish poem and Brahms wrote an 'Edward' based on the *alt-schottische* ballad of that name. But Fauré and others have borrowed the term without regard to its implications. The other musical misuse of the word is its application to the sentimental song which eminent singers were paid to

popularize at special 'ballad concerts'. A lady calling herself
Claribel was early in the field in the middle of the nineteenth
century. At the end of the century they were still flourishing
though not always of such abysmal inanity. They were known
as royalty ballads or shop ballads, though actually intended
for the drawing-room. They rejoiced in titles like 'Because',
'Beauty's Eyes', 'Love's Rhapsody', 'Down the Vale' or sometimes of a heartier kind such as 'Stonecracker John' or 'The
Deathless Army'. It was *de rigueur* that God should appear in
verse 3. They may have originated in narrative songs like
Braham's egregious 'The Death of Nelson'. This sort of ballad
has been indulgently described as 'not so much a form as a
phrase of English song'. It did not survive the First War and the
advent of broadcasting.

So then out of ball, ballett, ballet, ballade and ballad it
remains to investigate the narrative ballad of tradition.

The shortest definition of a ballad is Gerrould's: 'The ballad
is a folk-song that tells a story.' Folk, song and story are three
vital ingredients; Gerrould subsequently adds three other
characteristics: its stress on a crucial situation, its presentation
of the situation directly and dramatically (as, e.g. in dialogue
between the actors) and non-involvement of the narrator, who
remains objective and offers few comments. This is as it may
be, but Gerrould claims that it gathers in one fold all European
balladry. The author who does precisely that, takes all Europe
(except Hungary) for his province, W. J. Entwistle, has a
formula which also includes the same essential ingredients, folk,
song and story: 'Any sort of traditional narrative poem sung
with or without accompaniment or dance in assemblies of the
people.' This allows the possible connexion with the dance and
stresses the communal element. Narrative then about some
stirring event is the first distinguishing mark of the ballad and
explains at once the existence of the broadside ballad and its
kinship with journalism.

Not all narratives, even when they have a musical refrain,
however, are ballads, for there is the *cante-fable*, which may be

and often is a prose narrative with interruptions of a sung tune, refrain or melodic formula. Adam de la Hale's *Le jeu de Robin et Marion* (thirteenth century), which is claimed as the birth of the French *théâtre comique*, of the dramatic pastoral and by some stretch of terminology of French opera, is a *cante-fable*, in which dialogue employing both verse and prose is interspersed with airy little songs of troubadour origin. But though the *cante-fable* plays so small a part in literature that few text-books say anything about it, modern examples have been collected. Two from the Isle of Man were published in the *Journal of the Folk-Song Society* for 1924, both of fairy-tale character, the first called 'Bollan Bane' which tells how a young musician got a tune from the fairies, and the other, 'The Lazy Wife' about outwitting a giant. Each is punctuated by a snatch of tune. Bollan bane is the Manx name of the mugwort, which was a charm against the supernatural; its three-fold invocation in the tune suggests that the young man knew it was a risky business stealing anything from the fairies [Example 54].

Example 54

The ballad differs from the *cante-fable* in being a narrative cast in verse such as can be carried on a strophic tune. Any such structure would seem to be more likely the work of an individual rhymester than of the folk, but Boehme's formula covers the case precisely: 'First of all one man sings a song, and then others sing it after him, changing it in the process.' There is, however, a communal element in the ballad. The ballads whether oral, broadside or literary are always called 'popular'. On this point

Entwistle had this to say 'The word (popular) does not involve the slur of vulgarity (what the eighteenth century was inclined to call "rude") nor need the word imply adherence to the mystical doctrine of the people's authorship, about which much ink has been shed. The audience drawn without abstentions from the whole community, conditions the minstrel's performance as reciter and creator.' He adds a further point that the ballad community tends to be the clan or local society rather than the nation, whose poems become epics rather than ballads.

The minstrel postulated by Entwistle may be a person of humble talent, the local versifier, as he certainly was in the following ballad from an island in the Mississippi River.

SILVER JACK

Sung by 'Dutch' Kistenmacker, lumberjack on Island 66 in the Mississippi Rover.

1.   I was on the drive in 'eighty,
        Working under Silver Jack;
    The same is now at Jackson,
        And ain't soon expected back.

2.   There was a fellow 'mongst us
        By the name of Robert Waite
    Kind of cute and smart tonguey:
        Guess he was a graduate.

3.   He could talk on any subject
        From the Bible down to Hoyle,
    And his words flowed out so easy,
        Just as smooth and slick as oil.

4.   He was what you call a skeptic
        And he liked to sit and weave
    Hipolutin' words together
        Telling what he didn't believe.

5. 'Hell' he said 'is all humbug'
   And he made it plain as day
That the Bible was a fable;
   And we 'lowed it looked that way.

6. Miracles and such like
   Were [all] too rank for him to stand;
As for him they called the Saviour
   He was just a common man.

7. 'You're a liar!' someone shouted
   'And you've got to take it back'.
Then everybody started;
   'Twas the words of Silver Jack.

8. Then he cracked his fists together,
   And he stacked his duds and cried
' 'Twas in that there religion
   That my mother lived and died'

9. 'And though I haven't always
   Used the Lord exactly right
Yet when I hear a chump abuse him
   He's got to eat his words or fight'.

10. Now this Bob he aint no coward;
   So he answered bold and free,
'Stack your duds and cut your capers,
   For there ain't no flies on me'.

11. And they fought for forty minutes
   And the crowd would whoop and cheer
When Jack spit up a tooth or two
   And Bobby lost an ear.

12. But at last Jack got him under
   And he slugged him once or twice
And straightway Bob admitted
   The divinity of Christ.

128

13. But Jack kept reasoning with him
     Till the poor cuss gave a yell
     And 'lowed he'd been mistaken
     In his views concerning hell.

14. Thus the fierce encounter ended
     And they riz up from the ground
     And somebody brought a bottle out
     And kindly passed it round.

15. And we drank to Bob's religion
     In a cheerful sort of way;
     But the spread of infidelity
     Was checked in camp that day.

This ballad of a fight was collected from a lumberjack in the mid-twenties and the protagonist was Jack Driscoll, called Silver because of his prematurely white hair, who died in 1895. It appeared in Hudson's *Folksongs of Mississippi* in 1936, and a version with a few verbal differences was published by John and Alan Lomax in *Cowboy Songs* in 1936. Alan composed a tune for it in the folk narrative style which he published in his *The Folk Songs of North America* in 1960. It is not therefore a true folk-ballad but only the raw material of one, since the process of evolution by oral tradition had not yet got to work on it. No tune was recorded of it though Hudson heads it 'Text secured by Mr A. H. Burnett of Rena Lara from the singing of Dutch Kistenmacker'. Hence Lomax's wish to perpetuate the ballad by providing one. The address is obviously to a local audience, and though some ballads have travelled half-way round the world the local significance is the source of that immediacy which constitutes their strong appeal.

Thus even 'Chevy Chace', the song of Percy and Douglas, of which Sir Philip Sidney said: 'I never heard the old song of Percy and Douglas that I found not my heart moved more than with a trumpet and yet it is sung by some blind crowder (fiddler) with no rougher voice than rude style', though it involves nationalist passions, is primarily local in subject and address. This 'Chevy Chace', probably the most famous of traditional ballads, was old in Sidney's time: it probably refers to the battle of Otterburn in 1388 in the reign of Richard II. An alternative account of the same battle is found in a ballad of that name (Child numbers 161 and 162) and both were taken by Child from Percy's *Reliques of Ancient English Poetry*. It is a perfect example of the 'old unhappy far-off things and battles long ago' which Wordsworth prescribed as the essence of romance.

Hence then the romantic character of ballads and the appeal they made in the romantic period in spite of their origin in events very near to ordinary life. Their romantic character was responsible for the revival of interest in the ballads by people like Sir Walter Scott and the poets of the romantic awakening. Hence too came the new ballads composed by Coleridge ('The Ancient Mariner') and Goethe ('Der Erlkönig'). Hence also the attention of the literary world and then of scholars, which caused the study of ballads – and of their origin – to be undertaken all through the nineteenth century. This scholarly interest had one unfortunate side-effect in that balladry became a purely literary study, and it was not until the folk-song revival unearthed folk versions preserved by oral tradition of many of these traditional ballads that the importance of the tune was recognized. Sharp was emphatic that tune and words belong together. He wrote: 'It is greatly to be deplored that the literature of the ballad has in the past attracted so much more attention than the music. Properly speaking the two elements should never be dissociated: the music and the text are one and indivisible and to sever one from the other is to remove the jewel from its setting.'

Ballads and tunes could, however, become separated from one another; borrowing went on, especially on the broadsides. Thus 'Chevy Chace' is usually now sung, as it was on eighteenth-century broadsides, to 'O ponder well', familiar from *The Beggar's Opera*, of which the original name seems to have been 'The Children in the Wood', but it was also sung to 'Peascod Time' and 'Flying Fame' – Chappell prints all three.

Another tune, apparently quite firmly attached to its ballad, 'Lord Willoughby', has a remarkable history and ended as a Bach chorale, i.e. as a sacred parody. The exploit of Peregrine Bertie, Lord Willoughby of Eresby, in securing the evacuation of English troops from the Netherlands after engaging the Spaniards in 1589 was celebrated in a black-letter ballad now in the Douce collection. It was printed in Percy's *Reliques*. Its tune, which had a great vogue in England from 1590 on to the middle of the seventeenth century, and in Holland, where it is found in song-books from 1603 onwards for half a century, comes to us from Thomas Robinson's *Schoole of Musicke* (1603) under the name of 'Lord Willobies Welcome Home' [Example 55). Under this title it appears in *My Ladye Nevells Booke* as a

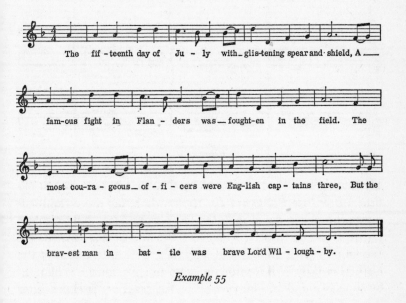

The fif-teenth day of Ju-ly with glis-tening spear and shield, A

fam-ous fight in Flan-ders was fought-en in the field. The

most cou-ra-geous of-fi-cers were Eng-lish cap-tains three, But the

brav-est man in bat-tle was brave Lord Wil-lough-by.

Example 55

piece for virginals with two variations by William Byrd. Exactly the same piece occurs in the *Fitzwilliam Virginal Book*

(No. 160) but here it is called 'Rowland'. The tune is in this form:

Example 56

The name 'Rowland' is traced by Claude Simpson in his *The British Broadside Ballad and Its Music*, where far more ramifications are tracked down than the few set out here, to a dramatic Jig on Roland, Robert, Margaret and the Sexton, which was known on the Continent and may have been introduced to the Netherlands by Will Kempe the actor in 1585, for the Willoughby tune is found in Dutch song-books, where it is called after Robert not Rowland. From Holland the tune somehow got to Germany and is found in C. P. E. Bach's collection of his father's chorales so – [Example 57] of which the words are

Example 57

'Keinem hatt Gott verlassen'. For the sake of completeness the morris dance tune 'Kempe's Jig' may be compared with Examples 55–57, for there are resemblances in the melodic contour, in the change to the second section of the tune and in the final cadence [Example 58].

Example 58

This is the sort of life history possessed by many ballads. They travel far, as 'Edward' for instance has done. They jump across the three main traditions, the oral, the broadside and the literary, as 'Barbara Allen' has done. Tunes and texts change partners. New names are acquired, as we have just seen. I takes all the scholarship of a Chappell, a Child, a Bronson (who is engaged in fitting surviving tunes to Child's standard collection) and a Simpson to keep track of them. Yet they are astonishingly persistent, and Bronson, who rightly decided that it would be a hopeless task to try to discover the tunes which Child had omitted to attach to his ballads, has had no difficulty in finding tunes currently being sung in the oral tradition, though he has been obliged to modify Child's texts, in fact to make a new 'Child'. Indeed he prints 200 versions of 'Barbara Allen'.

The ballad of hard-hearted Barbara Allen is indeed as tough in growth, persistent in currency and wide in distribution as any. Pepys records that he heard Mrs Kipps sing 'her little Scotch song of Barbary Allen' under date of 2nd January, 1666. This Scottish version which was first printed in Ramsay's *The Tea-Table Miscellany* in 1724, begins:

> It was in and about the Martinmas time
> When the green leaves were a'fallan
> That Sir John Graeme o' the West Countrye
> Fell in love wi' Barbara Allan

and contains the verse explaining her coldness by her having been slighted when healths were being drunk in the tavern.[1] Percy printed both his version and the more familiar one that begins:

> In Scarlet town where I was born
> There was a fair maid dwellin',
> Made ev'ry youth cry Well-away
> Her name was Barbara Allen.

Chappell adopted this version and provided a tune 'from tradition', the rather square tune in three-four time that everyone

[1] This explanation is very bluntly put in a version found in Virginia in 1930 by Dorothy Scarborough of Columbia University:

> Recollect, recollect, recollect, young man
> When I boarded at your tavern
> You drank, you walked with the ladies round
> And you slighted Barbara Allen

knows. But when Cecil Sharp came upon the ballad in his early collecting days in Somerset he found a much more flexible tune, and no less than twenty-seven variants of it most of them in five time [Example 59].

In — Scot-land I —— was born and bred, In

Scot-land I was dwel-ling, When a young man on — his

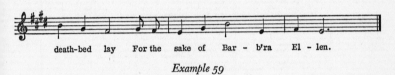
death-bed lay For the sake of Bar - b'ra El - len.

Example 59

Sharp also collected a score of version in the Appalachian Mountains of America, all in alternating threes and twos to the bar or other irregular rhythms. They are in the oral tradition and have various openings:

> In yonders town where I was born
> There lived three maidens dwelling
> The only one that I called my own
> Her name was Barb'ra Allen

and

> 'Twas in the merry month of May
> When all gay flowers were blooming
> William on his death-bed lay
> For love of Barb'ra Allen

and from an old negro woman who had been a slave what was obviously a corruption:

> Sweet William died choked up in love
> I'll die for him in sorrow (*bis*)

135

The variety is endless. A nineteenth-century broadside reproduced in Mr Leslie Shepard's book is headed:

The True Ballad of Barbara Allen's Cruelty

and opens:

> In Scarlet town where I was bound
> There was a fair maid dwelling
> Whom I had chosen to be my own
> And her name it was Barbara Allen

This version makes no mention of being slighted in a tavern but ends with Barbara's repentance and atonement:

> So this maid she then did die
> And desired to be buried by him,
> And repented herself before she died
> That ever she did deny him.

This cursory examination makes clear the vicissitudes of a ballad preserved in all three traditions, the oral, the broadside and the literary. The only problem that is not resolved is what happened to the tune. Claude Simpson in his extremely full collection of music from the broadside ballads says:

'For a brief period at the end of the seventeenth century a small percentage of broadside sheets included music. Doubtless this development is related to the increasing importance of new stage tunes and the exploitation of the theatrical popularity to float new songs and ballads. Whether or not this is the sole explanation the tunes printed were more likely to be new than old. . . . Among other casualties we must regret the absence of tune directions from versions of such familiar traditional ballads as 'Barbara Allen' and 'Lord Thomas and Fair Eleanor' which appeared in print during the seventeenth and eighteenth centuries. Lacking such information we cannot determine the continuity, if any, between tunes used then and now.' Perhaps

Chappell knew the tune from currency, i.e. oral tradition, or maybe he got it from anthologies of songs from the Pleasure Gardens. Anyhow the family resemblance of his tune to those that Sharp collected is presumptive evidence that there was a continuity. This broadside tradition represents on the whole the townsman's literate tradition, whereas the folk tradition was preserved by the less literate countryman. The ballad seller goes back at least as far as Shakespeare's Autolycus and his sheets performed some of the functions of the modern popular newspapers. They told topical tales of crimes and executions, political and even theological rumpuses, personal tragedies and anything of news value such as appeals to urban proletariates. The sheets, often adorned with a woodcut, were hawked at fairs and on stalls in the markets. Modern instances are the sheets sold in the public-houses of Portsmouth in 1940 about the evacuation of Dunkirk and one about the battle of Narvik that was picked up by an English sailor in Hong Kong. Broadsides that did not contain ballads are reproduced in Mr Shepard's book about the present Queen Elizabeth's coronation issued by Scottish Nationalists and a sheet containing a song, 'Words by John Brunner, Tune: Miners' Lifeguard' used by the Aldermaston Marchers. But traditional ballads were for centuries part of the stock-in-trade of the ballad printer.

Many of these printers are known by name, for the ephemeral wares defied the ravages of time and friability partly by being pasted on the walls of taverns and dwelling house as mural decorations, partly by the hoarding instinct which forbore to destroy anything with a picture on it. Izaak Walton is often quoted for the ballad as mural decoration. In the chapter of *The Compleat Angler* in which he describes how to make a chub eatable the fisherman says to his companion, 'I'll now lead you to an honest alehouse where we shall find a cleanly room, lavender in the windows, and twenty ballads stuck about the wall', and where the hostess knows how to cook the fish that is all needles and wadding. Several large collections have survived and are preserved in libraries, of which the chief are the

Selden collection in the Pepys Library at Cambridge, the Roxburghe in the British Museum, and the Douce in the Bodleian at Oxford. Private collectors in the present century have been Lucy Broadwood, Frank Kidson and Leslie Shepard, who has written a book about them (1962). The printers, who were legion, belonged to the humbler branch of the craft. Kidson (in the *Folk-Song Journal*, no. 7, 1905) lists their names century by century, giving the addresses, such as 'at the signe of the Mermayd', 'Printed and sold in Aldermary Church-yard'. The two names known to non-experts are those of James Catnach, who set up in Seven Dials in 1813, and Henry Parker Such, who had a business of newsvendor as well as printer in Union Street, Borough, from 1849. Catnach indeed was socially important enough to have a history of his press written – by Charles Hindley in 1887. Hindley describes how Catnach auditioned ballad writers and singers, and how in this way he acquired a stock of over 4,000 ballads. Broadsides were also printed in Edinburgh, Preston, Leeds, Manchester and Liverpool.

The broadside is by definition a single unfolded sheet of paper and other things besides ballads might be printed on it. Those printed in the sixteenth and seventeenth centuries were set in an old Gothic type called Blackletter, but a change to roman type about 1700 produced what are known in distinction as White letter broadsheets. It was customary to adorn broadsides with a woodcut, but no printer could afford fresh woodcuts for all the new ballads he printed and so he chose from stock such as seemed most nearly appropriate to the subject, or if he had nothing suitable he used any old block he had purely for decoration. The broadsides were sold for a halfpenny in the nineteenth century. After 1900 and the arrival of Lord North-cliff's popular press the broadside declined, but is not even now quite extinct, as we discover when some event strikes the popular imagination.

As a source of texts of traditional ballads the value of the broadside is obvious. There is no conscious touching up by a

literary editor who has to think about his text, but there is less
room for corruption than in the oral tradition in which a singer
may forget, misunderstand a word and plunge desperately for
the nearest in sound to it that comes to his mind. The broadside
is important too in that it brings the urban population into
touch with folk-song. The town with its shifting population was
not so suitable a medium for the preservation of a song or
ballad by oral tradition as the countryside, but folk-song is not
entirely a rural product: it belongs to the whole population,
though the educated classes had a more precarious access to it
and a less secure hold on it.

The literary tradition, which differs from the other two in
that it aims at permanence and involves the work of an editor
who must select and tidy up his texts, has of course a known
history. It begins with Percy's *Reliques of Ancient English Poetry*.
In 1765 Thomas Percy, subsequently Dean of Carlisle and then
Bishop of Dromore, published the first edition of his *Reliques*,
of which the core and the primary impulse was derived from a
manuscript that had come into his possession while he was still
a young man. This is his own account of its acquisition:

'This very curious old manuscript, in its present mutilated
state, but unbound and sadly torn, &c., I rescued from destruc-
tion and begged at the hands of my worthy friend Humphrey
Pitt, Esq., then living at Shiffnal in Shropshire, afterwards of
Priorslee near that town; who died very lately [the note is
dated 7th November, 1769] at Bath (viz. in summer 1769).
I saw it lying dirty on the floor, under a Bureau in ye Parlour:
being used by the maids to light the fire. It was afterwards sent,
most unfortunately to an ignorant Bookbinder, who pared the
margin, when I put it into boards to lend it to Dr Johnson.
Mr Pitt has since told me that he believes the transcripts into
this volume, &c., were made by that Blount who was author of
Jocular Tenures, *&c.*, who he thought was of Lancashire or
Cheshire, and had a remarkable fondness for these old things.
He believed him to be the same person with that Mr Thomas
Blount who published the curious account of King Charles the

2nds escape entitled *Boscobel, &c.*, Lond. 1660, 12mo, which has been so often reprinted. As also the *Law Dictionary* 1671, folio, and many other books which may be seen in Wood's *Athenae* ii. 73, &c. A descendant or Relation of that Mr Blount was an apothecary at Shiffnal, whom I remember myself (named also Blount). He (if I mistake not) sold the Library of the said Thos. Blount to the above-mentioned Mr Humphrey Pitt: who bought it for the use of his nephew, my ever-valued friend Robt Binnel. Mr Binnel accordingly had all the printed books, but this MS which was among them was neglected and left behind at Mr Pitt's house, where it lay for many years.' The attribution to Blount has been questioned but the handwriting confirms the date as about 1650, thus pushing the history of the ballads back a further hundred years, although some of them must even then have been current for centuries. Indeed some refer to historical events and persons, such as the battle of Otterbourne (1388), Thomas Lord Cromwell (1540, minister of Henry VIII), Fair Rosamund (mistress of Henry II, 1177), the murder of the King of Scots (Darnley, husband of Mary, Queen of Scots, 1568). Others refer to legendary characters like King Arthur and his knights and the exploits of Robin Hood.

Origins

The publication by Bishop Percy of his *Reliques* naturally provoked the question, where did all this anonymous poetry come from? It could not just grow, though the metaphor of the wild-flower was applied to it, and growth, as we have already seen, is a major factor in its creation. But how did the ballad start? The controversy that was waged through the nineteenth century and beyond revolved round four main theories, the minstrel, the courtly poet come down in the world, the local versifier, and the community acting homogeneously, but it was conducted by philologists and literary critics without benefit of musicians. But the musician's question, how does the folk-singer get his tune, complicates the controversy about origins. We can leave on one side divine inspiration which was lightheartedly invoked by the folk-singer who said to a collector 'When you've got the words God Almighty sends the tune', except to note that the singer's attention will be primarily directed to organizing his narrative and that the tune he uses may be an amalgam of his memories of the tunes that he knows. If this is so it possibly excuses, partly though not wholly, the literary critic's dismissal of this part of the problem in the phrase 'gets fitted with a tune somehow'.

There is no need to chronicle all the battles in the Ballad War,[2] nor to note all the refinements on the main theories by a long line of scholars from Joseph Ritson, who attacked Percy, on through the German philologists, Grimm and Boehme, the Danish Gruntvig, the Scots Motherwell and Andrew Lang, and the Americans from F. J. Child onwards through F. B. Gummere, G. H. Gerould and Evelyn Wells. But the main outlines of the controversy need to be stated, because Cecil Sharp called attention to the musical factor that had been omitted from it and the musicians were naturally concerned with the texts which shaped their tunes.

Bishop Percy began his essay on the Ancient Minstrels in England: 'The Minstrels were an order of men in the middle ages, who subsisted by the arts of poetry and music, and sang to the harp verses composed by themselves or others. . . . The Minstrels seem to have been the genuine successors of the ancient Bards, who were admired and revered by our ancestors. . . . And though as their art declined many of them only recited the compositions of others, some of them still composed songs themselves and all of them could probably invent a few stanzas on occasion. I have no doubt but most of the old heroic ballads in this collection were composed by this order of men; for although some of the larger metrical romances might come from the pen of monks or others, yet the smaller narratives were probably composed by the minstrels who sang them. From the amazing variations which occur in different copies of the old pieces it is evident that they made no scruple to alter each

[2] D. K. Wilgus's word in *Anglo-American Folksong Scholarship*.

other's productions; the reciter added or omitted whole stanzas according to his own fancy or convenience.'

Three points emerge from this: Percy regarded the ballads as the compositions of anonymous poets; they differed from normally composed poems in the existence of variant versions; there was a tradition within which the minstrel authors worked. Sir Walter Scott supported the view that the ballads were the work of minstrels or perhaps sometimes of a local self-taught versifier.

Motherwell (1827) on the other hand seems to favour the doctrine of communal authorship and, though unlike Ritson he is respectful to Percy, he is critical of editorial tidying up of texts, which he believes to be, like the language in which they are sung, an emanation evolved from the popular mind by popular usage. The nearest he gets, however, to a formulation of the doctrine goes no further than this: 'They (i.e. collections of ballads printed as they orally exist) convey to posterity that description of song which is peculiarly national and character-istick; that body of poetry which has inwoven itself with the feelings and passions of the people, and which shadows forth, as it were, an actual embodiment of the Universal mind, and of its intellectual and moral tendencies.' What a good thing the Collective Unconscious had not been heard of at the time, for this is vague enough! The full statement without hedging of the communal theory of origin was made by the German philologists, the brothers Grimm of fairy-tale fame. For them, *Das Volk dichtet* – it is the people, 'the singing, dancing throng' that is the poet. This brings in the dance, which, as in the carol, accompanies the rhythmic refrain, and this dance element maintained a place in later discussions of communal origin, as also did the somewhat similar attribution to the *cante-fable*.[3] But the Grimms also said that the folk-song composes itself, *Das Volkslied dichtet sich selbst*. The difficulty of maintaining such a doctrine is its vagueness – a folk-song is a specific thing, a poem and a tune, and, even if its inspiration is in the total com-

[3] See G. H. Gerould, *The Ballad of Tradition*, pp. 214–15.

monalty, how does it become concrete? Other German literary critics were not slow to attack it, notably Schlegel. Sharp briefly reviews the controversy, stating also the views of Uhland and Boehme, and though he says that they are not consistent and face both ways he gives it as his view that Boehme made the best statement, in which both the individual creator and the creative folk are assigned their parts: 'First of all one man sings a song and then others sing it after him changing what they do not like.' An advantage of this formula is that it is equally applicable to verse and tune.

The communal theory was supported by Andrew Lang, writing in the *Encyclopaedia Britannica* (11th edn., 1911), who invoked for it the support of anthropology and the comparative method. 'The vexed and dull controversy', he wrote, 'as to the origin of Scottish folk-songs was due to ignorance of the comparative method and of the ballad literature of Europe in general. . . . These minstrels are a stumbling block in the way of the student of the growth of ballads. . . . This theory (of wandering minstrels) fails to account, among other things, for the universal sameness of tone, of incident, of legend, of primitive poetical formulae, which the Scottish ballad possesses, in common with the ballads of Greece, of France, of Provence, of Portugal, of Denmark, and of Italy. The object of this article therefore is to prove that what has long been acknowledged of nursery tales, of what the Germans call *Märchen*, namely, that they are the immemorial inheritance at least of all European peoples, is true also of some ballads. Their present form of course is relatively recent: in centuries of oral recitation the language altered automatically, but the stock situations and ideas of many *romantic* ballads are of dateless age and world-wide diffusion.' True, no doubt, but still it does not really account for the concrete song or ballad, 'The Seeds of Love' as Sharp heard it or 'Lamkin' as Child put it into pigeon-hole no. 93. So the controversy has rumbled on among American scholars and a history of it has been written by D. K. Wilgus of Rutgers University, U.S.A. What, however, all allow is that it is the tradition of oral delivery that contains the essence of the thing. And the tunes confirm it by their distribution and variation.

A modern view of the origin of a folk-tune, which pushes the analysis a stage further back than the hypothetical first singer, is that of the Hungarian musicologist, Bence Szabolcsi, who in his *History of Melody* traces the evolution of vocal utterance from the intonations of speech through three-note chanting to pentatonism, which with its wider range of pitch and the possibility of modal organization makes genuine tune possible, on further to the diatonic and even chromatic melody of classical and romantic Western music of Europe. Folk music is a pervasive factor in this evolution and the feature of folk music which leads him to a new conception of melodic structure is its variants, the fact that there is no single, original or authentic version of a folk-song. To this conception he applies the Arabian name *maqam*, which means formula – (among other meanings, the original having been the platform on which the Arab singer stood). The melodic formula chosen by the singer has an outline, a terminal point and perhaps a prominent feature. Within the formula the singer extemporizes his song and in so doing uses vocal ornaments for expression or exuberance of feeling or for sheer virtuosity and the fun of doing it – thus another feature of folk-song is accounted for, ornament. Bence tells of a certain Hungarian village that would accept certain variants as its own form of expression and entirely exclude others; and although variant formation is nowhere the result of conscious intellectual effort, the village singers were well aware, as one woman said that 'there are many versions of these village songs', or, as a gypsy put it, 'it can also go like this'.

This theory has to recommend it that the words to be uttered are the starting-point of a song, that the song must be cast within a tradition, that there is room for invention within the tradition, that such invention in performance produces variants, that behind the variants there is enough consistency to establish its identity and that ornament, a feature of all monody, arises naturally in the individual singer.

Bishop Percy's *Reliques*, which he amplified from other sources, (notably Sir David Dalrymple, ordinary broadsides and old printed collections of poetry) also started a general interest in ballads which previously had been looked down on as a vulgar product and a debased form of art – indeed Percy apologised for his editorial handling of them 'in the present state of improved literature'. He provided no tunes for his *Reliques* and it was left for a later scholar, the organist and antiquary, Dr E. F. Rimbault to bring out nearly a century later in 1850 *Musical Illustrations to Percy's Reliques.*[4] Percy's editorial methods were impugned by the antiquary Joseph Ritson (1752–1803), who even doubted the existence of the famous manuscript, on which as a matter of fact Percy did keep a tight hold and which was only published by F. J. Furnival in 1867.

The impact made by the publication of the *Reliques* was immediate and far-reaching. Sir Walter Scott described its effect on him:

'I remember well the spot where I read those volumes for the first time. It was beneath a large platanus tree in the ruins of what had been intended for an old-fashioned arbour in the garden. The summer day sped onward so fast that, notwithstanding the sharp appetite of thirteen, I forgot the hour of dinner, was sought for with anxiety, and was still found entranced in my intellectual banquet. To read and to remember was in this instance the same thing, and henceforth I overwhelmed my schoolfellows and all who would harken to me with tragical recitations from the ballads of Bishop Percy.' Hence came the next landmark in the literary tradition of balladry, *Minstrelsey of the Scottish Border* which Scott published in 1802. It has been said that poets make bad editors, and Scott even

---

[4] Rimbault has seventy-four songs and ballads whose tunes he obtained 'chiefly from MSS and early printed books, deciphered from the obsolete notation and harmonized and arranged according to modern usage.' Rimbault was aware of the problem of harmonizing modal tunes.

while noting that the 'learned and amiable prelate used to restore the ancient ballad by throwing in touches of poetry so adapted to its tone and tenor as to assimilate with the original structure', followed much the same practice himself. While the practice has been criticised as bad editorial ethics it has to be borne in mind that a text has to be constructed out of a number of variants and that it is the business of an editor to edit or he overloads his pages with unreadable textual criticism.

When Lockhart prepared a new edition of *Minstrelsey* in 1833, a year after Scott's death, he printed some tunes: 'The airs of some of these old ballads are for the first time appended to the present edition. The selection includes those which Sir Walter Scott himself liked the best; and they are transcribed without variation, from the MSS in his library.'

With *Minstrelsey* the question of the provenance of the ballads came up and a rich thesaurus of specifically Scottish narrative ballads, both historical and romantic, was added to the literary tradition, such as 'Helen of Kirconnell', 'The Queen's Maries' and 'The Douglas Tragedy'. Between the two editions of Scott's *Minstrelsey* another editor took up the tale of Scottish balladry, William Motherwell, who in 1827 published *Minstrelsy Ancient and Modern* with a first-class introduction and historical notes. This introduction is notable for containing a catalogue of the previous compilations in which ballads have been assembled of which he lists no less than thirty-three, beginning with one printed in Edinburgh in 1508. His second collection is none other than the book of sacred parodies published by the Wedderburn brothers in 1567. The fact that popular secular tunes were borrowed for pious purposes – why should the Devil have all the good tunes? – means that a hymn-book can sometimes throw light on the traditional songs of its period. Anne Gilchrist dissected *Ane Compendious Book of Godly and Spirituall Sangis Collectit out of Sundry parts of the Scripture with sundry other Ballats changet out of prophaine Sangis for avoyding of sin and harlatry, with augmentation of sundrye Gude and Godly Ballates etc.* Motherwell, however, is overcome with horror at the very idea of a sacred parody: 'that patchwork of blasphemy, absurdity, and gross obscenity, which the zeal of an early Reformer spawned under the captivating title of 'Ane compendious Booke of Godlie and Spirituall Songs'' is neither comprehended under the description of Song as we are now in quest of, nor do its miserable and profane parodies reflect any trace whatsoever of the stately ancient narrative ballad.'

Here he goes too far. Miss Gilchrist while admitting that the narrative ballad of the Wedderburns' day would not lend itself easily to parody, none the less discovers one in their book, *The Constancy of Susanna*, which was the story of Susanna and the Elders found in ballad form in the sixteenth century and on broadsides, of which there is one in the Roxburghe collection. She also found that the 'Dawn Song', warning lovers to part, was turned into a hymn which was sung to the tune 'Hey, tutti, taitie', i.e. to what we now sing to 'Scots wha' hae wi' Wallace bled'.

Motherwell mentions a few earlier collections of Scottish songs in which a few ballads are to be found, Allan Ramsay's famous *Tea-Table Miscellany* of 1724 contained five ballads, including besides 'Bonny Barbara Allen', 'The Bonny Earl of Murray' and 'The Gypsie Laddy'. In the same year Ramsay brought out two small volumes which he called *The Evergreen, being a collection of Scots poems wrote by the Ingenious before 1600*. David Herd published his *Ancient and Modern Scottish Songs, Heroic Ballads &c.* in 1769, which he says on his fly-leaf were 'collected from Memory, Tradition and Ancient Authors'. . . . After Motherwell came publication of other collections, Peter Buchan (1825 and 1828) specialized on the north-east of Scotland, including the locality bearing the same name, Buchan, as his own. A modern scholar[5] puts the contribution of Aberdeenshire and neighbourhood as 'at least fifty per cent of all traditional song lore collected in Scotland'. William Christie produced two volumes of *Traditional Ballad Airs* in

[5] Kenneth S. Goldstein and Arthur Argo, *Folk-Song in Buchan* (by Gavin Greig), Folklore Associates, Pennsylvania (1963).

1876 and 1881. Interest continued to mount all through the nineteenth century, spreading to Europe, where the outstanding scholar was the Dane Svend Grundtvig, and to America, where Francis James Child of Harvard compiled the great collection of 305 ballads which was so far definitive that his numbering has been retained, like Köchel's numbering of Mozart's compositions, as the standard catalogue ever since, in spite of all the additional material that has emerged since 1898, when the last volume of *The English and Scottish Popular Ballads* appeared. The literature of the subject is enormous. At every stage there has been criticism of the last man's editorial ethics. Sharp's adventures in England and the Appalachian Mountains of America brought the tunes back into the centre of the picture. Professor Bertrand Harris Bronson began in 1959 to go through Child and print tunes for the ballads in his canon. While Sharp was publishing his finds from oral tradition an older Scottish collector, another Aberdonian who had combed Buchan, Gavin Greig (1856–1914),[6] posthumously injected into the stream of ballad literature *Last Leaves of Traditional Ballads and Ballad Airs* in 1925. This was an edition by Alexander Keith of 108 ballads with tunes extracted from a lifetime's collection of 3,050 texts and 3,100 tunes. The volume contains some not printed before. Goldstein and Argo's volume (1963) adds the texts of some 600 songs which Greig had contributed to *The Buchan Observer* between 1907 and 1911, without tunes, which could not very easily be reproduced in a newspaper. Greig, like Sharp, returns to oral tradition. It is therefore possible to say, as William Montgomerie does in a 'Sketch for a History of the Scottish Ballad', contributed to the *Journal of the English Folk Song and Dance Society* (1956):

'The folk-songs in the Greig collection are practically untouched. Greig's work was done by hand, with a pen. With the recording machine his work is being completed, at least on the recording side. We have come full cycle, from pure oral tradition, past the improved ballad as literature to be read and

[6] Further account of Greig's work will be found in Chapter 9.

recited, past the accurately printed ballad of the scholar to be studied, to the original ballad reunited to its tune to be sung again.'

There could hardly be a neater summary of the history of the ballad revival nor more succinct formulation of the trinitarian doctrine of tradition.

CHAPTER SEVEN

English Folk-Melody

(1) Oral, Broadside, Industrial

What are the characteristics of English folk-melody that make
it sound English? It ought to be possible by technical analysis
to distinguish features of mode, interval, rhythm and cadence to
allow some generalization to be made with the same degree of
applicability as enables us to predicate a falling fourth as a
common feature of Russian melody, a rising sixth and twice-
repeated-note cadence of Irish, the augmented second of the
Near East, the absence of anacrusis as a feature of Finnish and
Hungarian tunes, syncopation of negro origin, and so on in the
matters of phrase-lengths, use of sequence, transposition and
motivic organization. We have been warned (e.g. by Sir Julian
Huxley) against trying to identify national characteristics with
racial origins in such a mixed population as that of modern
Britain, though language is allowed to have a powerful influence on melody. Nevertheless we recognize in the British
Isles not only the Celtic fringe and the Gaelic that was spoken
in Scotland, Ireland, Wales, Cornwall and the Isle of Man,
but some more psychological, even ethical, characteristics that
differentiate the Englishman not only from the Frenchman and
the German but also from the Scot or the Welshman. Are these
reflected in our national music?

Three things struck the early collectors and those musical
people who joined the Folk-Song Society or became interested
in the revival movement: the first was aesthetic not technical,
the extraordinary freshness of the tunes, fresh perhaps in comparison with more succulent German melody. One possible

technical feature that might be responsible for this quality was their generous compass, rarely less than an octave, more commonly exceeding it by a tone, a third or even a fifth; and an octave leap in the course of the melody was not unknown. The second fact that stared them in the face was its self-sufficient monody, from which its modality, a very noticeable characteristic to those nourished on the classics, was seen to be due.

Monody is the normal condition of folk-song but it is not absolute. Even African music shows cases of part-singing as well as its famous counterpoint of drums. The Yugoslav style of singing consecutive seconds has been mentioned. And even in modern English folk-song a tradition of adding a lower part is occasionally encountered in some families, the best known example being the Copper family of Rottingdean, of whom the brothers Thomas and William sang to Mrs Lee, the first secretary of the Folk Song Society, before 1898, and who are succeeded in 1960 by Ron and Bob, cousins who contributed 'The Twelve Days of Christmas' and 'Twankydillo' to modern LP records[1] in an unacademic kind of harmony. So much being granted, however, it is still a fact that English folk-song and English folk-dance tunes are essentially monodic. The piano-accordion has in part usurped the place of the violin as accompanist to the morris dance and the 'squeeze-box' has added a few chords to give a lift to the rhythm, but the tune is in England, as it is in Scotland where the bagpipe has added its drone, basically a fiddle tune and therefore monodic. If it appears superfluous to emphasize the monodic character of English folk music, it is worth recalling that Chappell, who knew a lot about English melody but little about oral tradition, which moreover he mistrusted, went so far in his final essay, in which he was trying to do exactly what this chapter is trying to do, namely isolate the English features, concludes it by saying that 'the great test of whether a tune is good or bad is, will it admit of a good base? [*sic*]' To this conclusion he leads up by arguing that 'wild and irregular melodies', tunes that 'resist all

[1] Folksong To-day, HMV DLP 1143; A Jug of Punch, HMV CLP 1327.

attempts at making good bases (basses) for them' are thoroughly worthless and ought to be thrown aside. It is this attitude which made Sharp and his fellow pioneers insist on the independence of the oral tradition from Chappell's documentation, and if they sometimes claimed that the oral tunes were better than the written ones it was because they suspected that tunes lost something of their essential character when they were squared up for being fitted with a good bass. There were therefore good historical reasons for asserting the essentially monodic character of the tunes they found prevalent among an unsophisticated, i.e. non-harmonic, peasantry.

In practice, monody means the use of the modes other than the modern major and minor, as described in chapter 2, including the pentatonic. Pentatonism is common in Scottish music but rare in English folk-song, according to Dr Maud Karpeles in her revised edition of Sharp's *Some Conclusions*, whereas it is fairly common in the Appalachian Mountains of America. The only pentatonic tune quoted in *Some Conclusions*, and in a different context, is 'Robin Hood and the Pedlar', which was collected by Vaughan Williams in Essex in 1904[2] [Example 60]. A different kind of pentatonism, in which a

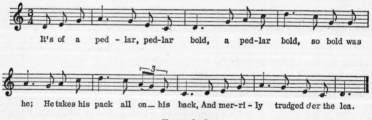

Example 60

semi-tone occurs is found in 'The Keys of Canterbury' collected by Sharp as already mentioned in chapter 2. The restricted compass of a fifth would seem to indicate that it is in essence a minor or at any rate Aeolian tune that happened not to need a

[2] *F.S.J.* No. 8 (1906), p. 155.

leading-note which might impede the non-stop circular re-
partee of the two singers – for it is one of those bidding-for-a-
bride songs best sung as a duet:

O Mad-am, I will give to you the Keys of Can-ter-
bu-ry, And all the bells in Lon-don shall ring to make us
mer-ry, If you will be my joy,— my sweet and on-ly
dear— And walk a-long with me an-y-where. —

Example 61

The Appalachian pentatonic tunes, however, suggest that they
are in some sense original, or earlier, versions of tunes in which
increased sophistication or a more impulsive artistry such as
produces ornamentation has caused the 'gaps' to be filled in
with passing notes, and strictly syllabic setting of words has
yielded to tied notes that make a more flexible, luxuriant
melody. This hypothetical evolution has been questioned, but it
seems inherently probable and best explains such a difference
as is shown in these two versions of 'The Cuckoo', one from the
Appalachians,[3] one from Somerset, both collected by Sharp
[Examples 62 and 63]. Example 62 is certainly beautiful in its
simplicity, but Example 63 is a more highly wrought melody,
such as the singer might have heard in an eighteenth-century
London theatre: the gaps have been filled, syllables have more

[3] *English Folk Song from the Southern Appalachians*, Vol. II, no. 140, p. 177.

The cuc-koo is a pret-ty bird, she sings as she flies; She brings us good tid-ings, she tells us no lies. She sucks all sweet— flow-ers to keep her voice clear; And she nev-er says cuc-koo till the spring of the year.

Example 62

O the cuc-koo she's a pret-ty bird, she— sing-eth as she flies. She— bring-eth good— ti-dings, she— tell-eth no lies. She— suck-eth white— flow-ers for to keep her voice— clear; And— the more she— sing-eth cuc-koo— the sum-mer draw-eth near.

Example 63

than one note and the rhythm has been made flexible with dotted notes. But the tune does not behave as though it had been up to London in one important respect: there is no implied modulation at the half-way cadence at the end of the third line. As already stated, the avoidance of modulation is almost a

154

litmus-paper test for the authenticity of a folk-song. On this point Sharp's experience and authority are decisive, and what he says is that folk-song 'so rarely modulates that we can almost say never modulates at all'.[4]

Modulates, that is, conventionally to the dominant. But occasionally one finds a song which seems as though it is on the point of modulating in the wrong direction, flatwards to the subdominant as in: 'The Brisk Young Widow' [Example 64]

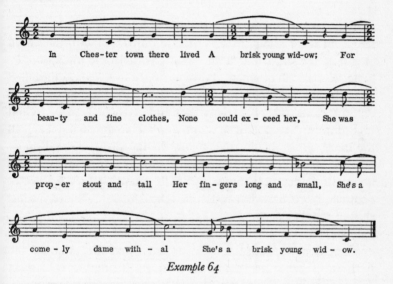

In Ches-ter town there lived A brisk young wid-ow; For beau-ty and fine clothes, None could ex - ceed her, She was prop - er stout and tall Her fin - gers long and small, She's a come - ly dame with - al She's a brisk young wid - ow.

Example 64

and the carol 'Come all you worthy gentlemen' [Example 65]. 'The Brisk Young Widow' is indeed an unconventional lady, fickle in her time-keeping, but she is emphatic that when she has

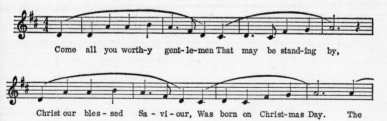

Come all you worth-y gent-le-men That may be stand-ing by, Christ our bles - sed Sa - vi - our, Was born on Christ-mas Day. The

[4] *Some Conclusions*, Ch. VI.

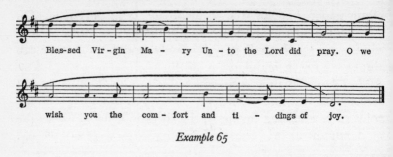

Bles-sed Vir-gin Ma — ry Un-to the Lord did pray. O we

wish you the com-fort and ti - dings of joy.

Example 65

switched from B natural to B flat she means it and sits on its strong beat for a long time, and is so impressed with the sound of it that she sticks to it in her final phrase in the tonality of C. 'The Worthy Gentlemen', however, only touch their flattened seventh once and have retrieved their balance by the next bar. All the same the effect is, if not indeed of a firm cadential modulation, at least of a momentary change of tonality, all the more noticeable in that it is in the flat direction and shows how the characteristically English feature of false relation comes about in Tudor polyphony and calls attention to a feature of Scottish, Northumbrian and some other tunes in which a similar shift of tonality occurs.

False relation occurs frequently in Tudor polyphony when one vocal part ascending uses a sharpened inflection of the sixth and seventh degrees of the scale while another vocal part descending uses the flattened inflection. They can even clash, but this liking for a contradiction between the parts is an English trait not favoured by continental composers and it persists from Byrd to Walton. But in monody no such contradiction is possible, only a blunt juxtaposition of two implied tonalities, when one phrase is simply transposed up or down to form its own counterpoise. A simple and well-known example is the Northumbrian folk-song 'Elsie Marley' [Example 66].

The sliding sequences, E flat, D flat, and maybe the octave leap in the second bar, though not in itself unvocal, rather suggest the influence of the Northumbrian small-pipe, a manually blown bagpipe smaller than the big Highland bag-

Di ye ken El - sie Mar - ley, hon - ey, The
wife — that sells the bar - ley, hon - ey? She lost — her pock-et and
all — her mon-ey A - back o' the bush i' the gar - den, hon - ey.
El - sie Mar - ley's grown — se fine, — She won't get up to
serve — the swine, — But lies in bed till eight — or nine. — —
Di ye ken El - sie Mar - ley, hon - ey?

Example 66

pipe. The latter according to Mr Francis Collinson is responsible
for a similar shift, down a tone and implying consecutive triads,
in a number of Scottish tunes, of which he quotes 'Tullochgorum' as an instance, in which this bar is repeated and varied
several times [Example C].

Example C

This feature of transposition of motif or phrase to make a
counterpoise to the original, though to be found in British

tunes, is not common compared with its occurrence in Czech and Hungarian tunes. Thus Kodály quotes from Bartók's collection (no. 243) an example that he says is universally known among Hungarians, 'Zörög a Kocsi' (The cart rattles) [Example 67], and he explains that this combination of a

Zö-rög a ko-csi, pat-tog-tat Jan-csi, ta-lán ér - tem jön-nek

Jaj, é-des a - nyám, sze - rel-mes daj-kám, de ha-mar el -visz-nek.

Example 67

pentatonic scale and a transposition structure is typical of the basic substructure of Hungarian melody. An English parallel, a five-note if not a pentatonic tune is the dance 'Nonesuch', which transposes its main phrase down a fourth [Example 68].

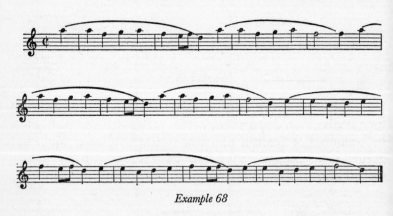

Example 68

Such transpositions, at different intervals, are fairly common in Czechoslovakian tunes. One example has already been quoted in chapter 3 'Tancuj' (Example 25) and one-bar transpositions were seen in Examples 26 and 27, and in Example 28 the Croatian tune used by Haydn in the London Symphony,

no. 104 in D. The Slovakian tune 'Pasol Janko tri voly' shows
an upward transposition of a fourth [Example 69]. Similarly in

Pa-sol Jan-ko tri vo-ly   u há - ja,   Pa-sol Jan-ko tri vo-ly   u há - ja

Example 69

the English country dance 'The Black Nag' there is an upward
shift of a fourth (and back) in the B music (i.e. the second part)
[Example 70] and sequence is of course often to be found, as in

Example 70

'Dargason' [Example 71]. But plainly there is nothing distinctively English in this occasional use of a structural feature
employed by various other national folk-melodies.

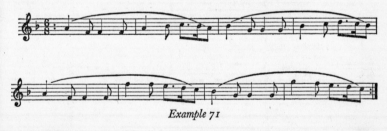

Example 71

Variable inflections and modality to be found in English
folk music give it some affinity, apart from historical anteced-
ence, with the art music of the sixteenth century, which indeed
seems to have lived nearer to folk art than that of later times.
Of the anonymous tunes that survive from the sixteenth century,
notably those in the virginal music of the period, it is not
possible to declare dogmatically that they are of folk origin but

M   159

most of those that occur in the Fitzwilliam and Neville collections have the smell of folk-song. The most conspicuous tune to have survived in both oral and printed traditions is 'Greensleeves', the most hard-worked tune of the seventeenth century. This has the suggestion of false relation, i.e. alternating flat and sharp sixths and sevenths in what is basically the Aeolian mode. It is in every way a remarkable tune: it has a compass of a tenth; it begins its second half with a flat seventh on a strong beat (cf. the 'Londonderry Air' for featuring the leading-note). Chappell gives its history from its entry at Stationers Hall in 1580, where it is called 'A new Northern Dittie of the Lady Green Sleeves', cites allusions to it by name in Shakespeare and Beaumont and Fletcher, notes its use in immediate borrowings of the tune for all sorts of words, including sacred parody. The version he prints is from William Ballet's Lute Book (*c.* 1600) as also does Simpson, both transposed up [Example 72].

Example 72

The inflections in this version are not identical with those of
Vaughan Williams's version that he put into his opera *Sir
John in Love* and so gave the tune a new twentieth-century
currency. But the tune, having been in print at any rate since
Playford put it into the seventh edition of *The Dancing Master*
in 1686 (reproduced by Simpson), has not produced many
variants, though Hammond found an odd one in Dorset in
1906 [Example 73]. However, the dance tradition has:

Example 73

Kidson and Neal produce this from a manuscript of 1838
[Example 74] and Sharp collected in Gloucestershire as

Example 74

accompaniment for the solo morris jig 'Bacca Pipes' [Example
75] in the Dorian mode, and a further variant from Somerset,
which he prints in *Morris Dance Tunes*, Set IV.

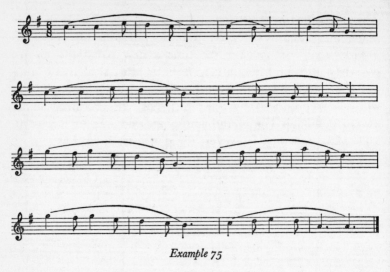

Example 75

Another Elizabethan tune with variable inflections is
'Rowland' or 'Lord Willoughby' already quoted in chapter 6,
Examples 55 and 56.

Of the modes Aeolian, Dorian and Mixolydian are in
common use, and their flat seventh was the feature that first
distinguished the newly collected folk-tunes from 'Old English'
and 'Traditional'. But the Lydian and the Phrygian are un-
common. The Lydian is the scale of the Elizabethan 'The
Woods so wild' [Example 76] and the Phrygian that of the

Example 76

beautiful Devon 'The Evening Prayer' already quoted [Ex-
ample 49]. The Ionian is of course commonest in English folk-
song and when combined with a jog-trot six-eight rhythm is the

vehicle for all the more cheerful, and often less distinguished, ballad narratives.

The revival of plainsong and folk-song at the turn of the century gave musicians a great deal of trouble when they came to harmonize their melodies, as they wished to do. The matter was endlessly discussed, e.g. in connexion with such a book as the *Cowley Carol Book* and by church musicians, including Stanford. Sharp had to devote two chapters to the subject in *Some Conclusions* and to put Brahms in the dock for his failure to observe the true character of the folk-melodies, of which he was fond, when he came to make settings of them. Experience and scholarship have now solved that problem, which is reviewed in chapter 9 below.

The structure of English folk-tunes is naturally determined largely by the words of the songs and the figures of the dance. The familiar quatrain pattern for strophic songs is the common A A B A, so are A B B A and A B A C, of which respectively Sharp quotes as examples 'The Banks of the Sweet Dundee' and 'The Sweet Primeroses', but more remarkable is the organic form of 'The Seeds of Love' [Example 77] in which each clause,

Example 77

five of them by means of repeating the last line of the quatrain, grows out of its predecessor A B C D E – like late Beethoven on a small scale.

Chappell prints a version, which he says is traditional and

came from Lancashire, which is plainly related to the Somerset version collected by Sharp – his first song incidentally – but though it repeats the last line, the form is more conventional, A B B A A – [Example 78] – hence the claim that the folk version is, if not better, at any rate more striking and interesting.

Example 78

Sharp notes two other features which struck him at the time he was collecting as unusual and characteristic. One was the use by the folk-singers of non-harmonic passing notes, i.e. quitted by a leap, and the other was the comparatively common use of five-in-a-bar rhythms as compared for example with the somewhat square tunes of Germany. His Somerset versions of 'Barbara Allen', 'Searching for Lambs' and most versions of 'The Bold Fisherman', all owe their singular charm to this rhythm, but since Sharp wrote comparative studies have shown that such five, seven and irregular rhythms are not peculiar to England.

It seems therefore not possible to isolate motifs, intervals and rhythms as characteristic to the extent that it is of other national folk-melody. Yet English tunes sound English. One broad class of them, like one broad class of English lyric poetry has a kind of pastoral air: Herrick and Housman both exhale the atmosphere of the English countryside. Playford's dance-tunes are more urban, but even they have the temper that used to be described in the adjective 'blithe'. There is something pre-Industrial about our folk music. It was from the peasantry and the merchant marine, before sail was driven from the sea by steam, that our corpus of folk-song was retrieved, and the subjects with which the songs dealt were predominantly rural, though the press-gang, highwaymen, executions, trades like cobbling and tailoring, provided material for the folk, as well as universal topics like love in all its variety, happy, unhappy, casual and faithful.

The towns after the Industrial Revolution did not wholly forget the songs brought in from the country, but for their own use mainly turned to the broadsides. Verses were turned out dealing with local topics, for which tunes were borrowed from various sources, including folk-song but often made up of strings of melodic commonplaces. Mr E. D. Mackerness pays some attention to the music of the town proletariat in his *A Social History of English Music* and speaks of the satirical broadsides of the period 1780–1850 in which the master-cutlers of Sheffield, puritans, teetotallers, *nouveaux riches* were attacked, and the effects of introducing machinery were sometimes deplored, but the building of railways and canals was often celebrated. The names of some of the local poets in the north of England are known, and the modern (i.e. post-1950) spread of urban folk-song connected with the names of Ewan MacColl and Peggy Seeger reproduces many of the features described by Mr Mackerness. The new words are the raw material of folk poetry, not yet folk because it is so far an individual composition unaffected by the oral tradition – like 'Silver Jack' on the Mississippi. Mr MacColl, for example, prints (in *The Singing Island*) a song written by a locomotive fireman of King's Cross in 1957. This song 'The Colour Bar Strike' is written in the folk tradition and though the versification is crude the heart is in the right place:

> The colour bar strikers soon went back
> Jim Figgins led the N.U.R.
> And when they asked for his support
> He said 'We'll have no colour bar'.

And the tune? A derivative from 'Searching for Lambs' [Example 79].

Example 79

Mr Mackerness records that the old love songs were sung as well as the modern satires, and Frank Kidson speaks of 'The Knight and Shepherd's Daughter', a trans-class ballad of marriage that is found in Percy's *Reliques*, being sung by Leeds mill-girls when they went on a 'fly-boat' outing on the canal. Mr MacColl's volume shows the same phenomenon, since among his courting songs he includes 'The Foggy Dew', 'Scarborough Fair', 'The Banks of Sweet Dundee' to tunes recognizably near to those traditionally known. Further evidence of the same sort is that remarkable old folk-singer who died at the age of 90 in 1962, George Maynard[5] of Copthorne on the Surrey-Sussex border. He had a big repertory, of which some eighty were recorded, which included both true folk-songs, including a slightly more florid version of 'The Seeds of Love' than Sharp's (cf. with Example 77) [Example 80], 'William Taylor', 'Rolling in the Dew', 'The Undaunted

[5] See *Journal of E.F.D.S.S.*, Vol. IX, no. 4, 1963.

O I sowed the seeds of love, For to blos-som all in the spring; I sow'd it all on one May morn-ing While the small birds they did sing, ____ While the small birds they did sing.

Example 80

Female' and other familiar songs, but also a ballad made up in the folk tradition for him by one of his friends about a poaching exploit – Maynard was a practised poacher – in which to a patter tune the story is told of a couple of poachers who were taken to Croydon for trial and to Wandsworth gaol to serve their sentences. Ewan MacColl similarly made up a song about a lorry driver's life to a slightly awkward tune (with an F sharp in the scale of A minor) which ended:

Bury me by Scotch Corner or on the road outside Carlisle
And I'll lie and hear the heavy stuff go tearing up the miles.

Still later *The Times* of 11th October 1966, quoted a case of three young men, one with a guitar, singing in St Vincent Street, Glasgow, a song provoked by the current redeployment of labour policy, which went:

Three nights a week and Sunday double time (*bis*)
We work all day and we work all night.
To hell with you, Jack, I'm all right
Three nights a week and Sunday double time.

Tune not specified. Rural and urban modern compositions in the folk-idiom. But a hundred years earlier the town population turned to the music-hall songs then coming into vogue. Mr Mackerness relates that the great days of the music hall, beginning in 1861 with the opening of the Oxford Hall in London, were preceded by popular sing-songs and concerts in public houses.

The most widely distributed of these music-hall songs was a pseudo folk-song called 'Villikins and his Dinah', which was often delivered to the early collectors without any suspicion that it was not like the other real folk-songs they were singing. Actually it was a burlesque of a folk ballad to what is essentially a folk-tune. This tune turns up as the basis to a large number of triple-time tunes to folk-ballads – Hammond collected a variant of it in Dorset in 1906 to the words of 'Peggy and the Soldier'. The music-hall 'Villikens and his Dinah' – the spelling of Vilikins varies a good deal – appeared in print *circa* 1850 when Sam Cowell included it in his *120 Comic Songs* thus:

Example 81
168

Note the element of facetiousness introduced into the words in order to enhance the comicality of that quaint thing, a folk-song from the country. But it continued to be sung by folk-singers everywhere – thus Helen Creighton had it sung to her in Nova Scotia in 1932. A similar and even more derisory parody is 'Joe Muggins', which follows the story and tune of 'Lord Lovel'. The parody is so outrageous that it is worth quoting in full, as it was sung by Daniel Copley, a carpenter who lived all his life (c. 1835–1927) in the Dartford district of Kent. The parallel with Sharp's version is hideously exact and the tune a near relation.

JOE MUGGINS

Joe Muggins he stood by his old donkey cart
A'stroking his old black moke
When up came his lady love, sweet Sally Belle
And thus to Joe Muggins she spoke, spoke, spoke.　(*Repeat for chorus*)

Where are you going, Joe Muggins, she said
Where are you going cried she
O I be a-going, you scamp Sally Belle
To Smithfield to sell my donkey, -key, -key.

When will you be back, Joe Muggins? she said
When will you be back, said she
About half past five, or six at the most
So yoo'll get me a bloater for tea, tea, tea.

Scarce had he been gone three hours or more
To Smithfield and sold his donkey
When the thoughts of his bloater came up in his head
Oh! I hope it's soft roed, said he, he, he.

So homeward he went on the Marylebone stage
Till he came to the famed Rose and Crown
And he saw there his lady-love stretched on the floor
And the people all fighting around, -round, -round.

He sent for two boxes of Morrison's pills
Seven dozen her throat he rammed down
Saying 'You won't get drunk in a hurry again'
As the pills she kept swallowing down, down, down.

Poor Sally she died from the pills, so they say
Which made poor Joe Muggins afright
He swallowed twelve dozen without delay
And gave up the ghost that night, night, night.

Joe Muggins was buried the very next day
And Sally in less than a week
And out of her ashes there grew a great carrot
And out of Joe Muggins a leek, leek, leek.

They grew and they grew to the top of the grave
Till they wasn't let grow any more
For cut up they were for to season the soup
That was given away to the poor, poor, poor.

LORD LOVEL

Lord Lovel, he stood by his own castle gate
A'combing his milk-white steed,
When up came Lady Nancy Belle
To wish her lover good speed (*bis*).

O! where are you going, Lord Lovel, she said
O where are you going? cried she
I'm going, my Lady Nancy Belle, strange countries for to
    see, see, see
Strange countries for to see.

How long you'll be gone, Lord Lovel she said
How long you'll be gone? cried she
In a year or two or three at the most
I'll return to my Lady Nancy, -cy, -cy
I'll return to my Lady Nancy.

He had not been gone but a year and a day
Strange countries for to see
But a strange thought came into his head
I'll go and see Lady Nancy, -cy, -cy
I'll go and see Lady Nancy.

He rode and he rode on his milk-white steed
Till he came to London Town
And there he heard the church bells ring
And the people all mourning around, a-round
And the people all mourning around.

Ah, who is dead? Lord Lovel he cried
Ah, who is dead cried he
An old woman said Some lady is dead
They called her Lady Nancy, -cy, -cy etc.

He ordered the grave to be opened a-wide
And the shroud to be turned around
And then he kissed her cold clay cheeks
Till the tears came trickling down, down, down, etc.

Lady Nancy she died as it might be to-day
Lord Lovel he died as to-morrow
Lady Nancy she died out of pure grief
Lord Lovel he died out of sorrow, -row, etc.

The one was buried in the lower chancel
The other was buried in the high'r
From one sprang out a gallant red rose
From the other a gilly flower, flower, etc.

And there they grew and turned and turned
Till they gained the chancel top
And there they grew and turned and turned
And tied in a true lover's knot, knot, knot, etc.

Copley's tune was

Example 82

which has a family resemblance to most of the known tunes to
'Lord Lovel'. Bronson[6] quotes no less than sixty in six-eight
time, most of which are from recent American singers, but a
number from British sources, including Sharp in Somerset in
1904, Gloucestershire in 1907, in Oxfordshire 1911, Clive
Carey at Thaxted in 1911, Percy Grainger in Lincolnshire in
1906 and two from Aberdeenshire *c.* 1850 and 1907. One of
Bronson's tunes comes from a book of comic songs, so it looks
as though the parody crossed the Atlantic. This is an unexpected
testimony to the hardiness of the traditional ballad and the
constancy amid all variants of the tune. Another such testimony
is to be found in Flora Thompson's *Lark Rise to Candleford*,
where she quotes the traditional 'Lord Lovel', though without
tune, as sung in the village inn of her north Oxfordshire hamlet
in the eighties. She also cites 'The Outlandish Knight' as an
out-of-date survival from a long line of grandfathers.

Further investigation of the industrial songs along the lines of
Mr Mackerness but reinforced by personal collecting in mining
areas has enabled Mr A. L. Lloyd[7] to write a new chapter in
the history of our popular music. He gives instances of new

[6] *The Traditional Tunes of the Child Ballads.*   [7] *Folk Music in England*, 1967.

subject-matter being poured into traditional forms by local versifiers. Thus he prints a dialogue ballad between a coalowner and a pitman's wife that was written at the time of a coal strike in Durham in 1844 to a tune of the 'Henry Martin' family. It began in the old 'as I went out all on the highway' manner and had a derry-down refrain but instead of a tale of erotic dalliance it turned into an economico-political argument about the difference between a coal-owner's royalties and a pitman's wage. Mr Lloyd records that this ballad was rediscovered in 1951 and had a second currency, but it does not seem to have lived for a hundred years as an oral folk-song. He has discovered and described a whole sub-literature of local songs in Northumberland and Durham, including workers' parodies of their own songs, songs of protest, and dialect pieces (these especially in Yorkshire and Lancashire, where incidentally the Bacup morris dance and the Easter custom of pace-egging survive). All this is of great sociological interest but Mr Lloyd admits that the industrial songs, for whatever reason, probably because they have not been subject to the refining process of oral transmission – or could it be that vulgarity is an urban product that tarnishes naïve and simple art? – are not artistically equal to their pre-industrial forerunners and he therefore differentiates them from authentic folk-songs by the name of 'workers' songs'.

Sharp and his fellow collectors in the south made a firmer distinction between what they collected from oral tradition in the country and the townsman's music than did Frank Kidson, who lived in the West Riding of Yorkshire where town and country interpenetrated – one walked from Shipley to Ilkley and thence into Leeds across open moorland – or than Stokoe and the collectors in the Newcastle area. The peasant and the industrial proletariat seemed different types, did indeed have some different tastes and, when it came to songs, preferred the more sophisticated products of the music hall to those that grandfather used to sing, but the difference and the distinction were not absolute nor exclusive. A further misconception that could not have been avoided till it was disproved by subsequent (up to half a century) events, was that folk-song was dying and that the collection of songs from the lips of old singers was 'only just in time'. It was all to the good that the revivalists acted under the stimulus of this imagined urgency. But folk-song has proved after all to be a tougher plant, as this urban currency and the post-1945 urban revival fifty years on has proved. Sharp found his *cache* of English songs in the Appalachian Mountains in 1917, which was also a safeguard against total loss. The story of American salvage is another bit of history related elsewhere (in chapter 5); it resembles the English story at any rate in having a post-war vogue among an urban population to account for. The plant is certainly tough enough to survive in the melting-pot of North America.

Mention of Northumberland brings up the question of regionalism in English folk-song. It was no more than the good manners of scholarship to record when, where and from whom a song was noted down. Certain localities attracted their own collectors: Lucy Broadwood began near her home in Surrey and Sussex, Cecil Sharp in Somerset because his friend Charles Marson had a country parish there, Ann Gilchrist was a life-long Lancastrian. It was no doubt with some idea of collating the scattered finds that *English County Songs* was published in 1893. Its editors, Lucy Broadwood and J. A. Fuller Maitland, who were cousins, aimed at getting specimens to represent every English county. But as collecting went on it became apparent that county boundaries had no significance for the currency of folk-songs. It was not only 'Barbara Allen' and 'The Golden Vanity' that were ubiquitous. Variants of the same song were found as far apart as Somerset, where Sharp found 'The Bold Fisherman', and Norfolk, where E. J. Moeran found it some years later – both were in five-four time – and before that it had been collected near Hitchin in Hertfordshire. This is not to deny that some songs have local attachments: 'The Derby Ram' comes from Derbyshire; the 'Helston Furry' belongs to Cornwall and nowhere else; ballads pick up local names and locally remembered tragedies. Indeed the Cumberland poet Norman Nicholson has said that one of the characteristics of the Border ballads is that they abolish the gap between generations, and that the landscape takes its meaning from inherited personal memories, i.e. the sense of locality is compulsive. But the geographical distribution of English folksong has very little significance with one exception – and of course the Celtic fringe. The exception is Northumbria, which has a corpus of songs, pipe-tunes and sword dances that are not found elsewhere in Britain.

The reasons for this regional folk music would seem to be, first, a racial one, that in its turn brings with it dialect and pronunciation. The second is the survival of the Northumbrian small-pipe – the Border country has lost its small-pipe[8] but the English pipe is still played and has an extensive repertory of some splendid tunes. There is also a concentration of sworddance traditions in the north-east of England – the distribution of sword dances is a special study in itself.

The racial strain that sets Northumberland, including Durham but not Yorkshire, apart from other regions of England, which are still roughly definable by the Saxon heptarchy, is Norwegian, to be distinguished from that of Danish Scandinavians further south. As if to underline this Norse dominance, in spite of all the mixing that has gone on for a thousand years, the rapper sword dance is confined to Northumbria and stops short at the Tees, whereas the longsword dances, which are not unlike it in pattern and ritual, belong to Mercia which was a Danish settlement.[9] W. G. Whittaker, while affirming the variety of type to be found in the various communities, pitmen, ashers, farmers, keelmen (i.e. boatmen, specially on coal tenders) and the existence of differences in dialect strongly affirms the singularity of Northumbria, likening it to Berwick-on-Tweed as being neither English nor Scottish, but both and neither.

[8] Francis Collinson, *The Traditional and National Music of Scotland*, 1966.
[9] Joseph Needham in *Journal of E.F.D.S.S.*, Vol. III, no. 1, 1936; *Collected Essays*: 'The Folk Music of N.E. England'.

The small-pipe, briefly mentioned in chapter 4, is a bagpipe blown with a bellows held under the arm with three (or four) drones and a chanter with nine (sometimes more – Tom Clough's pipe had seventeen) holes and a stopped end which allowed staccato playing and breaks in the sound such as is not possible on the Scottish bagpipe. Tunes played on this pipe showed the characteristic already noted of an implied harmonic shift up a tone and back again. A splendid example is the dirge 'Noble Squire Dacre' [Example 83], 'Elsie Marley' is a song

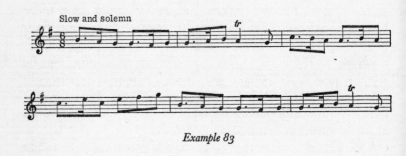

Example 83

which behaves in this way – as already quoted in Example 66 above.

Whittaker comments on the unusual succession of sixths (and he might have added octaves) in the tune, which he attributes to its pipe origin, and identifies Elsie Marley as the spoilt wife of the innkeeper of 'The Barley Mow' near Chester-le-Street who was pilloried by some local wag in the late eighteenth century. But there are plenty of true song-tunes; 'The Keel Row' is the one that has come south and is known to all. Love songs are 'Blow the Wind Southerly', which Katheen Ferrier used to sing, 'The Waters of Tyne' has an obviously local provenance. 'Dollia' from Tyneside is an example rare in English folk-song of a lullaby, in which the mother gossips to her friends about the regiments coming up and down the great North Road, while she dandles her child [Example 84]. Another song – two songs actually – peculiar to this tradition is the wry, gentle, lament of

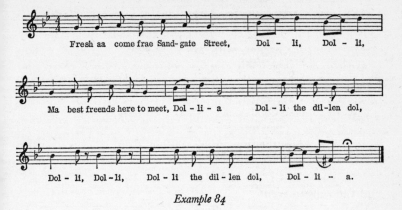

Fresh aa come frae Sand-gate Street, Dol - li, Dol - li,

Ma best freends here to meet, Dol - li - a Dol - li the dil-len dol,

Dol - li, Dol-li, Dol - li the dil - len dol, Dol - li - a.

Example 84

old age, 'Sair fyel'd, hinnie', self-pitying but **too** strong to be
sentimental:

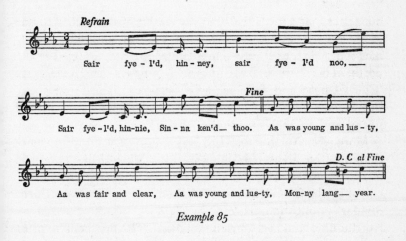

Refrain

Sair fye - l'd, hin - ney, sair fye - l'd noo, ___

Fine

Sair fye - l'd, hin-nie, Sin - na ken'd ___ thoo. Aa was young and lus - ty,

D. C al Fine

Aa was fair and clear, Aa was young and lus-ty, Mon-ny lang ___ year.

Example 85

The words of 'When This Old Hat Was New' may be quoted
instead of the tune

O what a poor old man am I
Come listen to my song

Four verses describe the good old days, of which the last is

> It's near to four-score years ago
>   The truth I do declare
> Oh, men they took each other's words,
>   And thought it very fair;
> Nae bonds nor bills was then required
>   Then words were a' so true;
> And that was in my youthful days
>   When this old hat was new.

and the refrain went:

> When this old hat was new, my boys
> When this old hat was new
> Oh, what a swaggering blade was I
> When this old hat was new.

Songs are found in the north on the nation-wide topic of thyme in the garden of love. 'The Oak and the Ash' and some Christmas songs such as 'I Saw Three Ships' are not confined to the north. There are ballads, of which among the greatest are 'Chevy Chase' and 'Binnoie', a fine version of 'The Two Sisters'. But in Northumbria there is a regional as well as a Border strand and an English strand of tradition.

Moreover, Northumberland was aware of it and did something positive about cherishing it. 'Elsie Marley' first appeared in a 'garland' of 1784, *The Bishoprick Garland or Durham Minstrel*, edited by the formidable Joseph Ritson, but no tune is specified. Similar publication of 'old' or 'famous' songs, peculiar to Northumberland and Durham followed. The first book to print tunes was a collection of *Tunes with Variations Adapted for the Northumberland Small Pipes, Violin or Flute* early in the nineteenth century. The composer, William Shield, was a Tyneside man who says he was taught Border tunes in his youth and used them in a text-book of harmony he published in London about 1815. By the middle of the century the matter of local tunes was taken up by the Society of Antiquaries of Newcastle-upon-Tyne. This was in 1855 when Chappell was at work in London, but delays of one sort or another prevented publication before 1881, by which time they had been anticipated by a Miss M. H. Mason, who brought out in 1878 *Nursery Rhymes and County Songs* with piano accompaniment to the number of fifty-eight. The animating spirit in the Society of Antiquaries was John Stokoe, and it is from his collection, *Songs and Ballads of Northern England*, for which piano accompaniments were provided by Samuel Reay, an eminent Victorian organist, that knowledge of them began to spread. Dr Whittaker criticizes the book not only for its harmony but also for a decline in Stokoe's scholarship, and it was with the mixed feelings of appreciation and reservation that he produced *North Countrie Ballads, Songs and Pipe-Tunes, for use, in home and school* (Curwen, 1922), in two volumes.

The names therefore of Shield, Stokoe, Mason and Whittaker have to be added to the pioneers whose work was described in chapter 5. It was not till Dr Whittaker (1876–1944), a New-castle man and first Professor of Music in its university, but known throughout the country for his work as a choral conductor and adjudicator, proclaimed the existence of the Northumbrian tradition by lectures and still more by his choral arrangements, that north and south fully realized that they belonged to one movement. The realization was helped in the first two decades of the century by Cecil Sharp's discovery of the living traditions of the sword dances of the north.

CHAPTER EIGHT

English Folk-Melody

(2) Functional

Ballads and folk-songs are works of art in their own right. They are both forms of *Gesamtkunstwerk*, products of a marriage (or some aestheticians say a rape) of two arts, words and music, which are roughly equal: in ballads the words are the dominant partner, in songs the melody is. But within musical folk art there are several categories in which the music is willingly subservient. They are the dance, which may be ritual or social; ritual itself in connexion with seasonal observances like harvest-homes and Christmas; shanties, where the function of music is to lighten labour and allied to them street cries, in which a vendor sings to make his voice carry and commend his wares; singing games and nursey rhymes, which belong to the folklore of childhood; and the carol, which has elements from balladry, ritual, theology, the seasons, poetry, dancing and all.

Carol and Wassail

As a matter of history the carol has had a revival of its own which has run parallel with that of the folk-song, though with mathematical impropriety the two lines converged in the first decade of the present century – Vaughan Williams's *Fantasia on Christmas Carols* may be taken as celebrating their handshake. Folk-song has a wider range of mood to cover; carol draws on a richer mixture of traditions. It is only as recently as 1958 that a full account of the carol, its revival and its extraordinary place in modern British life has been written. There is no mystery about it and some few people, myself among them, inspired to this as to so many other things in music by Sir Hugh Allen, began to explore the origins of the Christmas carol, of which the importance in our present community life is probably best indicated by the broadcasting to the world from King's College, Cambridge, of the Service of Nine Lessons and Carols on Christmas Eve.

But until Dr Erik Routley published his book *The English Carol* there was no means for a musician, a parson, a literary man, a chorister or just a plain man, to acquaint himself with all the lore behind this phenomenon, the carol revival which has conquered agnostics and Presbyterians – for Scotland, which Calvinistically for 400 years rejected Christmas and concentrated on the celebration of New Year, has capitulated in a single generation.

This is to speak of the Christmas carol, but 'carol' has a wider connotation and it was not, at least until the present century, restricted to Christmas. What then is a carol? The dictionary says a dance-song, a ring dance with a vocal accompaniment and this is historically correct, as appeared in chapter 6 *à propos* of that other dance-song, the ballad. The burden which is the distinguishing feature of the carol survives in the modern carol, such as 'The Holly and the Ivy', 'In Bethlehem City', 'The First Nowell', 'God rest you merry', all that is left of the dance. But this element is responsible for the gaiety which is proper to the carol – did not Percy Dearmer attempt to define it in the three adjectives 'simple, hilarious and popular'?[1] This gaiety makes it an appropriate song for any festal occasion, such as the beginning of spring on May Day or harvest-home. It is only by a gradual decline of the agricultural festivals that it has acquired its special connexion with Christmas. The corpus of English folk-song contains many examples of May Day carols:

> O I've been a rambling all this night
> And sometime of this day;
> And now returning back again
> I brought you a garland gay.

[1] Preface to *Oxford Carol Book*.

or this fragment of 'The Moon shines bright' sung by children at Rushden in Northamptonshire on May Day, 1905[2]:

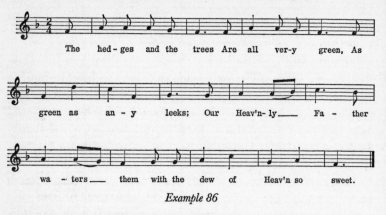

The hed-ges and the trees Are all ver-y green, As green as an-y leeks; Our Heav'n-ly___ Fa - ther wa - ters___ them with the dew of Heav'n so sweet.

Example 86

But in point of fact the carol has more and more tended to crystallize the special emotions of Christmas and New Year, although soon after the Reformation their theme was more often the Crucifixion than the Incarnation. Thus in Kele's *Christmas carolles newely Imprynted* (*circa* 1545)[3] there are only two Christmas carols proper, though there are several hymns to the Virgin and one or two for St Stephen, Holy Innocents and Circumcision, which are part of the twelve days' festival of Christmas. The Crucifixion is a more frequent subject, though there are a couple of ribald and a couple of comic songs in what was evidently a kind of community song-book – indeed the woodcut on the title page is a picture of the three crosses on Calvary, and the opening carol of the third section follows the refrain

> Gaudeamus synge we, in hoc sacro tempore
> Puer nobis natus est ex Maria Virgine

with a verse

> Mary moder come and se
> Thy sone is nayled on a tre

[2] *F.S.J.* No. 7, p. 132.
[3] Modern facsimile print from Harvard, ed. Edward Bliss Reed, 1932.

182

thus connecting the two events exactly as in 'The Holly and the Ivy'.

Kele and his predecessor Wynkyn de Worde, who issued a collection with the same title in 1521, of which the 'Boar's Head Carol' (*Caput apri defero*) survives, testify to the flourishing state of the carol, which has indeed been demonstrated ever since R. L. Greene made his great book in 1935,[4] by the publication in *Musica Britannica* in 1952 of 119 polyphonic settings of fifteenth-century carols, English, Latin and macaronic (i.e. with Latin interpolations in a vernacular text). Polyphony on this plane is far removed from folk-song, but the fifteenth century was the great age not only of carols but of mystery plays. The carol marks the same tendency to emancipate religious feeling from too restrictive ecclesiastical influence and to humanize it. Hence the appearance of Joseph, Herod, three Wise Men, shepherds in the fields and so on as very human people like the good citizens of York, Chester or Coventry who impersonated them in the mystery plays. The ambiguous position of Joseph, for instance, which was always an old man's part appears in the 'Cherry Tree Carol' [Example 87]. Mary asks for a cherry from the tree, Joseph refuses to

Jo-seph was an old man, And an old man was he, When he married Ma-ry In the land of Gal-i-lee.

Example 87

reach it for her – 'Let him pluck thee a cherry That brought thee now with child' – the child in the womb bids the tree bow its branch and Mary retorts to Joseph 'See, I have cherries at command'. This is a legend of wide distribution and great persistence. In the East Joseph is represented as an old man

[4] *The Early English Carol*, Oxford.

with a beard, tired from his journey, troubled and puzzled, cold and worn out. In the West the picture of him is variously modified: he is sometimes represented as helping to look after the child, but more often in the French carols[5] he is an object of ridicule, the *père putatif* who

> D'un air obligeant et doux
> Recevait les dons de tous
> Sans cérémonie

Wasn't he jealous?

> Saint Joseph, dites-le nous
> Quels sentiments eûtes-vous
> Quand vous vîtes la grossesse
> De la divine Princesse
> N'en fûtes-vous point jaloux?

English carols do not go as far as this: Joseph is merely (*a*) bearded, (*b*) unkind but not cruel. Thus the Chester play has:

> Whatever this olde man that heare is,
> Take heede how his head is hoare.
> His beard is like a buske of bryers
> With a pound of haire about his mouth and more.

The Coventry play contains as incidental music the well-known lullaby carol, where

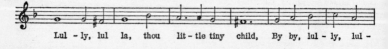

Lul - ly, lul la, thou lit - tle tiny child, By by, lul - ly, lul -

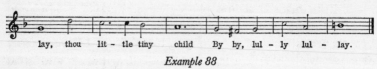

lay, thou lit - tle tiny child By by, lul - ly lul - lay.

Example 88

[5] See J. R. H. de Smidt, *Les Noëls et la tradition populaire*, Amsterdam, H. J. Paris, 1932.

is sung by the women of Bethlehem, just before the slaughter of the Innocents. The tune is dated 1591.

But to return to Joseph. In the Coventry play Joseph enters as the Angel Gabriel departs. He reproaches Mary, is reproved by the Angel, and is reconciled to Mary. So too in a French *noël* 'Joseph est bien marié'

Example 89

as also in our own 'When righteous Joseph wedded was' found in Gilbert's 1822 carol book [Example 90]:

Example 90

When righteous Joseph wedded was
To Israel's Hebrew maid
The Angel Gabriel came from Heav'n
And to the Virgin said:
Hail, blessed Mary, full of grace
The Lord remain on thee
Thou shalt conceive and bear a Son
Our Saviour for to be.

With a burden sung to the second part of the tune with a slightly varied cadence

Then sing you all, both great and small,
Nowell, nowell, nowell.
We may rejoice to hear the voice
Of the Angel Gabriel.

A Cornish folk-singer telescopes the 'Cherry Tree Carol' and 'The Holly and the Ivy' in a most curious amalgam, changing from the one to the other at the fifth verse but using 'The Holly and Ivy' refrain throughout [Example 91]. No very certain

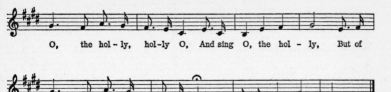

O, the hol - ly, hol-ly O, And sing O, the hol - ly, But of

all the trees that's in the wood It is the hol - ly.

Example 91

deductions are to be drawn except that, though there is a
strong case for arguing that the carol, unlike the folk-song, has
an ecclesiastical origin, the traditions have become inextricably
mixed and for this reason the designation 'traditional' is the
appropriate one. This particular sort of conflation from Cornwall, however, is very rare and looks like an individual idio-
syncrasy. Yet there is a similar telescoping of a wassail tune to
the twelve joys of Mary with 'The Holly and the Ivy' burden
in a carol collected from gypsies in the New Forest by Alice
Gillington [Example 92].

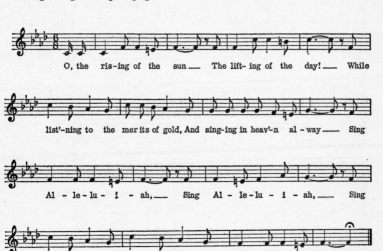

O, the ris-ing of the sun — The lift- ing of the day! — While

list'-ning to the mer its of gold, And sing-ing in heav'-n al - way — Sing

Al - le-lu - i - ah, — Sing Al - le-lu - i - ah, — Sing

Al - le-lu, the heav'ns are true, Sweet blest Al-lu u - ay. —

Example 92

Other carols that involve apocryphal legends are 'The Bitter Withy', 'I saw three ships' (of the skulls of the Magi being taken to Cologne) and 'King Herod and the Cock'. From a German mystery play we have taken (Oxford Carol Book, no. 77) a song of the crib;

> Joseph lieber, Joseph mein,
> Hilf mir wiegen mein Kindelein

to the gently swaying lullaby tune *Resonet in laudibus*, which Brahms was to set with viola obbligato. Also from a Leipzig manuscript of 1570 and there described as *uraltes* is the supremely beautiful *In dulci jubilo*, which was set as a chorale by Bach, as a noble part-song by R. L. Pearsall and maltreated by Helmore and Stainer, who set it to a jingle 'Good Christian men rejoice' that doubled its speed. The macaronic words had been translated by the Wedderburns for their *Gude and Godlie Ballates* of 1540. The rhymes of the Latin and the vernacular must be preserved, so that the old and the new pronunciations of Latin must be used according to the translation, the old Erasmian pronunciation as English when singing Pearsall, the new Ciceronian if singing Woodward's translation in the *Cowley Carol Book*. The word 'macaronic' means paste, like the *pasta* macaroni, which will seem a less mundane metaphor if we remember that we use 'interlarded' in the same sort of literary context: the carol text is interlarded with Latin tags of clerical origin. This clerical element is a further contribution from the Middle Ages to the carol tradition. Besides hymns of the Church – hymns made a further contribution four centuries later, e.g. *Adeste fideles* – the Middle Ages contributed lullabies taken from the worship of the Virgin by the Catholic Church.

The traceable history of the English carol is longer than that of folk-song, except in so far as the Wassail songs proper to New Year go back to immemorial and essentially pagan origins, at least in fact to the fourteenth century. But Sidgwick and Chambers propound the opposite theory to an educated origin and say that the Church took over popular songs and sanctified them, i.e. carols are sacred parodies. Both theories would seem to contain the truth for, as indeed we have already seen, the traditions cross and recross. If we continue this history from the point we have reached with the publication of Kele's *Christmas Carols newely Imprinted* and its immediate predecessor, Wynkyn de Worde's book with the same title of 1521, we find that as the sixteenth century advanced Protestantism grew more and more Puritan and the carols more and more solemn and further and further from the wassailing songs with their barely veiled paganism. The Reformation had removed the Virgin and the female source of inspiration of the carols and tended to turn Christmas back into a pagan feast with much eating and drinking, mumming, singing and games. But Puritanism by the seventeenth century took a stand against festivity altogether, so much so that the Long Parliament ordered Christmas in 1644 to be observed as a fast and in 1647 abolished it altogether. In 1656 a tract stigmatized Christmas Day as 'The old Heathen's Feasting Day in honour to Saturn their Idol-God, the Papists's Massing Day, the Profane Man's Ranting Day, the Superstitious Man's Idol Day, the Multitude's Idle Day, Satan's that Adversary's Working Day, the True Christian Man's Fasting Day. We are persuaded, no one thing more hindereth the Gospel work all the year long than doth the observation of that Idol Day once in a year, having so many days of cursed observation with it.'

However, as Mr Laurence Whistler writes in his book about the English festivals[6] 'to believe that the Puritans destroyed Christmas is like believing (as many do) that Dickens or the Prince Consort invented it.' The Prince Consort was responsible for establishing the German Christmas tree in England in 1841 and Dickens published his small novel, *A Christmas Carol* (in which there is only a single reference to a single carol), in 1843. Mr Whistler continues 'Christmas lives: loses one habit, acquires another and sometimes falls back into his ancient ways.

[6] *The English Festivals*, 1947.

Thus for example in Georgian times he allowed noble and bourgeois alike to reject this loveliest music, the carols.'

But they were still not dead, for in 1838 William Howitt a Quaker author wrote, 'Carols are not calculated to stand the test of these days: the schoolmaster will root them out', which rather looks as though the tradition, like folk-songs, was flowing underground among the illiterate. Anyhow, revival was on the way to neutralize the schoolmaster's rooting-out process. Five years earlier in 1833 William Sandys, F.S.A., published *Christmas Carols ancient and modern, including the most popular in the West of England, with the tunes to which they are sung*. The West of England connexion may have come from his predecessor in the field, Davies Gilbert, a Penzance man, an M.P. and a President of the Royal Society, who in 1822 published *Some ancient Christmas carols with the tunes to which they were formerly sung in the West of England*. Neither Gilbert nor Sandys were musicians enough to attempt four-part harmony though they provided a bass of sorts, but they were musicians enough to include the tunes, 'A Virgin most pure' (to a variant of the usual 'Virgin unspotted' tune) and 'While shepherds watched their flocks by night' to a psalm tune other than the usual Winchester Old (in Gilbert) and 'The First Nowell', 'To-morrow shall be my dancing day', 'God rest you merry', 'I saw three ships' and the 'Cherry Tree Carol' (in Sandys). The next publication of importance was *Carols for Christmas-tide* by Thomas Helmore and J. M. Neale in 1853, which contained a dozen Christmas carols 'set to Ancient Melodies by the Rev. T. Helmore, M.A., the Words, principally in imitation of the original by the Rev. J. M. Neale, D.D.' Helmore was not a very good musician, but Dr Neale is an important figure in the English carol renaissance.

John Mason Neale (1818–66) was a high-church parson – so high in fact that his ritualistic practices inhibited his promotion in the Church of England and brought down on him the strictures of the Bishop of Chichester while he was warden of Sackville College at East Grinstead. The Oxford Movement one way and another contributed to musical enlightenment; one way was through hymns and another through carols. Neale, translated some hymns from early Christian literature, of which 'Jerusalem the golden' won universal popularity, and wrote others that also found a place in *Hymns Ancient and Modern*. Such were 'O happy band of pilgrims' and 'Art thou weary?' and presumably 'Christian dost thou see them?' which was allegedly a translation but of which no original has been found. To him was presented in 1852 by the British minister in Stockholm a Swedo-Finnish song book called *Piae Cantiones*, upon which Neale fell with avidity.

This collection was made at Abô (Turku) by Didrik Petri, who published it in 1582 and revised it in 1625. He was a Protestant and editing it entailed some doctrinal tampering with words which enabled it to be used in the Reformed Church of Sweden and Finland right up till late in the nineteenth century. The book contains songs of which seventeen are for Christmas and the rest for various Church feasts, school life (*vitae scholasticae*) and two for spring (*tempori vernali*), of which one *Tempus adest floridum* is none other than 'Good King Wenceslas'. *Carols for Christmas-tide* came out in the following year and introduced from *Piae Cantiones* 'Earthly friends will change and falter', 'Christ was born on Christmas Day' (to *Resonet in laudibus*), 'Good Christian men rejoice' (to *In dulci jubilo*, most unsuitably) and 'Good King Wenceslas'. The 'imitations of the origin' of the title-page were not always close: 'Good King Wenceslas', for instance, involves a change of season from spring to winter and *In dulci jubilo* loses its Latin interlardings – fortunately it was known independently in Bach's and Pearsall's arrangements as already noted. Its beauty was too much for either Luther or Petri to reject. The dance element proper to the carol is preserved in the legend that the original words were sung by angels to a mystic, Henry Suso (1366), who was caught up into a heavenly dance with his angelic visitors. Neale did not exhaust the treasures of *Piae Cantiones*, for Woodward in his *Cowley Carol Book* (1900) introduced *Puer nobis nascitur* [Example 93] and *O quam mundum, quam jucundum*

Example 93

which he changed into 'Up good Christian folk and listen' and *Ecce novum gaudium* 'Here is joy for every age'.

In thus inducing Latin and foreign carols into England Neale established the non-folk tradition. He explained how and why he came to do it in his preface to his 1853 book: 'It is impossible at one stretch to produce a quantity of new carols, of which words and music shall be original. They must be the gradual accumulation of centuries, the offerings of different epochs, of different countries, of different minds to the same treasury of the Church. None but an empiric would venture to make a set to order.' Theodoricus Petri Nylandensis had acted on the same principle in compiling *Piae Cantiones*. And it is plain to us in the mid-twentieth century how much we owe to Neale for formulating and acting on it.

The next stage in the revival was the book published by Bramley and Stainer, both of Magdalen College, Oxford, in 1865, *Christmas Carols New and Old*, which has been in continuous use for a hundred years – though not even now superseded it has been supplemented by a shift partly of taste and partly of dogmatic emphasis. The high-church movement won men's minds round to that affinity with mediaeval Christianity that has, to the point of paradox, persisted into increasingly agnostic generations. It made anti-Romanism less virulent so that the Virgin and the Babe, who had inspired Renaissance painting, might once more be acclaimed in song in an English church. Between Helmore's and Stainer's books the practice of carol-singing had been reviving, as is testified to by Stainer's own preface 'The time-honoured and delightful custom of thus celebrating the Birthday of the Holy Child seems, with some change of form, to be steadily and rapidly gaining ground. Instead of the itinerant ballad singer or the little bands of wandering children, the practice of singing Carols in Divine Service, or by a full choir at some fixed meeting is becoming prevalent. Among the Carols here given are some which are best suited for the old simple mode of rendering; others which require more ample means for their performance. Some from their legendary, festive, or otherwise less serious character, are unfit for use within the Church.' In the last class he would no doubt put the Yorkshire Wassail song that he prints. We can see the pattern forming of our present riches through the intertwining of the various traditions. Among the traditional old carols he gives 'The Virgin unspotted' and 'The Holly and the Ivy' (to a tune described as Old French), those made known by Helmore and Neale like 'Good Christian men rejoice' and 'Good King Wenceslas', some then quite new like 'When Christ was born of Mary free' and 'See amid the winter snow', which are good Victorian as well as Dykes's bad Victorian part-song 'Sleep Holy Babe', on which Dr Routley pours out the vials of his scorn.

For the record it must be added that during the middle of the century carol singing must have been gaining ground as Stainer said, for several collections were published. There was E. F. Rimbault's *A Little Book of Christmas Carols* – it was little, containing only five carols, but with their tunes – in 1846; the same editor issued a larger collection of thirty-three carols, *Old Christmas Carols* in 1863 (to judge from its deposit date at the British Museum): this was published at half a crown by Chappell, a fact which has sometimes erroneously led to its attribution to William Chappell, but of which the social significance is contained in Rimbault's preface where he says 'The good old custom of carol singing is making excellent way in our English villages' — was Chappell not going to sell it in towns? — 'and pleasant it is to see the revival of this delightful pastime'. There was W. H. Husk's *Songs of the Nativity, being Christmas Carols, Ancient and Modern*, containing eighty carols that came out in 1868. Miss Dean-Smith's *A Guide to English Folk Song* (1954) lists these and some other smaller collections. None, however, had the impact or the influence of Bramley and Stainer.

The folk-song revival began to weave its thread into this expanding pattern of carols and carol singing in the first decade of the present century as Lucy Broadwood, Cecil Sharp, Vaughan Williams and others unearthed Christmas songs from the oral tradition. Their finds included besides what might have been expected, such things as 'Cherry Tree Carol', 'A Virgin most pure' and some excellent Wassail songs, a number of very odd, i.e. incongruous-seeming carols. Thus gypsies in Hampshire sang 'In Dessexshire as it befell'[7] in which sabbatarianism taken over from Jews by Christians has run mad, a sabbatarianism that one associates with puritanism, but in this case taking the opposite view of Christmas Day from the seventeenth century's. [Example 94]

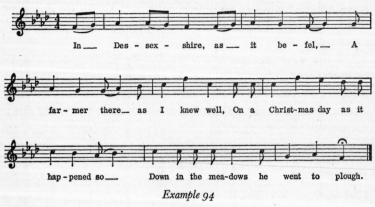

Example 94

[7] Collected by Alice Gillington before 1910.

2. As he was a ploughing on so fast
   Our Saviour Christ came by at last;
   He said 'O man, why dost thou plough
   So hard as it do blow and snow?'

3. The man he answered the Lord with speed
   'For to work we have great need,
   If we wasn't to work all on that day
   We should want some other way.'

4. For his hands did tremble and pass to and fro
   He ran so fast that he could not plough;
   And the ground did open and let him in
   Before he could repent his sin.

5. His wife and children were out at play;
   And all the world consumed at last.
   And his beasts and cattle all died away
   For breaking of the Lord's birthday.

This astonishing rhyme has all the marks of a ballad rubbed down to its stumps by oral tradition in its telescoping of events, its use of folk expressions 'on so fast', 'all that day', its rejection of all but essentials and these limned in with vivid strokes like 'So hard as it do blow and snow' and the Scotch snap feature of the Aeolian tune. A version of this story to quite a different tune was found in Herefordshire by Mrs S. M. Leather and Vaughan Williams, though the text of their singer was even more abbreviated and corrupt, the first verse going –

> On Christmas day it happened so
> Down in the meadows for to plough;
> As we were ploughing on so fast
> Up comes sweet Jesus His-self at last.

Fifty years on Mr Fred Hamer took down from a singer in Shropshire this same carol with identical words, save for some corruption in the last verse. To his surprise he found that this singer, May Bradley, was the daughter of Mrs Leather's singer, Esther Smith.

The Herefordshire carols of this collection contained instances of unintelligibility, e.g.

> Christ made a trance one Sunday at noon
> All with his own dear hands
> He made the sun clear all of the moon
> Like water off dry land

and of involuntary conflation of more than one ballad. But if this erosion by unretentive memory is to be debited to the folk-carol the credit offset is eloquently stated by Sharp who praises 'the unconscious art of the peasant. For his peculiar and most characteristic qualities, mental and emotional, are precisely those which in this case are most needed – his passion for simple, direct statement, his dislike of ornament and of the tricks of circumlocution, his abhorrence of sentimentality, and above all his courage in using without hesitation the obvious commonplace phrase, of words or music, when by its means the required expression can be most easily realized.' Sharp issued a small volume of twenty-one such carols collected in various parts of England in 1911; Vaughan Williams followed with a similar book of eight carols in 1919. These were the pure fruits of oral tradition and they at once entered the now full flowing stream of carols.

The Wassail songs belong not to Christmas but to the New Year and are derived ultimately from fertility magic through two channels; the Roman Saturnalia, from which we derive the season's special food, kissing games, dressing-up and charades, the exchange of gifts, parties and fortune-telling and the burning of candles, and north European Yule, from which we get ghosts and ghost stories, the yule log, fires and brandy snap-dragon, holly, ivy, mistletoe and Christmas trees. Besides these universally observed customs there are some local ones, such as serenading the apple trees in cyder-making districts, which involves not only folklore but folk music, namely the Wassail songs, of which a fair number survive from Yorkshire, Gloucestershire, Somerset and Cornwall. They have nothing religious about them, but a fair mixture of pagan elements, sympathetic magic, fertility worship through the wassail bough, apple trees and mistletoe, the *quête* (that survived, without the music, in the Christmas box to be collected on Boxing Day until the wars, rationing, better wages and even legislation combined to kill it by mid-century), and of course good wishes for the New Year.

The word 'wassail' is said to have originated in a toast proposed by Rowena, daughter of Hengist the Jute, who came to England *circa* 449 at the invitation of Vortigern, King of Kent, to help him drive off the Picts and the Scots, but who took a liking to England and would not go away, who indeed subdued his host and employer. Rowena toasted Vortigern in the words 'Waes hael, Koyning', which is to say 'Health to you, O King'. Wassail songs are therefore essentially toast-drinking songs. Two sorts may be distinguished: those like the Somerset examples in which there survive elements of magic and fertility rite, and those like the Yorkshire examples which are *quête* songs:

We are not daily beggars that beg from door to door
We are the neighbours' children whom you have seen before.
We have a little purse, it is made of leather skin,
We want a little sixpence to line it well within.
Bring us out the table and spread it with a cloth
Bring us out the bread and cheese and a bit of your Christmas
　　loaf.

and in return

God bless the master of this house, likewise the mistress too,
And all the little children which round the table grew.

Our ___ jol - ly was-sail, our ___ jol -ly was-sail, Love and joy come to you and to our was-sail bough; Pray God bless you and send you a hap - py New Year, A New Year, ___ A New Year, ___ Pray God bless you and send you a Hap - py New Year.

Example 95

After each verse came a long burden [example 95]. Vaughan Williams collected a similar Wassail song[8] in south Yorkshire with an Aeolian mode tune, similar in that it was a *quête* song associated with greenery and wassailing and having a burden to each verse:

> For its Christmas time when we travel far and near
> May God bless you and send you a happy New Year.

Of the incantatory type Sharp collected an Apple Tree Wassail in Somerset [Example 96], the singing of which was followed by a spoken ritual formula and shouting, stamping and firing-off of guns. In some Wassail songs, where apples are not the appropriate crop to invoke – 'a drop or two of cyder will do us no harm' – the farm animals are toasted by name, Cherry or Dobbin, as in the Gloucestershire Wassail.[9] The *Folk-Song Journal* for 1929 printed five Wassail carols from West Cornwall

[8] Printed in *Eight Traditional Carols*, Stainer and Bell, 1919.
[9] *English Folk Carols*, C. J. Sharp, 1911.

Old ap - ple tree— we'll was - sail thee,— And hop - ing thou wilt bear,——— The Lord does know — where we shall be To be mer-ry an - oth - er year.—— To — blow well and to bear well, And so mer - ry let us be,——— Let ev' - ry man— drink up his cup— And health to this old ap-ple tree.——

Example 96

which were variants of tunes known elsewhere and showing minor corruptions of the words. The collector, J. E. Thomas, noted that the Cornish St George plays usually end with some verses of the Wassail song – a sign perhaps for passing round the hat. The Wassail songs with their ramifications into folklore are, more than the Christmas carols, true folk music.

Folk-Dances

Also with its roots in folk custom and connexions with wassailing, the *quête*, the mummer's play, but still strong in its independence is the folk-dance, which has brought in another though smaller stream of English folk-melody. Its revival was concurrent with the folk-song revival, but it was the work of one man, Cecil Sharp, and occupied only a quarter of a century. Sharp saw his first morris dance on Boxing Day 1899; he died in June 1924. In that time he uncovered pretty well, though not quite, all the surviving lines of dance traditions – some of the team dances had to be pieced together from the recollection of a single old man. The conscious revival of the dances, which has often been criticized, ridiculed even, as artificial and by now unnatural, has had as a side effect the restoration of a number of traditional teams to activity and brought in a few more survivors. The criticism of unnaturalness has this much truth in it that most English folk-dances – no one ever brings these reproaches against Scottish dances – are a peasant art and so out of touch with townsmen's taste. This at least applies to the male ritual dances, the morris and the sword dances, but only partially to the mixed social dances, though indeed they are called country dances.

The dances which Sharp saw at Headington on that historic Boxing Day were 'Laudnum Bunches', 'Bean Setting', 'Constant Billy', 'Blue-eyed Stranger', 'Rigs o'Marlow'. On the next day he took down their tunes from William Kimber (d. 1961).[10] 'Laudnum Bunches', which would seem to be a corruption of 'Lads a' Bunchum', a crudely descriptive title found in other localities, is distinguished by having three strains A B C, all suitably repeated, in which a Scotch snap is a feature, though it would seem to be derived from Purcell rather than Scotland or Hungary. The C music contains alternating measures of six-eight and nine-eight time to fit the figures of the dance. 'Bean Setting', which is a stick dance that contains vestigial remnants of fertility magic has its A music in twelve-sixteen time, its B music in six-eight, with some interpolations of nine-eight again in order to accommodate the clashing of sticks and thumping the floor. 'Constant Billy', another stick dance, is more regular, for the very good reason that it is a borrowed song-tune, none other than that used by Pepusch for 'Cease your funning' in *The Beggar's Opera*. First printed in 1726 it was said by Sir Henry Bishop to have been composed by Geminiani. It could equally have been a folk-song, but with its

[10] All these tunes are accessible in Sharp's albums of piano arrangements for dance accompaniment.

sequential construction it does not altogether sound like one. 'Blue-eyed Stranger', which is a handkerchief dance, sounds more like a fiddle-tune: it is a crisp two-four, compactly organized melody consisting of variations on three principal motifs. In 'Rigs o'Marlow', which is a stick dance, the Purcell-ish Scotch snap dominates the A music and dotted note rhythm the B, with two emphatic crotchets at the cadences for the clashes of the sticks. It may be observed that in the majority of cases it is impossible to guess at the origins of the names of the tunes, even more so than in the similar case of the names of hymn tunes. The borrowing of song tunes is common in English folk-dance, frequent for country dances, common for sword dances which took what fitted, but less so in morris dances, in which the tunes are on the whole tailored to and fairly firmly attached to their dances. The reason for this is not far to seek, the sword dances are in their general nature *moto perpetuo*, but the morris dances contain not only the clashes of sticks and the clapping of hands but what are technically called capers, which call for a slowing of the rhythm, which in many cases is brought about by using a phrase of the tune in augmentation, at least that is how Sharp was obliged to notate it in, for instance, 'The Rose' [Example 97]. However, since the musician will adapt

Example 97

the tune to the dance by variations of tempo or using parts of a phrase, the association of a particular tune with a particular dance is not absolute, and song tunes are to be found requisitioned, for example 'Princess Royal', which occurs in three variants in the Bampton and Abingdon traditions and, for a morris jig, sounds like a derivative of 'The Arethusa', the sea-song by William Shield (1748–1829). If it is, the pressure of folk influence towards modal forms has got to work on it. Many morris tunes besides 'Princess Royal' are found in variants in several traditions, such are 'Shepherd's Hay' (Bampton and Headington), 'Constant Billy' (Adderbury and Bampton), 'Bacca Pipes' (Bampton and Brackley) both versions of 'Greensleeves', 'The Old Woman tossed up in a Blanket', one version in common time, another in six-eight.

The morris dance is notable for its preservation of ancient folkloristic elements in its tradition. Thus it is essentially a spring or Whitsuntide dance and therefore rooted in fertility magic; some of its figures suggest conflict; small bells strapped to the legs, flowers and ribbons in the hat and handkerchiefs to be waved are relics if not of a national costume at least of a ritual vestment; its name is derived from Morisco, though the Moorish element that is left is the element of disguise, again to serve ritual, which is sometimes achieved by blacking the faces of the dancers, of whom there are usually six to a team. It is found in distinctive but obviously allied traditions only in the Midlands. As there are authoritative books on the English folk-dances[11] there is no need further to expound their choreography or their folklore here.

In the sword dances which are confined to the north-east the ritual significance is the death and resurrection of the turn of the year – the 'lock' or 'nut' formed by the intertwined swords placed round the neck of the fool, who is one of the stock characters attending the dance team, is clearly a vestige of human sacrifice, or at least symbolical sacrifice. Its season is the New Year and it was once a part of the mummers' play of St George. Its team may consist of five, six, seven or eight men. Its swords are of two sorts, the Northumbrian 'rapper' which is short, has a handle at each end and is therefore more like a scraper than a sword – 'rapper' may be a corruption of 'scraper' – and the longer stiff wooden (or iron) sword with hilt and point used in the Yorkshire traditions. The tunes used for the score or so traditions that survive, or have been revived, are mostly not rigidly attached to their dances but rather depend on the discretion of the team's musician. Sharp found that the Yorkshire dancers gravitated to 'Brighton Camp' ('The girl I left behind me') but that the Grenoside (near Sheffield) team always performed to the same tunes, each to its allotted figure, jig, hornpipe, reel, roll, all except the first in much dotted-note rhythm. Elsewhere he found that the proper tunes, possibly small-pipe tunes, had been lost and that any Scottish or Irish jig tune would serve if the tempo was right: dancers and fiddler (or concertinaist, accordionist) knew each other and when each should be the controlling agent.

The connexion of the sword dance with the folk-play is

[11] E.g. by Douglas Kennedy and Violet Alford, subsequent to Sharp's original *Morris Book*.

responsible for what is called a calling-on song, in which the captain of the side introduces the members of his team to their audience. These songs are not of much distinction except this primitive strain from Earsdon (Northumberland):

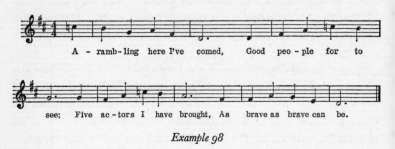

A - ramb-ling here I've comed, Good peo - ple for to see; Five ac-tors I have brought, As brave as brave can be.

Example 98

The Horn Dance of Abbots Bromley in Staffordshire, which is neither morris, sword or country but partakes of the nature of all three, yet is unique in its horns, enormous reindeer antlers, instead of swords, sticks or handkerchiefs, has an eerie tune with a strange history that helps to weave the spell cast by this strange ritual processing and posturing. When Sharp first saw the dance, of which the season is Wakes Week in September, it had no special tune, but his interest and the resulting publicity elicited from a resident a tune which he had noted down as far back as 1858 from the fiddle-playing of the local wheelwright, named Robinson.[12] This is a remarkable tune in three sections, Aeolian on G with a middle section shifting but not modulating to C. In performance it is accompanied by strokes on a triangle [Example 99].

The country dance is a purely social affair for mixed couples. Its known history in Britain began in the reign of Henry VII and its last appearance in English ball-rooms was probably in the first decade of the present century, when I for one danced Sir Roger de Coverley, a longways for as many as will. It was gradually extruded by the polka and the waltz from about

[12] The story of four tunes for the Horn Dance is told in a book by the headmistress of the Woodard school in the town.

Example 99

1840, for Fanny Horsley, Mendelssohn's Kensington friend, records[13] that she was dancing them at London parties in 1834 along with quadrilles. Whereas English folk-song may be legitimately described *à la* Marx as a class phenomenon, the property of the peasantry as long as there was one – indeed then as in the modern urban revival it embodied social and political protest: 'Sent him to the cruel wars, to be slain, to be slain' – the English folk-dance crossed all class barriers, as dancing of every sort always seems able to do. There is the well-known reference to country dancing in a letter from the Earl of Worcester to the Earl of Shrewsbury under date 19th September 1602, which runs 'We are frolic here at Court: much dancing in the Privy Chamber of Country Dances before the Queen's Majesty, who is exceedingly pleased therewith.'

[13] Rosamund B. Gotch, *Mendelssohn and His Friends in Kensington*, O.U.P., 1934.

The Inns of Court saw them in their celebrated masques during the first quarter of the seventeenth century, and then at the half-way mark came Playford and his *The English Dancing Master*.

Playford has his own niche in English musical history and his staggeringly successful dance manual suddenly reasserted its influence by engaging the interest of Cecil Sharp in 1910, who thereupon revived the dances of which he had unravelled the notation and grafted them on to the few traditional dances which he had already found alive in Derby, Devon, Somerset, Surrey and Warwick. He published eighteen of them with their tunes in *The Country Dance Book*. Sharp's successor as Director of the English Folk Dance Society founded by Sharp in 1911, Mr Douglas Kennedy, regards Sharp's deflection from traditional to printed records as an aberration, on the grounds that Playford's dances imply, indeed demand, a less athletic, more polished, which is to say sophisticated, treatment than the countryman's country dance. They invited the attention of the dancing master by the beginning of the eighteenth century; the fiddlers who played them made their own manuscript books of tunes[14]; and so the folk character of the dances was refined away, though it obviously continued to survive in the country since Sharp found it alive in the twentieth century. Mr Kennedy's point, though sound enough as far as it goes, overlooks this classless character of the dance: naturally the same dance, let us say 'Sellenger's Round' will not look the same when danced by farm workers, school children, fashionable youth or elderly office workers, but it belongs equally to them all, a national possession. It is here that the term 'traditional' becomes valuable: there is art which is communal but not folk, of which Scotland provides instances in its piping tradition and country dancing, both of which contain made-up elements, tunes and variations, steps and figures; these the Scots rightly

---

[14] The *Journal of the Lakeland Dialect Society* for November 1939 contains an account by Anne Gilchrist of 'Some Old Lake-Country Fiddlers and their Tune Books'.

call traditional. Similarly Playford's country dances are, if not
folk, at any rate traditional.

There were, however, more country-dances of folk provenance than Sharp, having become absorbed in Playford, discovered, and they have since been revived. One such is the fine
Northumbrian tune 'Morpeth Rant', which feels more like a
fiddle than a pipe tune [Example 100] in which a little is made

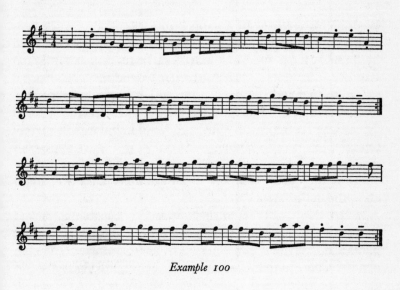

Example 100

to go a long way quite satisfactorily. 'The Triumph' on the
other hand owes its quality to its rhythmic variety, thematic
abundance and variation of its constituent figures [Example
101]. Song tunes were impressed for dancing. Thus 'Haste to the

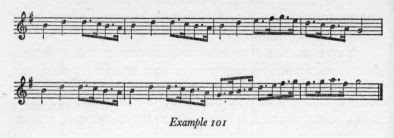

Example 101

'Wedding' is ascribed by Chappell to a chime for church bells and by others to a Vauxhall Garden song probably composed by James Hook. One of Sharp's early tunes was 'Brighton Camp' (which goes to 'The girl I left behind me'). 'Galopede' on the other hand is a dance tune with a bump at every two-bar cadence of a thrice repeated note – when Irish song tunes use this thrice repeated note they do not bump but merely represent a feminine ending to a line. A few tunes undergo a momentary change of rhythm to accommodate a figure of the dance – 'Step and Fetch Her' is an example. They are almost all in the major mode.

In all this wealth of melody it is not possible to isolate features such as Scotch snaps, augmented seconds, three-bar phrases, and say that they determine their unmistakably English quality. Come to that, we talk about the English character and generalize about its difference from the French or the Dutch character, but to any distinguishing quality one predicated, one would have to admit an immediate flood of exceptions. If the song tunes sound, maybe because of their modal character, pastoral or reserved or even wistful, the dance tunes sound happy-go-lucky. Sometimes English people are happy-go-lucky and care-free, or at any rate used to be.

Shanties and Sea Songs

Sea songs are of two sorts, songs about the sea and songs sung at sea by sailors. Folk-song has both sorts. Any maritime nation is bound to amass legends of the sea, histories of voyages, wrecks and battles, sailors' yarns about foreign parts. And its sailors living together in a confined space will sooner or later, now and then, break into song either to pass the time or to lighten labour. English folk-song has the ballads of 'Henry Martin' and 'Ward the Pirate' dealing with piracy, 'Spanish Ladies' with navigation, 'Admiral Benbow' with battle and 'The Captain's Apprentice' with life at sea. The Hebrides has 'Kishmul's Galley', Nova Scotia and Newfoundland have songs about their fishing fleets, Normandy celebrates its ports – and their imports ('Des pommes, des poires, des gros navets' for refrain) – Havre and Dieppe; Sicily, which is rich in sailors' songs, has shanties and songs by their womenfolk.[15]

Songs about the sea and sailors, which may range from a ballad about a sailor from over the sea to mermaids and conscripts, women in travesty aboard ship, are naturally to be found in most people's folklore, but especially in those in which the sea impinges on national life. The songs actually sung by sailors aboard ship, though not in the Navy, are also of two sorts, work songs and leisure songs. The latter are technically called forebitters, songs sung in the fo'c'sle; the former sung on deck are shanties. John Masefield, who, as is well known, went after training in the *Conway* to sea in sail and knew the Pacific as well as Cape Horn and the Atlantic, gave an authoritative description from first-hand experience in 1906:[16]

'The sea songs in general use in merchant ships are of two kinds. There is the working song, or shanty, which is sung as an aid to labour during the performance of certain tasks. And there is the sea-ballad or sailor's folk-song, which at sea is sung in the second dog-watch; and in port at night after supper.' The latter are as a rule of less interest and merit than the shanties which since the disappearance of sail from the seven seas have achieved a new independent life as folk-songs, but what he says of them is worth quoting before embarking on our main concern, the sailor shanty.

'The songs sung in the sing-songs, or sailors' concerts, have

[15] A. Favara, *Canti della Terra e del Mare di Sicilia* (Ricordi).
[16] *Temple Bar*, Macmillan, January 1906.

lost much of their distinction. The old sea songs, proper to the sea, have given place to a great extent, to the peculiar lyrical mechanics of the music hall. The old songs may still be heard, but they are dying out [N.B. again], for the sailor has lost much of his individuality. The English sailor is generally to be found in steam-ships, making short passages. He is no longer cut off from his fellow men for many months at a time. . . . Music is the one enjoyment of the sailor at sea. In the second dog-watch, in sunny latitudes, after supper, when the work about decks has ceased, the sailing-ship's forecastle hands hold a concert, or sing-song. Sometimes they gather together on the forecastle-head, but more generally they sit about just forward of the fore-rigging, on the fore-hatch, to "sing their longing songs of home". Their repertories are limited but they never tire of the songs they have. They prefer a song with a chorus, so that all can take part in it. If the songs have no chorus, they generally repeat the solo part. . . . Of the songs I have heard in these sea sing-songs very few were beautiful. The old naval ballad of "Spanish Ladies" was sometimes sung, and this old song was certainly the best of all I heard. There are several versions of the ballad.' There are indeed: he quotes one in G major from Davis and Tozer's *Sailors' Songs or Chanteys* of 1887 which was quoted by Captain Marryat in one of his novels, but Sharp's version is a hexatonic tune in the Aeolian mode and is a capstan shanty. Which shows what one would expect, that, though there is a distinction between the work and the leisure songs, they do spill over – indeed 'Spanish Ladies' was sung in the Navy, where they do not sing shanties at all.

In the corpus of shanties themselves distinctions used to be observed between hauling, pump and capstan shanties, but in the most recent and, one dare say, definitive collection by Stan Hugill[17] this last of the Shantymen, who in his time rounded the Horn in that capacity, says that such classifications are too rigid because different ships had different usages in this matter. His book makes it unnecessary to go deeply into the

[17] *Shanties from the Seven Seas*, Routledge, 1961.

subject here. But certain general conclusions have been reached as a result of the studies that have been made successively by Captain W. B. Whall (1912), Cecil Sharp, Sir Richard Terry (1921), C. Fox Smith (1927) and in America by W. M. Doerflinger (1951). First the name, then the origin and history, then world distribution and something about words and the tunes themselves.

The word has had various spellings, chanty, chantey and shanty. The derivation from French *chanter* seems obvious, but since *chant* in English was pronounced with a hard *ch* and the sailor's practice was a direct imitation of the French soft *ch* the spelling has finally hardened into an initial *sh*. A desperate attempt was made to derive it from *shanty*, meaning a little shed, on the strength of a strong negro element in the tunes which came from the presence of negro watermen in the West Indies. They had a custom of rolling their huts or shanties on low platforms on wheels to the sound of a song with chorus led by one of their number sitting astride the roof. He was a shanty-man, so was the song leader aboard ship; hence shantyman for the singer and shanty for the song. This really does not bear consideration but while the matter of the spelling was in debate the possibilities had to be exhausted for the origin of the term. It should not be called a sea shanty which is pleonastic but, if qualified, a sailor shanty.

The shanty of both Atlantic sea-boards as we know it seems to have been a nineteenth-century creation. The steersman of a Greek trireme may have marked the rhythm of the oars with a song and the usefulness of music for concerting effort is so obvious and universal that one cannot doubt that it has been so used continuously from time immemorial, but the shanty, the song in which solo and chorus alternate in such a way as to be applied directly to hauling sails or to keep a capstan turning, came in possibly in the late eighteenth century, when the East India Company started its operations, but only in a big enough way to attract attention after the Napoleonic Wars when the seas were clear again and ships were growing bigger. Masefield, it is true, says in the article already quoted that 'Haul the bowline' 'was heard aboard a Dover trader during the reign of Henry VIII and may be several centuries older', but he does not give his authority, and 'Amsterdam' appears in Thomas Heywood's Elizabethan drama of 'The Rape of Lucrece'. But after 1815 and until the seventies, when steam began to supersede sail, the practice of shantying grew and with it the repertory, in which it seems certain there is a West Indian, i.e. negro element, as may be heard in 'Clear the track let the bulgine run', bulgine being negro for engine, and 'Johnny come down to Hilo' which is about 'a big buck nigger and a [Bar] Badian beauty,' which exploits a short-long metre – one can hardly call it syncopation. It lingered on with the grain ships from Australia into the present century and of its gradual extinction Mr Hugill tells the story. Sharp had collected fifty-seven shanties from John Short of Watchet in Somerset who at the time, i.e. in the first decade of the present century, was seventy-six years old. Sir Richard Terry (1865–1938) heard them sung to him by relatives as a boy on Tyneside and later heard them in West Indian ports – he brought out his collection of them in 1921 (Curwen). The *floruit* of the shanty was therefore 1835 to 1865, a mere thirty years and mainly in British and American ships.

But it is not to be supposed that Norwegian and Italian sailors cannot sing. Masefield says on this: 'They may be heard in ships of every nationality, but it is thought that they are most common in American and rarest in French ships. The most beautiful chanty I have ever heard was sung by a Norwegian crew. I have heard two Greek chanties of great beauty and I am told that the Russians have at least one as beautiful as any of our own.' Hugill includes in the last section of his book German, Norwegian, Swedish, French, Welsh, Finnish and pidgin-English with Chinese and Hindustani words. In confirmation of Masefield's note on the scarcity of French shanties Hugill quotes the chief French authority, Captain A. Hayet, as saying that there are only eighteen genuine *chansons de bord* of which thirteen are capstan and halyard shanties – but Hayet's standards are strict and exclude shore folk-songs.

This raises the question of origin – texts and tunes. The texts are admittedly of less value than the tunes and than the texts of ordinary folk-songs. Being functional they need only a commonplace 'I thought I heard the old man say' or 'Oh a long farewell' to start and a call 'With a heave ho haul' or an onomatapoeic 'Ah-ho, way-oh, are you most done' for chorus refrain. Moreover, if there is a thread of story left over from some ballad about a public or a legendary figure like 'Reuben Ranzo' half of the shanty is going to be improvised by the shantymen who can therein work off criticism of the officers or put in a bit of cheerful obscenity. A resourceful shantyman, moreover, can use a shore folk-song, a stock ballad or part of a hymn as the skeleton for a new shanty, words and tune, so long as its shape and rhythm conform to the required pattern. Sharp thought that the music, which though simple is of striking quality, could come from the stock of peasant tunes in the singer's head – and indeed he cites 'Blow away the morning dew' and 'Sweet Nightingale' as instances of songs which have been impressed for nautical service. Popular songs might equally be turned into shanties. But an even more likely and more copious source of supply might be from the ship's fiddler who was on the strength of the smaller ships of the Royal Navy and of the East India Company's boats. This theory of the fiddler as the predecessor of the shantyman who put forward by Miss C. Fox Smith[18] and supported with the plausible argument that in shanties, unlike folk-songs, the tunes came before the words – 'Nobody would have been likely to make up such trivial doggerel'. The fiddler on the other hand would have a lot of tunes to draw on much as the maker of broadsides had, and she quotes an actual case of a shanty at the time of the Crimean War being made of nonsense words sung to the tune of the Huntsmen's Chorus in *Der Freischütz*! But whatever their raw material blown together from all sorts of sources, whether identifiable or not, these tunes

[18] *A Book of Shanties.*

were forged into a unity, often of the highest melodic quality, as in such a shanty as 'Lowlands away'. If this tune is examined it will be found to have a compass of a tenth – in spite of their being sung by untrained male voices the shanties in general had a big compass: 'Shenandoah' spans the interval of an eleventh, as do 'The Liverpool Girls' and 'Bound for the Rio Grande' and 'Sally Brown' a tenth – and its rhythmic organization is an alternation between two and three time. In sum the shanty owes its appeal to its direct and compelling rhythm and to melodic lines that have the buoyancy to keep them afloat in a high wind and words that vary easily between mere vocables to snatches of poetry and pungent caricature.

Other Sea Songs

The fishing community also has its songs though they are less attached to the work in hand or to deep-sea community life. Sicily, for instance, has many such songs. The Nova Scotian and Newfoundland fishing communities are still at the stage of composing their own ballads and fitting them to traditional tunes or to a tune strung together of melodic commonplaces. Thus a sealer's song popular in Newfoundland is full of local allusions, family names and slang (e.g. dog hood = ferocious male seal) which could only have been made up by the local rhymster, is sung to 'The girl I left behind me'. Another Newfoundland sealing song of eleven verses describing the events of the voyage, including the massacre of seals

> From east to west for miles around
> The ice was crimson dyed
> . . . .
> Twice seven thousand pelts was flagged
> Beneath the setting sun

was included, along with a similar jog-trot ballad of sealing from Nova Scotia, in Helen Creighton's Canadian collection[19]

[19] *Maritime Folk Songs.*

published in 1962, though the songs may be half a century old.

Whaling also had produced its balladry. But the book from Massachusetts that has made it available to landlubbers[20] took its texts not from singers but from log books, and its tunes, though certainly used with the associated poems, 'have no scholarly value' as they were taken by the editor from all sorts of sources, old song-books, books of fiddle tunes, sheet music, and sometimes trimmed to fit. Still, here is a picture of a closed community showing folk-song in one of its stages of gestation from conception to birth, and though there are in it songs from the British Isles, folk-songs like 'The Mantle of Green', 'The Turkish Lady', 'The Happy Boy', and also folk-songs of a maritime flavour like 'The Dark Eyed Sailor', 'Tarry Trousers' and 'The Silvery Tide', a group of nineteen deals specifically with whales and whaling. 'The Greenland Whale' becomes quite technical, spotting the whale, launching the boats and alas!

> There was harpineery and picaneery
> And boat steerary too,

losing a man overboard.

The interest of songs of this category is more sociological than artistic; they afford one more meeting-point of music and anthropology, which is a legitimate function of folk music.

Cries and Calls

Since they can certainly be put into musical notation the street cries which, at least until the middle of the present century, when the racket of modern roads roared them down, were traditional in English life, come under the heading of functional music preserved orally: they are music, that is, not shouts. The official Town Crier, as well as the vendor of muffins, lavender or fish, needs to put tone behind the words he utters to make them carry. In doing so he will use different pitches and almost before he knows what he is doing he is making a tune,

[20] *Songs the Whalemen Sang*, by Gale Huntington.

not, however, a formal melody, for, though there may be repetition of motif or the call itself may be repeated whole over and over again, there is no structure, at most only a single line, a so-called stichic tune, or a freely improvised string of phrases as in yodeling. Shepherds' calls are the commonest from the countryside – Wiora quotes examples from Norway, the Salzkammergut, Sweden, southern France, Bohemia, Estonia and Moravia – street hawkers' salesmanship from the towns. In England examples of the latter survive, or at least are preserved in poems, from the fourteenth century, and in the sixteenth century cries of London were used for fancies, i.e. quasi-madrigals by Weelkes, Gibbons and Deering. Vaughan Williams incorporated primrose and cockles cries into his opera, *Hugh the Drover*, and a snatch of the Westminster lavender cry into his *London Symphony*. The *Folk-Song Journals* of 1910 and 1919 contain examples of cries hawking the following miscellany of goods: lavender, primroses and other flowers, fly-papers, wicker chairs and wicker baskets, toy lambs, hearth-stones, fish, watercress, cockles and mussels, feather brooms, fire logs, small coal, knives to grind and chairs to mend, rags and bones, lumber and old iron to buy.

These snatches of tune vary in length. They were evolved from the words, yet the words tended to disappear into mere vocables, and by the end of the nineteenth century, when Lucy Broadwood paid attention to the cries, the words had been so eroded that it was often impossible to tell what the wares were and one had to look into the barrows or baskets to find out. The criers themselves seemed unaware that the cries were unintelligible: they had become a personal possession, an individual tradition. They were also, the longer ones, part of a communal tradition in so far as the lavender cry of one hawker bore a resemblance to the lavender cry of another, or to a primrose cry heard in the spring instead of the summer. Thus the primrose cry heard in Westminster in 1898 [Example 102] is basically the same as the well-known lavender cry heard by the same person in July 1903, also in Westminster. It serves to show the

Example 102

structure of a cry rather more than half-way to becoming a tune, two three-bar phrases balancing one another with a one-bar phrase repeated twice as coda. But many cries are no more than the length of this coda.

Addison contributed a piece to the *Spectator* of December 1711 on the Cries of London, an amusing spoof application for the iob of Comptroller-General of the London Cries, which should bring some order into the hubbub caused by the large numbers of street vendors competing for sales with cries that are either too high pitched or too low, sung too fast or too slow. He preferred slow ones which were in his opinion more tuneable – 'Nor can I forbear being inspired with a most agreeable melancholy when I hear that sad and solemn air with which the public are very often asked "If they have any chairs to mend".' Dr Johnson at a later date wrote '. . . the attention of a new-comer is generally first struck by the multiplicity of the cries that stun him in the streets'. In his monograph on London Cries Frederick Bridge reproduces the poem 'London Lackpenny' once attributed to John Lydgate *c.* 1400 and as frontispiece a painting of 1761 by J. Dixon of a dentist in action or 'Teeth drawn with a Touch'. In Deering's Fancy one of the cries is 'Touch and go! Touch and go! Ha'ye work for Kind-heart the tooth drawer? Touch and go!' Deering also composed a similar piece based on 'Country Cries.' Altogether six of these fancies for voices and viols exist. Lucy Broadwood compared her collection of Westminster and Chelsea cries with those in Orlando Gibbons's 'Cries of London' and found that, though the merchandise had changed, some of the tunes were recognizably similar after three centuries: brooms might be substituted for oysters and fire logs for white turnips but the same corpus of tunes had been drawn on, showing that there is even in this fragmentary folk art a continuous oral tradition that has only been extinguished in the last fifty years.

It is not to be supposed that musical street cries were confined to London, but they are from the nature of the case an urban form of folk-song found most commonly where business is to be done. Examples from Norwich and Brighton are noted in the *Folk-Song Journal* and sixty years later a Bedfordshire song incorporating a cry of 'Turkey Rhubarb' has been published in Mr Fred Hamer's collection *Garners Gay*.[21] Nor are they confined to Britain: Charpentier quotes three in his picture of Paris in the prelude to the second act of *Louise*. Dr Picken quotes Chinese examples, though he does not specify the merchandise, in the *New Oxford History of Music*, where they show a stage in the evolution of the scale structure of Chinese folk-song. And Rodney Gallop has this street cry of a Portuguese orange seller:

Example 103

Street cries are thus of interest as charming phenomena, as of some social significance and as material for musical analysis. But they are not of any great artistic value in themselves as ballads and carols are.

---

[21] Mr Hamer kindly supplied me with examples of cries he had himself heard from the lips of street vendors, in whose families they had been traditional. These were whitening stones for door-steps from the Pennines, home-made fly-papers and a splendid catalogue of the virtues of the herring.

Nursery Rhymes and Singing Games

If there was any need to demonstrate the strength of oral tradition the children's ditties of the nursery, the playground and the party would provide it. Books do exist in which words are printed and simply harmonized tunes of singing games are to be found for mothers and nurses of modest keyboard technique. Iona and Peter Opie's *Oxford Dictionary of Nursery Rhymes* says the last word on its subject but few words on the tunes, except the important statement that the nursery rhyme (in America 'Mother Goose song') 'by tacit and universal consent may be either said or sung'. Alice B. Gomme collected up the traditional games of the British Isles in a dictionary[22] and also published small books containing a few rhymes with tunes in the nineties. In 1933 Sir Percy Buck published a music book of nursery rhymes, containing a few French examples among its hundred-odd songs set out for singing to piano accompaniment with all extant verses, which serves as a useful corpus for reference. But no one needs to consult a book if she wants to play with her babe or amuse the youngsters at a party; she knows the rhymes and games already, has known them as long as she can remember. Wilma Muir, however, describes how as a schoolgirl she was initiated into the tradition of half a dozen games, 'Father, Mother, may I go', 'We are three Jews', 'Have you any bread and wine', which she quotes with their tunes as preserved in a playground tradition by the girls themselves at an Aberdeen school, and, a nice proof of the secret freemasonry of that tradition, the words were sung not in Scots dialect but in what they took to be English and therefore something slightly removed from ordinary life. There is indeed a touch of magical incantation in all these children's rhymes.

Their origin has been shown to be in the most varied, and unlikely, sources. For the nursery rhymes the Opies list adult jocularity, fragments of ballads and folk-songs, customs and

[22] *Dictionary of British Folk Lore: Part I, Traditional Games*, 2 vols. 1894. Following E. F. Rimbault.

rituals, street cries, tavern and barrack-room choruses, from scholars, wits and the stage – anywhere in fact except from children or things written for them. One conclusion to be drawn from this is that whatever the case for folk-song being the creation of oral tradition, in this branch of folklore the origin is ultimately to be sought not among the folk, if by folk the peasants and the proletariat are meant, but among the educated classes, from whom they have filtered down, shedding as they go their original meaning and assuming a different function.

What about the tunes, though? How old are they? Where did they come from? It is hard to say. Some seem to be so close a fit to the words as to be almost formed by the combined sense and rhythm of the words: 'Here we go round the mulberry bush', a circle of tonic chord up and dominant chord down; 'Hush-a-bye, Baby', a rocking six-eight of the interval of a major third, but the tune extended – this is very common – by shifting it up a tone or two; 'Jack and Jill' going up hill and bumping down like Sisyphus's *laas anaides* (λᾶας ἀναιδής)[23] 'Oranges and Lemons' from the very sound of bell chimes. A few can be traced a stage or two back: 'Girls and boys come out to play' to a country dance of the early eighteenth century; 'Simple Simon' and 'Lucy Locket' to the American 'Yankee Doodle', which is half a century later (but we must be careful: some Americans say that 'Yankee Doodle' came from 'Lucy Locket'); 'Three Blind Mice' further back to Ravenscroft's *Deuteromelia* (1609). They vary in structure from what is surely the simplest tune in the world, 'Bye, Baby Bunting', two bars of five notes spanning the interval of a fourth simply repeated to make an even number of phrases, to something as complex as 'Old King Cole' (A B C B) in sixteen bars.

There is no great musical or aesthetic interest in these tunes, except that they are perfectly tailored to their words and the actions of the choosing and counting games to which they belong. Their lack of artistic as opposed to anthropological interest

[23] κατα πέδονδε κυλίνδετο λᾶας ἀναιδής ('Down to the bottom rolled the contumacious stone'), *Odyssey*, ii. 598.

had a curious legal consequence. When in 1948 the Inland Revenue undertook a revision of local authority rating it proposed to remove Cecil Sharp House from the exemption from paying rates which it enjoyed under the Scientific Societies Act, 1843. A decision in favour of the English Folk Dance and Song Society by the Lands Tribunal was reversed in the Court of Appeal. The Master of the Rolls (Raymond Evershed, who had as a matter of fact an active interest in music and should therefore have known better) observed during the hearing of the appeal that he could not regard 'Ring o' Roses' as a work of art. Since the aims of the Society, set out in its Articles, included the preservation of singing games it was not entitled to the exemption which it had previously enjoyed, though the Lands Tribunal had accepted both the artistic and the scientific (i.e. anthropological) value of the work of the Society. 'Ring o' Roses' thus cost the Society a thousand a year!

CHAPTER NINE

The Fringes

Norse and Celtic

Scotland

Something has already been said about the efforts that were
made to collect from oral tradition the native music of Scotland
and Ireland, before it had been thought of for England, and
incidental comment on the character of this Celtic folk-song
has fallen from time to time by the way. But a good deal more
needs to be said if anything like an adequate picture of what
has been found in the British Isles is to be offered to an ethnomusicologist from Europe or America. In view of the previous
history, which goes back well into the eighteenth century for the
Celtic countries – the Isle of Man had almost nothing to show
till the end of the nineteenth – it has been more urgent to con-
centrate on English folk music, but it is still necessary by way of
context, as well as coherence and completeness, to attempt some
account of the music of the Celtic fringe as also for non-Celtic
Scotland, though more summarily since a scholarly account is
now available in Mr Francis Collinson's *The Traditional and
National Music of Scotland* (1966). Traditional and national note,
not folk, though the book certainly deals with Scottish folk-song,
but compared with England, where regionalism exercises only
a small influence, Scotland presents a tangled skein of traditions.

First of all there are two languages, representing different
racial strains, the Lowland Scots dialect of English and the
Gaelic spoken in the Highlands and the Islands. These are
quite distinct, though there is a certain limited amount of interchange between their songs. There is more regionalism than in

England or even Ireland: thus the Border and Aberdeenshire are strong in balladry; the Lowlands, with Edinburgh for head-quarters, are noted for all the familiar Scottish airs known further south for a couple of centuries; the Hebrides have preserved the Gaelic songs of the west in all their purity. These embrace ancient heroic lays, labour songs of agriculture and the sea, laments, fairy-tale ballads and dialogues. The Western Highlands also have a tradition of Gaelic poetry and song. The Border ballads got into print a long time ago, as already described in chapter 6, and were popularized by Sir Walter Scott. The ballads of Buchan (Aberdeenshire), which of course include versions of the traditional Border classics that got into Child's collection, are still alive in oral tradition,[1] the so-called bothy ballads being one current in this pure stream. The name associated with this copious tradition is Gavin Grieg (1856–1914), who made a collection of some 3,000 traditional songs and ballads of the district.

The Lowland songs are copious and have a long history in print from *Orpheus Caledonius* (1725), on through Thomson's collections seventy years later, for which he enlisted the help of Haydn, Beethoven, Pleyel, Kozeluch and Weber, to provide settings. They – some of them picked up new verses by Burns and also gathered into their fold songs by aristocratic ladies – are probably today, and certainly were half a century ago, better known among English people than their own folk-songs. Knowledge of the Gaelic songs came much later, for though some printed collections were circulating in Scotland – e.g. John Mackenzie's *Sar-Obair*, a collection of verses (1841) and Patrick McDonald's *Highland Vocal Airs* (1781) – it was only in the mid-nineteenth century, according to Miss Broadwood,[2] that a more determined attempt was made to preserve these varied songs of an oral tradition. Miss Frances Tolmie of Skye

---

[1] As I discovered to my astonishment at the Edinburgh Festival of 1956 when Jeannie Robertson of Aberdeen sang 'Edward' to a native tune – no tune for it having been previously known to exist in Britain.
[2] See *Journal*, F.S.S., Vol. IV, Pt. III, 1911.

contributed 105 of such songs to the 1911 *Journal of the Folk-Song Society*; the later work of the Kennedy Frasers made them widely popular throughout Britain and still more recent work has been done by Mr and Mrs J. L. Campbell of the islands of Bara and South Uist and by the School of Scottish Studies.

But having separated out these strains of Scottish song one is left, in the case of the Lowland music, with a vast mass of anonymous and traditional music that may not be folk music. These familiar songs have been in print a very long time, which does not in itself preclude folk origin though it removes them from the remoulding process of oral tradition; they have been subjected to various degrees of additional processing; they have many of them passed through the crucible of Robert Burns's mind, which was a very good crucible, for he was, according to Mr Collinson, a folk-song expert and not at all destitute of an ear for music, as has been alleged, but it none the less transformed native song, and in some cases even injected English tunes into the Scottish stream. The nature of this problem of authenticity may be posed by the well-known and beautiful tune 'The Lass o' Patie's Mill',[3] [Example 104]. This *sounds* traditional but hardly folk, either in words or tune. It is beautifully though too elaborately constructed: it has too many slurred notes, most syllables have two notes apiece; it is, as did not fail to be observed, too Italianate in its cantilena for folksong, though, to be sure, it is free from an implied dominant modulation at the half-way cadence. Its history is that Allan Ramsay wrote the words or at any rate printed them in his *Scots Songs* of 1718 (songs=poems). They were fitted with a tune that was attributed to David Rizzio, Mary Queen of Scots' lover, and published in *Orpheus Caledonius* of 1725 and the song has been sung ever since, its tune having even been borrowed by Gaelic song-makers. The attribution of the tune to Rizzio has been scouted, but its possibly sixteenth-century origin has been allowed and an authority of Frank Kidson's standing has

[3] Of which Mr Collinson quotes a Gaelic much simpler and folkier version (*op. cit.*, pp. 33–4) as well as the ornamented version from *Orpheus Caledonius*.

The lass o'— Pa - tie's mill — So bon - nie — blythe — and —

gay —— In — spite — of — all my skill ———— She

stole — my — heart — a - way —— When ted - ding — o' — the —

hay ———— Bare-head - ed — on — the — green — Love —

midst — her — locks — did — play, — And — wan - ton'd — in her e'en.—

Example 104

recognized 'the influence of a court musician'. This sort of
historical annotation can be, indeed ought to be, appended to
every single song in a good collection of Scottish national songs,
such as, for instance, *The Minstrelsy of Scotland*, which contains
200 such songs and was edited by Alfred Moffat with copious
notes.

There is folk-song in non-Gaelic Scotland, among the
travelling tinkers who go berry picking in season, says Mr
Collinson, among the bothies of Aberdeenshire, as Mrs Muir
testified, and in families like that of Jeannie Robertson who
produced that version of 'Edward' which so startled me at the
Edinburgh Festival. But most of the familiar Scottish songs,
including those with words by Burns, or as in the case of 'Lizzie
Lindsay' with a tune from Burns – where did he get it? – are
best regarded as traditional. Many may well have been folk-
songs at one time but they have been stabilized in the Scottish

national tradition and are no longer folk-songs in the same sense as the more recently retrieved Gaelic songs which *are* folk-songs. The same applies to the dance tunes, of which there are many manuscript and printed collections, such as those of Niels and Nathaniel Gow in the late eighteenth century and the Athole collection of reels and strathspeys printed as late as 1884 and recently reissued. There is indeed an immense wealth of such traditional and national music. But its folk character is denied by Gavin Grieg (of whom more later), an expert whose word should be decisive. In his address to the Buchan Field Club in 1905 he takes the same line as Sharp was contemporaneously taking in England about the nature of true folk-song. 'Folk-song', he says, 'by a kind of social gravitation always seeks the lowest level and keeps it' – an opinion with which Mr A. L. Lloyd would agree. 'It is necessarily of the people and for the people and all attempts to raise it are soon met by a certain invincible inertia, for it cannot transcend the average lyric sense and sanction of the plebs. . . . Your folk-songist knows what is what – knows his own mind. . . . If folk-song could have been raised Burns was the man to do it; but not even *he* succeeded. He has not given the people a new and higher type of folk-song, he has only reinforced and enriched in measureless degree a kind of song that, however it may all along have hung on the horizon, has never quite been folk-song.' So we call it national and traditional.

What then about national characteristics? Their generally wide compass, more often a tenth than an octave and often stretching to a twelfth, is one cause of the lyrical quality that marks Scottish song, pentatonism (not inconsistent with wide compass: cf. 'Auld Lang Syne' which has a range of a twelfth) was noted as a characteristic by Burney and it has survived in a pure state in the Gaelic music, but is of course neither universal in Scotland nor peculiar to it. Modal tunes are found, as in England. Mr Collinson notes as another feature of frequent occurrence the tonal shift already noted, by which the final note is not always in the main tonality, or a phrase is repeated at a different pitch as in many Czech tunes, in the English 'None-such', the Northumbrian 'Elsie Marley' – Mr Collinson concedes possible bagpipe influence and instances the Scottish 'Tullochgorum'[4] – as producing a juxtaposition of tonalities, as the jargon used to have it, instead of a modulation or the maintenance of a single tonality.

Then there is the Scotch snap. High words have been exchanged about this. Lucy Broadwood, writing a preface to the Tolmie collection of Gaelic songs, which she put into the *Folk-Song Journal* of 1911, says that the strong accent on the first syllable of Gaelic words combined with their weak endings ('as elusive as the French mute "e"'), 'was observed and misunderstood by Lowland Scottish and English musicians of the late seventeenth century and onwards', who are thus responsible for the 'odious' snap. Mr Collinson will have none of this and asserts that the snap (of which he finds the epithet 'Scotch' so spelt odious) is characteristic of both Highland and Lowland tunes, though plainly the accentuation of the two languages is not identical. If a single instance may be allowed to confirm his point 'The Bonny Earl o' Murray' can speak for the Norse side of Scotland and another 'Lament for Diarmid' from Skye for the Gaels [Examples 105[5] and 106], or more markedly in

Ye Hie-lands and ye Low-lands, O where hae ye been? They hae slain the Earl o' Mor-ay, And laid him on the green, He was a braw gal-lant And he rode— at the ring, And the

[4] Cf. above p. 157.   [5] *F.S.J.*, 1911, p. 248.

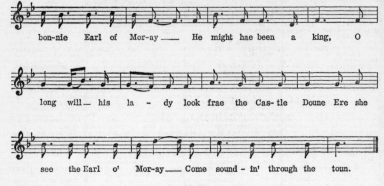

Example 105

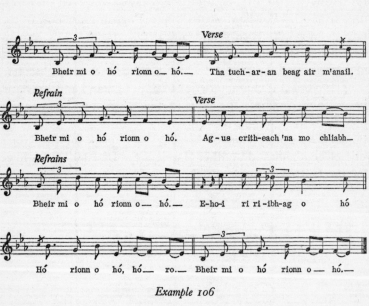

Example 106

'Oran don ghunna', a song about a gun collected by Lucy Broadwood at Arisaig in Invernesshire in 1905 [Example 107].[6]

In this respect then all Scottish folk-song would seem to be at

[6] *F.S.J.*, 1932, p. 47.

Example 107

one, though this particular device has not so strong a compulsion behind it as the Hungarian language exercises on its employment in Hungarian folk-tunes. In Gaelic it is less harshly accented in accordance with the smooth lilt of the language, and even in 'Green grow the rushes, O', the natural accentuation of the words makes it run lightly off the tongue. In the Aberdeen collection it occurs less frequently but is certainly not unknown. The dance tunes are full of it. Here is an instance taken at random from the Athole Collection, a strathspey tune called 'Mr George Anderson', in which the snap is not confined to the first beats of the bar [Example 108].

229

Example 108

The Aberdeen tradition has continued to flow naturally, while the stream through Edinburgh has been canalized. It still flows, but it was tapped round the turn of the present century by Gavin Grieg, an old-style dominie who spent his whole life (1856–1914) near Aberdeen, and working with him the Rev. J. B. Duncan (1848–1917). They too had their predecessors in the field of collecting, notably Peter Buchan (a surname as well as a place-name) who had published a couple of volumes of *Ancient Ballads and Songs of the North of Scotland* as far back as 1828. His editorial integrity was impugned but was defended by Alexander Keith in his preface to Gavin Grieg's *Last Leaves of Traditional Ballads and Ballad Airs*, published posthumously in 1925. This collection of 109 ballads, all with their Child numberings, is a classic. In it each ballad has an introductory note, following Child's example, in which historical and comparative matter is marshalled, references made to other versions or to the appearance of the ballad in any of the other Scottish collections of Buchan, Herd, Motherwell and Kinloch – and indeed to English versions as well. Selected versions from Greig's more ample collection are printed below with name of singer, place and date of acquisition supplied and then a note on the tunes, which in many cases are different from those already known and in some cases supply a vacancy in other collections. 'The Dowie Dens o' Yarrow' affords an example of the scrupulous scholarship, the wealth of cross-reference and the attention to the melodies which Greig brought to his task [Example 109]. Child (no. 214), he says, obtained

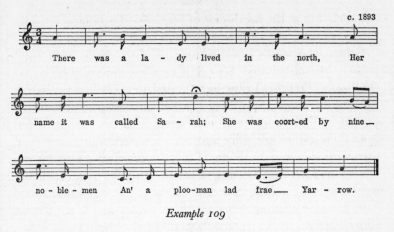

There was a la - dy lived in the north, Her
name it was called Sa - rah; She was coort-ed by nine —
no - ble - men An' a ploo-man lad frae — Yar - row.

Example 109

nineteen versions from print or manuscript but 'we' (i.e. Grieg)
have here eleven from tradition since the ballad was a favourite
in the north-east. They are, however, so nearly related as to be
properly regarded as variants of one version – so he only prints
one. He found only one tune for it, which he also found used
with other ballads, but he noted twenty-two versions, printed
six of them and observes that they 'give an exceptionally good
idea of how folk-airs may combine variety in detail with un-
changing melodic substance'. Example 109 is representative.
What strikes the eye of the reader is the prevalence of tunes
comprised of a single strain of eight bars or sometimes twelve.
Keith, Grieg's editor, notes this and offers it as an explanation
of the reason why the Christies, father and son, who in 1876
published the first considerable collection of ballads with their
tunes, *Traditional Ballad Airs*, come under fire as already
mentioned for too much editing, not only of the words but of
the tunes by extending them with second strains. He notes that
Grieg's experience, unlike Sharp's, was that text and tune
were not indissolubly connected, since a singer in Aberdeenshire often used the same tune for more than one ballad and
members of the same family might provide different tunes for
the same ballad. Grieg claimed only a very few as indigenous
to Aberdeenshire and thought there were no more than 300

folk melodies in the north-east of Scotland. These facts illumine the living tradition and the way it has been preserved.

Grieg, who was a distant kinsman of the Norwegian composer, also contributed a weekly article containing texts but (naturally) no tunes to the local newspaper *The Buchan Observer* between 1907 and 1911. They contain much discursive information as well as ballad and song texts from his collection but from their nature are more informal. They constitute, however, such a mine of lore that some of them were reissued in forty-two sets by the Carnegie Trust, and in 1963 two American scholars[7] went through the files, collected up the whole series and issued it in a single volume between stout covers together with an address given by Grieg in 1905 to the Buchan Field Club. Duncan's collection was deposited in the Library of Aberdeen University and is only now in the decade of the sixties being tapped with the consent of Duncan's grandson in the *Journal of the English Folk Dance and Song Society*. The oral tradition was also tapped in a publication of *Bothy Songs and Ballads* by John Ord in 1930 and was described in operation by Willa Muir in her *Living with Ballads* in 1965. There are still folk-singers in Aberdeen, as was shown so vividly in the Pleasures of Scotland show at the Edinburgh Festival already mentioned, of whom Jeannie Robertson has become famous for her repertory, learned from her mother who was a travelling tinker, and for her traditional style of singing.

Celtic

Another uncontaminated oral tradition of folk-song to balance that of north-east Scotland was the Island tradition of the north-west. The Hebrides preserved into the radio age something of the way of life, including arts and crafts, the Roman Catholic religion and Gaelic speech, of previous centuries insulated by the sea. Though to be sure the sea can join as well as separate, for Norse influence dating from the voyages of the Vikings is

[7] Kenneth S. Goldstein and Arthur Argo, Folklore Associates, Halboro, Pennsylvania, 1963.

traced in the legends and the songs of the Hebrides by Gaelic scholars. Also of course a good deal of Gaelic song is common to both Highlands and Islands. But the character of Hebridean song is so marked that in the present century it has stolen the limelight and in the mind of south Britain at least is regarded as the main representation of the Gaelic song of Scotland. This was largely the work of one remarkable woman, Marjory Kennedy Fraser, though she was neither the first nor the most learned, nor even a native, propagandist for Hebridean music. But she combined in her single person as collector, editor and singer, three kinds of musical ability, and the circumstances of her life – birth in the Highlands at Perth (1857); marriage to A. J. Fraser which gave her a daughter, Patuffa, who learned to play the clarsach; and descent from the notable Scottish singer, David Kennedy, which gave her a sister who was also a musician – reinforced the appeal of a compelling personality. She had accompanied her father on the piano as a child; she was trained as a singer in Milan and Paris; had an interest in folk-song aroused by Ducoudray's collection of Breton folk-song; she visited the Outer Hebrides in 1905 and published three volumes of *Songs of the Hebrides* between 1909 and 1921. She toured widely giving lecture recitals and so spread the knowledge of a little-known but still living tradition. She has not escaped the reproach levelled at Tom Moore, Robert Burns, even Bishop Percy, and other editors who have 'improved' texts or tunes or both, since some of her adaptations are too free by scholars' standards. Thus for instance Mr Collinson quotes the waulking song which Mrs Kennedy Fraser turned into the splendid sea-song 'Kishmul's Galley', or as he says, 'on which she based her song Kishmul's Galley. The notes will be found to be the same, but of different rhythm to Mrs Kennedy Fraser's song.' But Mrs Kennedy Fraser herself refers to the variability of the tunes according as the singer is a good or an unmusical one and she found, as all collectors do, that variants belong to different times and different places. 'In selecting from different versions', she says, 'we should be careful to perpetuate the most strongly characteristic, the most faithful to the type, and to reject such as are at variance with the modal character of the air'. She had the root of the matter in her and her piano (or harp) accompaniments certainly come within the canon proposed by Vaughan Williams that they 'be made with love' and are no less certainly effective without over-elaboration. If in arranging the songs for performance by others than folk-singers she went beyond the collector's strict ethics — in 'Kishmul's Galley' she fitted words from Barra to the tune sung on Mingulay — she probably took the best versions as being most characteristic and made a conflation from them, which is only an extension of any collector's practice in arriving at a central version of a tune which a singer varies from verse to verse.

She had a contemporary who was earlier in the field and, not having performance in view, was more scholarly in her method. This was Frances Tolmie, born in Skye in 1840 of a family that claimed to have come from Scandinavia with the Viking ancestors of the Macleods. Some hundred songs of her collection were published in the *Folk-Song Journal* of 1911. Apparently she encountered in 1900 Dr George Henderson, the Glasgow professor of Celtic studies, who urged her to set down on paper the fruits of a lifetime's immersion in Gaelic lore and music. He also introduced her to Lucy Broadwood, at that time editing the *Folk-Song Journal*, who herself went collecting in Arisaig in Invernesshire in the summers of 1906 and 1907. Some of these Arisaig songs were published posthumously[8] in the last of the old *Folk Song Journals* (1931) and the first of the new *Journal of the English Folk Dance and Song Society* (1932). A still later collection of over a hundred songs mainly from South Uist was published by Margaret Fay Shaw in 1955 and some gramophone records of folk-songs in the Isle of Barra were made by her husband, J. L. Campbell.

What immediately strikes the student of these collections is that a large proportion of the songs are labour chants for milk-

---

[8] As I know to my cost since I had to see them through the press as successor to Miss Broadwood as editor.

ing, churning, reaping, sowing, that the ballads are not those of the other side of Scotland but deal either with characters of Celtic mythology, Diarmid and Deirdre, or with local events, shipwrecks and false loves, or with magic and the stuff of fairyland. There are also of course songs of occasion, dirges, sea lilts, part-incantations, even of Christmas (the religion is more of Rome than Calvin), Hogmanay and Hallowe'en. But unique to the Hebrides is the *puirt a beul*, the mouth music, which in the absence of an instrument was used as the accompaniment for dancing. Musically pentatonics and hexatonics are common; so are the modes and the circular construction of verse and refrain which leaves tonality in suspense. Generalization about compass is unsafe, for if one observes, as one is bound to, the large number of tunes that are enclosed within the interval of a fifth or sixth, one equally finds, if one scans Miss Tolmie's or Mrs Campbell's tunes, plenty of octaves, ninths and tenths. Mrs Campbell quotes one tune of four whole tones only F to B and so without tonality, 'O eadar an dà chraicionn', but as this is a Hogmanay *quête* song it may well be, like the Chester Souling Song which only once steps a tone outside a minor third, essentially an incantation. More like a tune but still short and made up of only four consecutive notes but this time comfortably in G minor, is a fragment of a 'Lord Rendal' kind of ballad with question and answer, verse and refrain, that Miss Tolmie got from a singer on Mull who in turn got it from her nurse who was a native of Eigg, 'Ciod è ghaoil?' (What is it, love?) [Example 110].

Example 110

235

Perhaps the low pitch of Hebridean voices noticed by Mrs Kennedy Fraser had something to do with the small compass. However, short tunes of narrow compass, little more than motifs that can evoke an answering motif and then juggle with it in various permutations, are a natural product of labour lilts, in particular the waulking songs which are the Hebridean speciality.

Waulking, which is a process of fulling cloth, has often been described.[9] Women get together, sit round a table, pound and pull at a roll of tweed in order to shrink the tweed to a state fit for the tailor, sing rhythmically as they work and after it is finished they give the roll a quick clapping finale. Then tea with a dram of something stronger. How idyllic is the picture of a small society and its handicraft, until one learns that the essential liquid in which the cloth is steeped is hot urine! Still, the no less essential songs are sweeter and their structure and tempo are determined by the work. Mrs Campbell gives some half dozen ways in which solo and chorus divide the text between them and observes that the character and speed of the songs alter as the cloth gradually acquires the right texture. Some waulking songs allow improvisation with teasing local allusions in the same manner as sea-shanties do. An example from Tolmie's collection shows several of these features, comical words about a youth rescued from the waulking tub and a structure by which a solo sings a one-line refrain, followed by a choral refrain of meaningless syllables to be followed in turn by the solo verse which carried the story, i.e. there are three elements, solo verse, solo refrain and chorus in which all present joined [Example 111] ('Chraobh an iubhair). The allocation of these three elements gives various structures to the waulking songs. Dr Andersson sets them out in his pamphlet 'Gaelic Music from the Isle of Lewis' and calls special attention to the one in which the second (or last) line of solo provides the first line of the next stanza. But this form, which helps the listeners to

[9] By Tolmie and Kennedy Fraser and by the Finnish scholar, Otto Andersson, in his pamphlet on *Gaelic Music from the Isle of Lewis*, Abo, 1953.

Example 111

learn a song by heart, is not peculiar to waulking songs but is found in Sweden, Denmark, Germany and Russia, and in an example, which he also quotes, from Serbo-Croatia as recorded by Bartók and Lord.[10] This song has sixty-five two-lined stanzas, twenty-two of which are linked stanzas thus:

3. Your mother has fallen ill
   And God knows that I shall not recover

4. God knows that I shall not recover
   For I have had a bad dream

5. I have had a bad dream
   That my brocade caught fire

All the collections, of which the first to be published was Patrick McDonald's *Highland Vocal Airs* (1781) and the most recent Mrs Campbell's (Fay Shaw) (1955), contain examples of laments for chieftains and heroes, lullabies, work songs from spinning to navigation, love songs and *puirt-a-beul*, which are rhythmically lively and verbally nonsensical. Here is an

[10] *Serbo-Croatian Folk Songs* (not *Heroic Songs*), I, p. 119, no. 12a, Columbia, 1951.

example collected by Otto Andersson in Lewis in 1936 of which the words are nonsensical 'very daft and very happy' [Example 112]. The salvage would seem to be complete now that the

Example 112

School of Scottish Studies continues the scholarly work of the ladies described above. Yet Patrick Duncan, writing 200 years ago, gave them a life of twenty years: 'In less than twenty years it would be vain to attempt a collection of Highland music.' Folk-song is always at its last gasp, but it never dies.

Ireland

Ireland like Scotland has its Gaelic-speaking inhabitants and the speaking of Erse has been officially encouraged since independence. But the bilingualism of its folk-song is not just a question of geographical distribution as in Scotland, rather it is the result of a historical accident that the bulk of Irish tunes were instrumentally preserved, their words were the concern of their poets and until the present century the field work of collecting was not undertaken by experts. A quotation from Vol. VI of the *Journal of the Irish Folk-Song Society*, a London body founded in 1904, describes the position:

'Irish song collectors have, as a general rule, most unfortunately worked in two separate sections. Musicians have gone about collecting and publishing Irish airs which, as in the case of the vast Petrie collection, have been divorced from the treasury of Gaelic lyrical poetry to which they were originally wedded. With the exception of dance music and certain harp and bagpipe tunes, all the airs in this and other collections of course belonged to songs. The words taken down by Eugene O'Curry have been apparently separated from the musical collection. As against this we have collections of Irish poetry, like Dr Douglas Hyde's love-songs of Connacht and the earlier Hardiman's *Minstrelsey*, without any record of music.'

The first collection of any size to be made in which tune, Gaelic words, English translation and notes were treated with adequate scholarship was the work of A. Martin Freeman (1878–1959), a London literary recluse whose Irish wife made him into a Gaelic scholar. Three journals of the Folk-Song Society, 1920–2, printed songs collected in Co. Cork in 1914, which according to Donal O'Sullivan is 'incomparably the finest collection published in our time of Irish songs noted from oral tradition'.

Something was said in chapter 5 of Bunting's pioneer activity in collecting tunes from all parts of Ireland – for he became interested in 'collating the airs of different provinces with each other' – which stemmed from a contest of harpers in Belfast in 1792. His first volume of *A General Collection of the Ancient Irish Music* contained sixty-six airs, of which the Irish titles but not the words were given; it was published in 1796 but was not a financial success. On the other hand Moore's *Irish Melodies*, for which some of Bunting's tunes were requisitioned and fitted with English words, was a distinct success and attracted wide-spread attention. So for his second publication in 1809, two years after Moore's song book, Bunting provided words, to obtain which he employed the services of Patrick Lynch, a Gaelic scholar who went round after Bunting to collect the verses. At this point politics intervenes painfully. The Belfast enthusiasts, who had been responsible for the harp contest and had engaged Bunting, consisted of the McCracken family, the Emmet family and Thomas Russell, who were members of the United Irishmen, the body that raised the rebellion of 1798 in the north and the uprising of 1803 in Dublin. Lynch was arrested and gave evidence of identification against Russell, who was executed, as also was Robert Emmet.[11] It seems likely that the bitter feeling, generated by Lynch's turning King's Evidence, was responsible for Bunting not carrying out his declared intention for his second book in 1809, 'to procure translations of some of the finest songs and for several of the airs best adapted for the purpose to give English words with an instrumental accompaniment', i.e. to copy Moore's example. But he also added 'to annex the original poetry in the Irish character'. What, however, he actually did was to bring out piano arrangements of seventy-seven airs with Irish and English titles (of which thirteen were repeats from the 1796 volume) and for twenty of them provide English words, of which twelve were translations of Lynch's manuscripts. For the third collection of 165 airs, published much later, in 1840, after Bunting had moved to Dublin, he was content with piano arrangements. The first two of these collections were reissued by the Irish Folk Song Society of London between 1925 and 1939. The editors, D. J. O'Sullivan and A. Martin Freeman, had at their disposal the original manuscripts of Bunting and Lynch. In an earlier number[12] of the *Journal* of the Society A. P. Graves explains how the events just summarized occurred: 'Mrs Milligan Fox (the secretary and moving spirit of the Irish Folk Society)

[11] Emmet is the subject of the lament in Moore's 'She is far from the Land.'
[12] Vol. XIV, 1914.

calling at Morley's, the harp maker, learnt that one of his customers had recently ordered an Irish harp on the ground that his grandfather had been a collector of Irish music. Mrs Fox inquired his name and address. The purchaser proved to be Dr Louis Macrory of Battersea who generously put a great amount of unpublished material inherited from his grandfather, Edward Bunting, at Mrs Fox's disposal. He furthermore added to her delight by informing her that there were other Bunting papers in a box in Dublin. This proved to contain a great number of the Gaelic originals of the tunes in the Bunting collection. Why had they been neglected for fifty years or more? Because Patrick Lynch, who had collected them round the country, had turned King's Evidence against Russell, one of his employers on this quest. Russell was sent to the gallows, the friendly company of song collectors was broken up and there was a strong feeling against the publication of manuscripts collected by Lynch the informer, and hence their suppression until their discovery by Mrs Milligan Fox.'

Yet neither Moore's example – he published ten sets between 1837 and 1854 – nor politics fully accounts for the continuing Irish practice of collecting songs without their words. Tunes were still noted from fiddlers, pipers, harpers and even from whistling, and only incidentally and unsystematically were the words recorded by George Petrie and Patrick Joyce. The latter often comments, 'I only recall one verse of this song', and his second book of tunes of 1909, *Old Irish Folk Music and Songs*, valuable as it is, presents a disconcerting spectacle of tunes with and without words, words sometimes in Gaelic sometimes in English, sometimes underlaid and sometimes printed separately below the tune. He had issued an earlier book in 1873, *Ancient Irish Music*, and another in 1888, *Irish Music and Song*, in which according to Donal O'Sullivan, Irish words were for the first time printed under the notes of the tune. Joyce had contributed many tunes to Petrie, whose complete collection numbered over 2,000 tunes. George Petrie (1789–1866) was the versatile son of a Dublin portrait painter, who began life as an artist but branched off into archaeology, and while ranging the countryside in these two pursuits encountered folk-song. He could play the violin and he took it on his subsequent song-collecting expeditions, by which he entertained his singers and checked the accuracy of his transcriptions. Dr P. W. Joyce (1827–1914) was a teacher, head of a training college for teachers, who also had wide antiquarian interests and a good ear and memory for tunes, as a glance at his last published book immediately reveals. This book also reveals still another of the complications that bedevil the story of Irish folk-song, which are such that it is almost impossible to write a single, factual sentence, without having to qualify or rewrite it. This particular complication is that Joyce has printed versions of English folk-songs – 'Brennan on the Moor', 'Searching for lambs', 'The Foggy Dew', 'The Mantle of Green' are a random selection. It would seem that the cross-channel traffic in immigrant labour is responsible both for Irish idioms affecting English folk-song, as has often been pointed out, and the occurrence of English songs in Ireland.

But the inter-relations of the three main collections – there were several others of equal value but less extent – Bunting, Petrie and Joyce, though they can be sorted out by the patient scholarship of an O'Sullivan, are complicated by the facts already noted, the use of instrumental sources, the haphazard connexions of words and tunes, the publication of parts of the collections and subsequent overlapping, but most of all by the Gaelic. As in Scotland, Gaelic was spoken in the west of the country, and English encroached from the east of a line drawn from Waterford to Derry. The encroaching was going on all through the nineteenth century, when our collectors were at their work. Bunting, as we saw, employed Lynch to obtain the Gaelic words. Moore frankly wrote new words which, unlike Burns's, had no relation to their originals. Joyce has a whole section of Irish songs with English words. Stanford was not a Gaelic speaker, but to him were handed three bound volumes of Petrie's collection containing 2,148 tunes, which he reduced to

1,580, edited and published in three volumes subsequently put together in 1906. He also drew on it for two volumes of songs designed for performance with words by A. P. Graves and provided with piano accompaniments by himself. A third volume of such Irish songs was derived from Moore's *Irish Melodies*, which he cleaned up with strong criticism of Moore's editorial ethics. Stanford's criticism, however, and his own editorial practice have come under critical fire in as much as he had had no experience of collecting in the field, as his successor Herbert Hughes had, and he was unable to check Petrie's sources, but the comparison of his version of 'She is far from the land' with Moore's shows the sort of cleaning up he had to do, see Examples 47 a and b in chapter 5, and his piano accompaniment sharpens the difference of the two versions when compared with the Haydnesque introductions and harmony of Sir John Stevenson.

The Irish Folk-Song Society began to publish its *Journal* in 1904 and to advocate by precept and example more strictly scholarly ways of preserving Irish folk-song, which that society had established for its own practice. In 1909 Herbert Hughes published the first of his four volumes of songs 'edited arranged and for the most part collected' by himself. He explains in his preface what he means by those three participles and the only aspect of then current notions which he disclaims is the modes – Irish songs, he says, are in untempered scales and use microtones but, having no appreciable contact with plainsong, are not modal. What they do show is variable inflection of the third and seventh degrees within the same tune, even a sharpened fourth (in 'Slowly the Shadows'). But even here again the words are loosely tethered, as Hughes has recourse to Yeats for 'The Maids of Mourne Shore' and Padraic Column for 'She moved through the fair'; two only are translations of the Gaelic but many are adaptations of ballads and fragments known to him from his youth. Significant of the English-Gaelic trouble is the very engaging 'I know my love' which was popularized by Barbara Mullen on a record. Hughes notes that in Galway and Clare the song was sung in alternate verses of Irish and English, but as he had been unable to obtain the Irish words he gives the version known in Limerick. It is a remarkable tune with the compass of a twelfth in *moto perpetuo* rhythm with one of its phrases transposed up an octave [Example 113]. Hughes also recognizes the cross-channel traffic,

Example 113

especially the migration and return of farm workers at harvest time. Thus in his Kerry collection (his last published in 1936) he says of 'The Star of the County Down' – it sounds local enough – must have 'had a travelling career'. It is in fact 'Lazarus', and of some other of these Kerry songs says 'they must have come from England generations ago in spite of the

Irish tang that is an essential ingredient. How and when they came to the heart of these Kerry mountains it would be interesting to discover, for there is no longer any considerable migration of labourers to English and Scots farms, such as was customary in the North (i.e. Ulster) at harvesting time, always a fruitful source of exchange in balladry.' This may offset the other claim that used to be heard, and was repeated not so long ago by Michael Tippett, that most English folk-songs are Irish.

Even when we come to Martin Freeman's utterly scrupulous collection from Ballyvourney the songs, which were sung to him in Gaelic by four singers, of whom three were illiterate and three bilingual and three nearly eighty years old, are such a hotch-potch that Freeman has to write an introductory note explaining why some of them are corrupt and some almost untranslatable. He found some few poems that were obviously and genuinely folk and he presumes that all of his rich haul of melodies must at one time have had their own verses, but, as he explains, in the eighteenth century over most of the south of Ireland a debased kind of poetry (Gaelic not English) acquired a vogue which became popular with folk-singers – 'conventionality, exaggeration, vagueness of meaning, looseness of connexion and multiplication of words' are how he describes them. Then he continues: 'Yet it is for these very qualities that they are prized by the country singer and his hearers. He has an immense respect for them as the compositions of learned people. Vaguely descriptive stanzas, consisting largely of compound words and obsolete and literary expressions, impress him tremendously, and he does not trouble to enquire into the exact meaning of the lines: his object is to remember them and sing them again. Any passage which is unintelligible, or nonsensical, is by the folk-singer generally accounted for by one of two expressions, "Old Irish" and "Poetry". Very likely he might not understand the original if he heard them; very likely he learned them wrongly at first; very likely the person who first made the poem known in the district read it wrongly, or got it from an inaccurate copy. It is no matter. The worse the corruption the greater is the singer's veneration for his text, since his inability to understand it is a proof of its high antiquity.'

Consequently he found it difficult to give a connected translation of some of them, and certainly 'inconsequential' seems to be the word to describe the sudden divagations of the sense between one verse of a song and the next. Indeed one of his songs contains the verse (as translated) (no. 20):

But I have not fully and clearly told my tale –
For I would not tell it falsely in any way –
It was the fairy-hosts of the sun that came towards me
And carried her away from me to the Round Hill of the Dark
   Woman.

This is part of a ballad 'Is fada ghom er buereav' (Long have I been troubled) which is one of a group dealing with a girl and a man meeting in one form or another of a love proposal to tunes having some family relationship, of which this one came from Conny Coehlan, the old man who provided half of Freeman's songs, a good and typical tune [Example 114]. We are told

Example 114
246

that there is a version of this poem in *The Poets and Poetry of Munster* (1849) attributed to a certain George Roberts, of whom nothing is known; that poem's eight verses has grown to twelve by means of 'transpositions, corruption and accretion and so have not only become incoherent but are well on the way to becoming a different song from the original'. In one of his versions, more ornamented but restricted in compass to an octave, the seventh degree is variously inflected sharp and natural. In many of these Irish ballads the girl sometimes stands for Ireland, and Mr Freeman found a whole category of song called *Aisling* which are Jacobite productions invoking the triumph of the Catholics and the slaughter of the English.

The best account of these divorces, misalliances, sudden and short marriages of convenience, or even long ones like those with Thomas Moore and A. P. Graves, is to be found in the introduction to the excellent anthology published in 1960 by Donal O'Sullivan, *Songs of the Irish*. Even so late he has to repeat the old statement that the tunes were noted independently of the words 'since the collectors of the tunes did not know Irish and the collectors of the words did not know music'. This is intended to be a representative selection and comprises fifteen categories, work songs, love songs, children's songs, drinking songs, humorous songs and so on. In it the Gaelic, identified in many cases by title as in Bunting, has been attached to its proper tune, a singable English version complemented by a more literal prose translation has been provided and historical or other suitable annotations appended. Is it then impossible in the light of this chequered history to analyse out of all these various collections the characteristic features of Irish folk-song, as the Scotch snap for instance is of Scottish? Not altogether, if definitions and discriminations are not pressed too rigorously. Thus one can say at once that the interval of the sixth, both rising and falling, is a common feature that gives a characteristic ethos to the melodic shape, the elaborate anacrusis and the twice repeated note at a feminine cadence are other fingerprints, a wide range, as compared for instance with French folk-song but resembling Scottish, gives a feeling of sweep and a power of expression – of this an extreme instance may be quoted from 'Shule Agra', where upward motion proceeds unchecked through the song's compass of a tenth [Example 115]. Octave leaps are to be found. But long

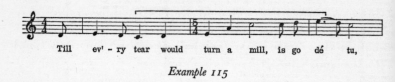

Till   ev' - ry   tear   would   turn a   mill,   is go   dé   tu,

Example 115

ago, indeed in Petrie's first publication *Ancient Music of Ireland* in 1855, a rhythmic feature was noticed in what Petrie called 'Narrative' airs. The term was retained by Joyce, who says that it is immediately recognizable by ear and eye. It consists of a crotchet or dotted note figure in a bar of three-four time, i.e. either

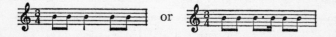

Joyce says that narrative airs are found in every collection of Irish music but seldom outside Ireland – its fingerprint is certainly not a common feature of English three-four time tunes.

Preoccupation with Gaelic song must not ignore the fact that English has been in use all over Ireland even among Gaelic speakers for more than two centuries, and the Irish do still sing folk-songs with English words. Thirty years after Martin Freeman made his haul of Gaelic in Co. Cork the B.B.C. sent a collecting expedition which put down a net in Ulster as well as the south. In a report of its haul[13] it was recorded that of 500 songs taken from over a hundred singers 140 were in Gaelic,

---

[13] Contributed to *E.F.D.S.S. Journal*, 1955 and 1956.

the rest in English – questions of origin and derivation being neglected as too complex and uncertain and not to be certainly determined – sixty-five were from the common stock of English-text songs found elsewhere in the British Isles, and of these sixty-five there were sixteen of Child's ballads still being sung. These included 'Sweet William's Ghost' (Child 77) to a variant of 'Dives and Lazarus', 'Edward', 'The Lowlands of Holland', 'The trees they do grow high'. It would appear from the samples available that Irish singers ornament their melodies more than English singers, that they preserve hexatonic and pentatonic scale structure and that the three repeated-note cadence is intrinsic, though many of the tunes are recognizably the same as their English equivalents to the same words.

The corpus of Irish tunes is very large and more homogeneous than the Scottish in so far as there is really only one tradition and not two. The subjects of the songs are the ones universally found in folk-song, though the absence of carols, such as form an important branch of folk-song in England, and of rowing songs such as are found in Gaelic Scotland, has been noted. Political songs often take the form of a love ballad in which the girl's name is a symbol for Ireland. The survival of the harp, itself a heraldic symbol of Ireland, which has a bardic tradition behind it, may have contributed something, perhaps the wide compass and the rhapsodic character, as found for instance in the 'Londonderry Air', to Irish folk-song which is not found outside the Celtic fringe.

The dance tradition of Ireland is chequered: political turmoil from Tudor times onwards seems to have prevented the practice of any national dance, and rather curiously Irish literature contains no references to dancing and the Irish language has no words for it. Of course Irishmen must have danced and Joyce prints tunes labelled jig, real and hornpipe, but none of these names is Irish – jig and hornpipe are English, and the reel Scottish. He also prints tunes labelled 'jig and song tune', as though the dance fiddlers borrowed song tunes for dancing, which is consistent with the rather odd fact that so many of the tunes in Bunting, Petrie and the other collectors were taken from instrumentalists. There is not, therefore, a wealth of dance tunes to be added, as in England and Scotland, to the corpus of the national folk music. But the Irish danced jigs, reels and hornpipes and imparted a national flavour to them. Many of these tunes are known by name outside Ireland – such as 'The Rakes O'Mallow' [Example 116] to which a four-hand reel is

Example 116

danced. Joyce devotes a short paragraph to the various kinds of dances in the preface to *Ancient Irish Music* (1872) and reprints it bodily in his 1909 book. The dance tunes that prevailed in the Munster counties, twenty-five or thirty years ago (i.e. *c.* 1845) he says were chiefly the reel, the double jig, the single jig, the hop jig and the hornpipe. The reel was in common or two-four time, the jigs in six-eight, the hornpipe in common or two-four time, played not quite so quickly as the reel. The hornpipe was danced by a man unaccompanied by a partner. And, as already stated, there are plenty of examples in his pages which followed.

Wales

Wales too is bilingual and in Wales the Celtic language has maintained an official status although, or perhaps because, the pressure of English speech from the east has been longer and harder. The Welsh are great singers – in their chapels, in their male-voice choirs, in their eisteddfodau and in their choral societies. They have also kept alive their tradition of harp playing and have by combining voice and harp produced a unique kind of descant singing which they call *penillion*. In this the harper plays a traditional tune and the singer extemporises a counter-tune, which need not fit exactly either as to an identical rhythm or a simultaneous start, but tune and descant, harp and voice, must end together. Penillion is thus a mixture of three survivals, an old bardic tradition of declaiming lays to the harp, folk-song which provides the canto fermo, and a native feeling for counterpoint that goes back to the famous quotation from Giraldus Cambrensis who in 1191 said, with some exaggeration, that in any company of Welsh singers there were as many contrapuntal voices, i.e. parts, as there were voices to sing them, the only condition being as in penillion that they fetched up together at the end and in consonance.[14]

The bardic tradition of harping encouraged a kind of melody derived from, or implying the harmony of chords. There is some documentary evidence[15] that a homophonic type of secular music was to be found in Wales during the polyphonic period of the Middle Ages. Hence the survival of arpeggio-form melodies like 'The Ash Grove', 'David of the White Rock', another of these bardic songs which like 'The Men of Harlech' are folk-song by adoption,[16] has a melody which is a spelling-out of an

---

[14] *in unam denique sub B mollis dulcedine blanda consonantia et organicam convenientia melodiam.* For 'the sweetness of B flat' I would suggest the translation 'in a plagal cadence'.

[15] Explored by Mr Peter Crosley Holland: see Grove and his article in *Music and Letters*, April 1942.

[16] And so make a dent in the definition sternly laid down in chapter 1.

elaboration of the chords of E minor, its dominant seventh and relative major [Example 117].

Example 117

The geographical distribution of the Welsh form of Celtic language, i.e. cymric, is to west and north, and North Wales, as the remaining stronghold of Welsh speech and culture, gave more support to so recent a movement as the foundation of the Welsh Folk Song Society in 1906, than did South Wales where less Welsh is spoken and where English cultural pressure has moved in more easily over a longer period. As in Ireland so in Wales, only more so, the true folk-song tradition, songs from England and the tunes of bardic origin just described have impinged on each other. As in Ireland too tunes were collected without their words. A book was published in 1809 by John Parry 'with appropriate English words, adapted for the voice with symphonies and accompaniements'. In the same year the Edinburgh publisher, George Thomson, raided Wales for his enterprise to which he had yoked Haydn and Beethoven, published his collection 'adapted to the voice, and united to characteristic English Poetry'. It was not till 1844 that a book

containing forty-three songs collected from the peasantry by
Maria Jane Williams, 'to which are added the words usually
sung thereto', was printed. Thereafter collection of a more
scientific character has gone on: Brinley Richards edited a
volume for the English market in 1879, which was current for
many years, and Joseph Parry, J. Lloyd Williams working in
collaboration with Arthur Somervell produced a useful selection with Welsh and English words in 1907–9. A. P. Graves
gave for Wales a representation of thirty-three Welsh tunes
with Welsh and English words in his *Celtic Song Book* (1928).
Graves turned out a large number of lyrics for Welsh editors
just as he had for Stanford's edition of Petrie's Irish tunes.
More recently W. S. Gwynn Williams has done excellent work
combining scholarship with practical use in mind, producing in
1961 a book of the best things that had appeared in the *Journal*
of the Welsh Song Society, *Caneuon Traddodiadol Y Cymry*
(Traditional Songs of the Welsh). I take from this book a
Wassail song which shows a rhythmic feature begotten by the
Welsh language, a Scotch snap that is neither Scotch nor a
snap but a much gentler intonation [Example 118]. This is a

Example 118

Mari Lwyd song, a *quête* song for Christmas, in which the carol singers demanded food and drink if the house of call could not give as good as it got in the way of an antiphonal stanza. Other and better-known songs in this rhythm are 'Y Deryn Pur' (The Dove), one of Maria Jane Williams's collection, in which it is rather less insistent,

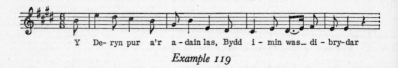

Y De- ryn pur a'r a - dain las, Bydd i - min was_ di - bry-dar

Example 119

the lullaby Suo-Gan, where the time signature is four-four [Example 120] and the love song 'Mae'nghariad i'n Fenws'

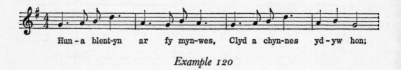

Hun - a blent-yn ar fy myn-wes, Clyd a chyn-nes yd-yw hon;

Example 120

(My sweetheart's like Venus) [Example 121].

Mae 'ngha - riad i'n Fen - ws, Mae 'ngha - riad i'n

fain; Mae 'ngha - riad i'n dly - sach Na blod - au y

drain; Fy 'ngha - riad yw'r lan - af, A'r wyn - na'n y

sir; Nid can- mol yr yd - wyf, Ond d'wed -yd y gwir.

Example 121

254

This of course is not the only pattern to be found: there are the usual six-eight patter tunes for ballads and some straight-forward melodies that could have grown over the border in England. There are indeed a few Welsh folk-songs with traditional English words – the first song in Gwynn Williams's anthology, culled from the *Journals* of the Welsh Folk Song Society, is 'Llangollen Market', which turned up, appropriately, at Llangollen Eisteddfodau in 1858, 1908 and 1958 with an English text about a girl whose lover has gone for a soldier, to a minor tune with a sharp seventh. In as much as folk-song has the fortunate property of its best being its most characteristic a glance through this representative anthology of seventy-four songs – representative in the sense that it contains songs, ballads, carols, lullabies, children's rhymes, and hymns – reveals some noteworthy though non-statistical features. The prevalence of the Dorian mode in the vocal as opposed to the harp-derived tunes was noticed by most observers. Here nos. 2, 3, 13 and 14 are pure Dorian; nos. 8 and 45 are hexatonic, the first with a flat seventh and the second with a penultimate sharpened leading note; no. 58 is in a major scale with a flat third, C with an E flat only in the signature and said by its contributor to be peculiar to the old Welsh music called *Gogywair*; nos. 18 and 19 pivot on two tonal centres, minor and relative major, as does no. 68 (tonic minor in a major key); variable inflections like the Irish are to be found in nos. 21, 25 and 73. Compass varies from a fifth in no. 6 to an eleventh in nos. 53 and 71.

Welsh folk-dances were knocked out by the puritan traditions and beliefs of the nonconformity which spread through Wales in the eighteenth century. A recent attempt by Hugh Mellor to uncover any lurking survivors produced meagre (his own word) results which he has set forth in a small book (1935). He found traces of the morris in North Wales, English country dances being danced in Merioneth in Central Wales, a four-handed reel in the Gower peninsula and of sword dances not a trace anywhere. For the disappearance of national dances, which must have existed though the literature is silent, and their tunes, John Wesley is not wholly to blame but also partly the harp, which is not a good instrument to dance to. No dance tunes are found in John Parry's collection of 1742, the first professedly Welsh collection and such as Mr Mellor encountered in his search are of no particular quality or interest. An odd situation, which a Welsh Folk Dance Society (*Cymdeithas Ddawns Werin Cymru*) is trying to retrieve by reconstructing what traces it can find into something danceable.[17]

The Isle of Man

Manx Gaelic has not, like Cornish, become extinct, but the compilers of the first modern song-book, *Manx National Songs* published by Boosey in 1896, say in their introduction 'The language being practically dead, songs with Manx words would not be generally sung', though they prefaced their decision to abandon it with the remark, 'For the most part the original songs were sung to Manx words and it may be thought that these ought to be given in this volume.' So once more we have salvage of a corpus of Celtic folklore conducted in several separate operations and once more the enthusiastic figure, though less scholarly than he believed, of Alfred Perceval Graves writing substitute verses – this as late as his *Celtic Song Book* of 1928.[18] The temptation of each subsequent generation of scholars to berate its predecessor is unseemly, for pioneers have no hindsight to guide them. What is evident in all the work of the Celtic revivalists is that they sought not only to preserve the vanishing heritage but to make it viable, to use a modernism with which they were unacquainted. Their efforts began with Dr John Clague, a Manxman who was a medical

[17] At the Albert Hall Folk Festival of 1968, a tap dancer found a harp sufficiently rhythmic for his accompaniment and one or two of these reconstructed dances were shown.

[18] I have in my possession a letter to me from Anne Gilchrist refusing to review the book, giving chapter and verse for examples of its insouciant scholarship.

practitioner and an amateur musician. He joined forces
with two brothers, J. F. and W. H. Gill in a systematic search of
the island between 1890 and 1894 and its fruits were published
under the musical editorship of W. H. Gill in the above mentioned volume and its sequel *Manx National Music* in 1898.

Gill had read a paper on Manx Music to the Musical Association in 1895, in which he noted that the only printed source
available to him was a small inaccurate collection of thirteen
tunes called *Mona Melodies* published in 1820, that the language
in the course of the last thirty years had been rapidly disappear-
ing, but that the oral tradition which he had at first regarded as
equally hopeless had yielded some material. This was what Dr
Clague had been collecting. From it 140 songs went into the two
Gill books, some of the remainder had appeared in a short-lived
publication of the Manx Language Society, and then in 1924
and 1925 a larger selection of ninety-seven miscellaneous songs
made by Anne Gilchrist was printed in the (English) *Folk-Song
Journal*. This contained, among fairy songs, love songs, sea
songs, narrative ballads and songs connected with customs, two
remarkable specimens of the cante-fable. One other publication
which helped in the identification of the tunes, since Clague's
manuscript was without words, was *Manx Ballads* (1896) by
Speaker A. W. Moore – incidentally J. F. Gill was a Deemster –
in which forty-five tunes were appended to seventy-four ballad
texts. It was from *Manx Ballads* that Mona Douglas and Arnold
Foster chose most of the twenty-four songs they successfully
edited with original words and translations and arranged (for
voice and piano and for chorus) in 1928–9 (Stainer and Bell),
though even here and at so late a date Miss Douglas found it
necessary to take one or two tunes from Clague and marry
them to words from Moore, so obstinately have the two traditions held apart. Moore also was useful to Miss Gilchrist in her
editorial work on the Clague collection, in which she made the
first serious attempt at comparative study.

What such comparative study revealed, as was to be expected
on an island which had welcomed (or resisted) successive waves

upon her shores of Irish and Scottish Christian missionaries, Norse kings and their lieutenants, English Plantagenets, the Stanley family of the Derby earldom, British bishops and officials and holiday-makers, was that the majority of Manx tunes are immigrants too, and at that not very long settled as folklore counts time, English, Scottish and Irish in that order of frequency.

The Isle of Man, however, has a certain number of songs known as distinctly Manx outside the island, 'The Sheep under the Snow', 'Old Mylecherane', 'Red Top-Knots', 'Hunt the Wren'. Probably less known is the exquisite 'Good-night Song' – 'Time to go home – Time to say Goodnight' –

Example 122

which was sung at the end of gatherings, notably at the end of the carol singing in church on Christmas Eve.

The 'Bollan Bane' cante-fable from the Isle of Man was mentioned in chapter 5. Another cante-fable,[19] 'The Lazy Wife', about a woman outwitting a giant uses a spinning-song as its refrain 'Snieu, queeyl, snieu', which as such is in the Douglas-Foster collection, in Moore and in Clague [Example 123].

There are dance tunes in the Clague collection according to

[19] Both are in the *Folk-Song Journal*, Vol. VII, No. 3, 1924.

Snieu, quee-yl, snieu, 'rane, quee-yl, 'rane; Dy
chooil-ley clea er y thie, snieu er my skyn,
Lhee-ish yn ol-lan, lhi-ams y snaie, 'S beg
fys t'ee yn ven lit-cher-agh dy re Moll-yn Droat my en-nym.

Example 123

Miss Gilchrist, 'but most of them seem to be of Irish or Scottish origin and some are well known in one or other of those countries under other names'. The Manx dance, however, which in more recent times made a great impression at the

Example 124

259

winter festivals of the English Folk Dance and Song Society at the Albert Hall was the Dirk Dance of the Kings of Man executed by a male soloist. This was a most impressive ritual of dedication in which the dancer first circles round holding the dagger before him, then lays it on the ground and dances round and over it, finishing with some final lunges of devotion towards it. But the tune for this, which fitted admirably in feeling and in rhythm, was borrowed from the Hebrides, a lullaby collected by Frances Tolmie in Skye in 1897 [Example 124].

CHAPTER TEN

Scholarship

Related Problems

The reader who has persevered so far will have realized that though folk music is an enclave of limited significance in the total art of music, like plainsong or Passion music or pedagogy, it spills over to involve other branches of knowledge sufficiently to have acquired a scholarship of its own. The emergence of the kindred subject of ethnomusicology has extended the field and called for new disciplines. Yet this vast field is cultivated only by individual students without any academic base from which to work. The English faculties of American universities have been active in balladry and an institute has been established in California to promote the study of ethnomusicology. Books have been written in the U.S.A. on negro and white spirituals. Archives of sound recordings were established in Berlin and Budapest before the wars, and we have now started to do the same thing in this country at Cecil Sharp House, the B.B.C. and the Institute of Recorded Sound. The University of London has since 1965 admitted folk music as an optional special subject for degrees in music and some theses have been presented for post-graduate degrees. The University of Leeds is extending its department of local studies in dialect and folklore to include folk music. But the School of Scottish Studies is the only institution to take the subject seriously, as it is at the Institut für Deutsche Volkskunde in Berlin.[1]

There have of course been individual scholars whose works,

[1] A chair of folklore has recently been established at Leicester and degrees are obtainable at Leeds and Edinburgh.

which is the foundation of existing and any future studies in this country, have appeared constantly in these pages, and there are others who have done field work abroad, like the Rev. A. M. Jones in Africa and Mr Peter Crossley-Holland in Tibet. But what is needed here in Britain, I venture to think, is an academic home to be found for the purpose of mapping the vast territory already explored, evolving methods of dealing with the material comparatively, co-ordinating individual research, and turning it into an academic discipline, which means how to teach it – for that would in itself put order into the study. It would discover techniques of organizing and marshalling the knowledge we already possess, techniques like graphs, statistics and percentages, diagrams, tables and systems of symbols, which I personally, who was brought up on words and who think in concepts, confess to find confusing, even unintelligible and certainly repellent, but which are now widely used in all the humanistic sciences like psychology, economics and sociology.

The *Journal of the Folk-Song Society* and its successor the *Journal of the English Folk Dance and Song Society* provide the foundation for any systematic study of English folk-song. Perhaps someone someday will convert its contents into a dictionary of tunes, a modern Chappell but dealing with the products of oral tradition. The work of collecting still goes on wherever it offers possible rewards and the field of research is wide open, as the annual Conferences of the International Folk Music Council bear witness. But what seems to me more pressingly needed is a more easily accessible, to musicians as well as the non-technical public, compendium of essential knowledge about a misunderstood subject. I have written this book as a preliminary essay towards this end, and I think that academic recognition in our conservatoires and university music faculties would be the quickest and surest way of achieving this aim.

In what follows I discuss some of the academic problems which have already arisen in folk-music studies, notably classification, editing and arranging, as some indication of what might occupy the attention of scholars.

Classification

Preservation was the first task of all lovers and students, singers and scholars, of folk-song. It appeared in all countries, the urge to write down for the sake of contemporaries and posterity the treasure, literary and musical, of the traditional ballads, of the seasonal songs, and the simple lyrics. Some were earlier than others in the field. Scotland and Russia in the eighteenth century, Ireland at the turn of the century, central Europe under the influence of the romantic movement in the middle and France, England and Hungary at the end of the nineteenth century. The harvest yielded by the movement for preservation turned out to be immense, more in fact than an ordinary musician can cope with in his own country. Individual songs then required annotation, for their texts often embodied all sorts of buried history, symbolism and allegory. Examples in English folk-song are 'Down by the Riverside', which goes back to the Gnosticism of the fourth century, 'Six Dukes went a'fishing' which started in the fifteenth century (though later origins can be argued for it),[2] 'The Dilly Song' ('The Twelve Apostles' or 'Green Grow the Rushes O!'), which is found in ancient and modern languages from Hebrew on and is theological. Flower symbolism of sex is found everywhere; it is an anthropologist's job to discover why the willow is a symbol of unhappy love (? because it weeps), thyme of virginity and the rose of constant and true love, just as it was to uncover the meaning of the golden bough. Thus the study of folk-song starts spilling in all directions.

But even the music itself must be put into some sort of organization if anyone is to cope with it. It is true that some folk-singers have carried an enormous repertory, thus Henry Burstow of Horsham in Sussex, from whom Lucy Broadwood collected in the first decade of this century, is credited with 400 songs, and George Maynard of Copthorne in Surrey fifty years later is thought by Ken Stubbs, who put 65 of them on tape,

[2] See *E.F.D.S.J.*, 1965.

to have known nearly as many. But Cecil Sharp's total is nearly 5,000, if some 1,700 from the Appalachian Mountains are included. What is one to do with 5,000 songs even if a good many are variants? Still more what is one to do if one is concerned to compare this English corpus with the uncounted songs of the two Scottish traditions, the two Irish traditions and the songs of Wales? Plainly folk-song needs a Linnaeus to classify its flowers. And not one Linnaeus, but one for every European tradition, ethnic, national and local, one at least for Africa and half a dozen for Asia.

Collectors for their own convenience began to divide their songs into categories according to text and function. Thus England found itself first with ballads and songs (i.e. roughly long narratives and short lyrics, though with plenty of half-way dialogue of love), and soon after with subdivisions of carols, shanties, singing-games and nursery rhymes. Bartók, who had nearly 600 tunes from the nineteenth century and 7,800 from the twentieth to dispose of, distinguished between older and newer styles, then between *tempo giusto* (earlier) and *parlando-rubato* and then a mixture which gave a freer and more complex kind of performance and thence of structure. He also adopted a system devised by Ilmari Krohn of Finland which reduced all tunes to the same tonic, classified songs by the number of lines to the verse, noted caesuras and tonics and compasses and so prepared the way for a method of indexing them. Less scientific is the spotting of resemblances, which leads to grouping in families. Melodic resemblances are mainly a matter of contour, and it may seem too casual to rely on somebody with a good head for tunes recalling that tune (a) is much like tune (b) and even bears some resemblance to tune (c), although the mode, or the time, is different. But this is how it all begins, and if we need a scientific justification for it we have it in the word *Gestalt*. For *Gestalt* theory explains why the identity of a tune is unaffected by its pitch or transposition; we do in fact apprehend tunes as entities, we perceive their *Gestalt* and we can therefore spot resemblances, as Kuhač did to the Croatian tunes in

Haydn's symphonies, as the Headington bricklayer did when he mistook 'Country Gardens' for 'The Vicar of Bray', as the Elizabethan 'Rowland' is recognizable as Bach's chorale 'Keinem hat Gott verlassen'. But as Dr Walter Wiora, the German musicologist, who has done more work on comparative melodic research than anyone,[3] said in a paper read in 1956 to the International Folk Music Council, we must proceed 'from toying with vague similarities to scientific method', and he proceeds to map out some lines, mentioning typological, morphological, genetic and geographico-historical, which are in fact only fine names for distinctions so far drawn, except the genetic, and on this Dr Wiora has an interesting theory about the interconnexion of all European folk-song.[4]

According to this there is much more unity in Europe than appears after concentrating comparatively on national differences, which are what strike one at first glance at a nation's folk-songs. 'What we meet everywhere are typical melodic and other *forms*, while the various nations' individualities are expressed more in colouration and modification of these basic forms, rather than in the forms themselves. Also, some nations are drawn more to certain such forms than to others, filling them, completing and changing them and giving them the stamp of their own styles and personalities.' It is not wholly clear what is meant by form, certainly something much more than the formulae A A B A or A B B A, but some of the examples are very remarkable in that they run to a dozen distinct but related tunes, not to be called variations since they are not derived from one basic melody but differing in the number of notes they use, their mode and their rhythm. Their basic resemblance is in fact one of contour, though it would appear that Wiora means more than this, since that would reduce it to the 'similarity' which he says is not enough. Thus he gives a Burgundian basse danse [Example 125] and proceeds via the Netherlands, Bohemia,

[3] Except the Hungarian, Bence Szabolesi, in his *A History of Melody*, 1948.
[4] Expounded in the introduction to Arno Volk Verlag's *Anthology IV*, English edition, 1966. The example quoted below is from No. 69.

Example 125

Spain, Rumania, Hungary (two), Moravia, to England's 'As I rode over Salisbury Plain' collected by George Butterworth in Sussex [Example 126], and adds two more remote versions from

As I rode ov-er Salis-bu-ry Plain, 'Twas— there I met a— young scam-ping blade, He— kiss-ed me and en-tic-ed me so— Till a-long— with him— I was forced for— to go.

Example 126

Nova Scotia and France. The trouble with this, though Wiora makes a strong case for his thesis, is that resemblances can (and do) become less and less appreciable. The attempt, however, is heroic, and if we can accept that each version is a version of the 'form', we are on the way to classifying *à la* Linnaeus the whole of European folk-song. For any one mind to hold such a vast number of tunes in one cranium shows an astounding melodic memory. With such he is able to proceed to his next point, which is 'Growth and decline, variation and transformation', to look for some deeper relationship, such as belonging to the same text or custom, or a historical connexion between the localities where the tunes are found, or the moulding by different communities, say Czechs and Scotsmen, according to styles and varying abilities of performers in those communities. His major premise is not easy to accept, but if it is accepted for the sake of the argument, he then accounts for the differences which are so striking (and indeed so interesting) by the play of local conditions, not merely folk music but art forms and styles of epochs, upon the basic material. 'Much of what is today considered as a peculiarity of the Scandinavians, the Hungarians or the people of the Rhine, used to be very widespread and now characterizes those nations or tribes only because they cultivated it more or because it survived with them for a longer time.' Here at any rate is a beginning, supported by sufficiently striking examples in 'a synoptic melodic table', of an international grouping by families of tunes.

But before international complications are tackled the need is felt for organizing single categories, such as ballad tunes, within a single tradition, the Anglo-Scottish-American tradition of popular ballads, for instance. Merely to index tunes, if a satisfactory way of doing so could be found, would be of practical utility and might further be a first move towards scientific classification. Various attempts have been made to reduce tunes to formulae for the purposes both of indexing and classification. Child's collection (edition) of the *English and Scottish Popular Ballads* has been the starting point for this operation of analysing tunes so as to group them into 'types', 'styles', 'families' – the terminology is fluid. Thus Sigurd Bernhard Hustvedt made for his own use a melodic index of the fifty-five ballad airs that Child himself had appended to his edition of the texts and published an account of it in 1936. Hustvedt says that he consulted systems of lexicography devised by Oswald Koller, Ilmari Krohn and Hans Mersmann before devising his own. To illustrate his system he took not a folk-tune but 'Drink to me only with thine eyes', which he reduced to 12 B A B 2 3♭ 68 U 8 a/beag. f/e. – r (g – e). This is its own self-condemnation: how on earth is anyone to read it readily enough for it to be of the smallest use to him? Literary men, e.g. Entwistle, lament the (to them) unintelligibility of ordinary musical notation, which after all has had a currency of a thousand years, but to ask musicians to learn several new kinds of algebra here and now is to be over-sanguine. However, Hustvedt's successor at Berkeley, Professor Bertrand Bronson, who has in fact completed the task to which Hustvedt set his hand when he made his first cut at Child, has made (at least) three contributions towards a system of classification. As far as the modes are concerned (discussed in chapter 2) he has devised a seven-pointed star to signify the seven diatonic modes, the external angles between them their hexatonic equivalents and the internal angles their pentatonic equivalents symbolized by the Greek letter π with an index number, thus π^3. This (for which see *Traditional Tunes to Child Ballads*, Vol. II or *All this for a song* (1962)) yields a formula for every case of modality crisp enough for immediate apprehension. He has also had recourse to a computer and put poor 'Barbara Allen' through it. By means of the computered cards so obtained, which no doubt we shall all learn to read one day, he has been able to divide Barbara Allen tunes into four unequal groups – English and major, Scottish and modal, American and pentatonic and American and corrupt.

A further stage would be to assign Barbara Allen to a family – as if she were not a family in herself! This has also been tackled by Professor Bronson[5] and by another American scholar, Samuel Bayard of Pennsylvania State College. Bayard prefers the term 'family' to 'type', though since Greek τύπος signifies a stamp and therefore the cut of a tune, it seems to me preferable to 'tune family', although 'family' permits various degrees of kindred and affinity. The characteristics that are thus typified

[5] 'Some Observations about Melodic Variation in British-American Folk Tunes', *Journal of the American Musicological Society*, Vol. III, No. 5, 1950.

are authentic or plagal range, opening phrase, mid-way cadence note and, inevitably, the ambiguous resemblance of melodic contour already discussed. For international differentiations I have always preferred[6] melodic behaviour to melodic contour and general resemblance, which triggered off the Haydn-Kuhač controversy, and by behaviour I mean features such as phrase-lengths, characteristic interval (augmented second or falling fourth), presence or absence of anacrusis, Bartók's *tempo giusto* and *parlando rubato*, syncopation and so on, as described in chapters 3 and 4. But within the nation 'type' or 'family' will do, and Bayard instances some of these by now established families – the Lord Randal Family, The Bailiff's Daughter Family, the Butcher-Bateman family. There are some forty such families, he says, already identified.

These are serious attempts upon an intractable problem but musicology has yet to find a reasonable, efficient and not too complex solution for it.

Editing and Arranging

The problems of editing arose immediately it was desired to transfer folk-songs from oral tradition to something less fluid and more amenable for study and dissemination. They were not solved all at once but they had to be tackled and in three generations an acceptable code of ethics was evolved. They still confront an editor when he is on the job. They embrace acknowledgment of source, accuracy of transcription and notation, treatment of variants of the tunes and of the texts, grammar, sense, metre, collation with broadside versions, propriety, sheer error, decadence, dialect and spelling.

There are no fixed rules in the business; editing is exercising judgment in matters of detail. It is an editor's business to edit, and, though he will certainly be criticized for what he decides, he must still have the courage to be wrong in his own way. It is not enough to print and publish material in its raw state without scrutiny. It is accepted nowadays, though not till the

[6] See *Man, Mind and Music*.

present century, that the source should be specified, singer's name, place and date of performance. It sounds simple, but the singer will have varied one or more of his melody notes in every verse; he will have corrupted one verse of the words into nonsense by non-understanding or misunderstanding; moreover his version is so like another's as to suggest a common source or a very firmly established tradition so that it is perhaps desirable to adjust their slight difference into what seems musically or verbally more feasible—should one then acknowledge a genealogy of sources? Moreover such editorial scruples can be carried to slightly ludicrous lengths. Thus an American collector in the Southern Appalachians dutifully records that

> Jesus is a rock in a whirly wind,
> A shelter in the time of storm.
> Hope my {mother / father / brother, etc. will be there,
> A shelter in the time of storm

was taken down by Miss Julia Stokes at Crossmore, North Carolina in July 1930 from the singing of Hetty Twiggs, aged ten, though no tune is given. It is a corrupt version of a Moody and Sankey hymn of no value whatever, except perhaps to show how corruption of a text can occur.

Scrupulosity of record was attempted by Percy Grainger when he tried to reproduce his singers' vowels in dialect spelling, but dialect spelling is a tiresome nuisance, though novelists sometimes use it as a help to characterization, since those to whom it is not natural will imitate it at the peril of making themselves foolish, and it is not easy to read. For Scots there is of course an established convention of quasi-phonetic spelling – e.g. 'Scots wha' hae wi' Wallace bled' – so here the difficulty hardly arises, save perhaps for a Sassenach singer.

It is considered legitimate to collate the text of a ballad with a broadside version, if necessary to restore a missing verse or a lacuna in the sense. There is no virtue in preserving a palpable error or an obvious misunderstanding. Mistakes in transcription have been known in serious publications. In the early days of the movement to retrieve ballads in the United States a book came out of Harvard University Press in which there were wrong time-signatures, impossible accidentals and dubious tonalities. On the other hand folk-singers do not stick rigidly to a regular pulse and the intervals of the equally tempered scale. So that a musical editor must develop a sixth sense of what is folk and what is idiosyncratic.

The question of propriety was briefly discussed in chapter 1 and the universality of sexual symbolism recognized a few pages back. Kodály testifies to the use of flower symbolism everywhere and always: 'But in the sixteenth century they did not arouse great moral indignation. A glance at a contemporary French or German song collection is sufficient to prove this. The songs were as current among the humbler classes as at royal courts: the greatest composers (e.g. Orlando di Lasso) set them to music in more refined form perhaps, but handling their subject with even more sophisticated candour.' Still, there *is* a problem here which is not solved by invoking complete candour or accusing a sensitive, or let us say good-mannered, editor with prudery. Prudery is not so much a matter of morals as of psychology. One has to recognize the existence alongside the most insistent of our instincts two others of similar biological value, modesty and disgust. It is the interplay of these instincts which forms the sentiments we have about our bodies, and which conditions the poetry and laughter, the inhibitions and expressions of sexual energy. There is nothing unnatural about the conventions, which vary from time to time, that regulate discussion about intimate (and therefore private) matters, rather are they a social convenience. An editor will therefore have some regard for social convenience as it obtains at any particular period, or in any particular society, or for certain kinds of occasion. The existence of frank and not so poetical eroticism in folk-song has been recognized by all collectors. Christie in his *Traditional Ballad Airs* says it was 'unpresentable'; Baring Gould altered it to make it presentable. Some folk-singers will not sing a particular song to a lady like Lucy Broadwood out of delicacy to avoid mutual embarrassment. An editorial decision on inclusion or exclusion, the text or its modification, will turn on the kind of publication intended, for a scientific society or an infants' school, a public concert-hall or a public house. The problem is real, even in what is now a tolerant period, but it is solved in practice by a hard straight look and a sense of what is fitting.

Then there is the question of the decadent or corrupt text and the degenerate tune, for if a folk-song can come up and evolve on the principle of the survival of the fittest by transmission, it can equally suffer from that 'erosion of unretentive memories and inaccurate ears' to which I have several times already referred. The many collections that have been coming from the United States and Canada for the past forty years provide instances of degeneration. 'Lord Rendal' (Child 12) is a common sufferer, but he has a wide circulation and is in essentials pretty stable. His names, however, are innumerable, which is not, however, a very serious problem: 'Tyranty', 'Sweet Nelson', 'Johnny Rilus', 'John Willow', 'Fileander', 'Henry my son'. But the ballad is quoted in a version from South Carolina by Reed Smith, who devotes a short chapter to this question of degeneration, in which, as he says, everything has gone so wildly wrong with Lord Rendal that his own mother wouldn't know him and that it 'wins a first prize for organic perversion'. It shows a surrealist metamorphosis of motives, bequests, poisons, medicines and sheer nonsense:

> What did you leave your dear mother for, Anzo, my son? (*bis*)
> She has plenty of kitchen furniture; make my bed soon,
> I am sick in my heart, I should fail and lie down.

> What did you leave your dear sweetheart for, Anzo, my son?
> Here is a red-hot iron will broil a bone brown
> She is the cause of my lying down.

What will you have for your supper, poor Anzo, my son
Make me a little breely broth soup,
For I'm sick in my heart, I should fail and lie down.

This was collected in South Carolina in 1913. From West
Virginia in 1916 there was a curt version – no tune – which ran:

Where have you been all day, Henry my son
Where have you been all day, my loving one?
Up sister's, up sister's; make my bed soon
For there's a pain in my side, and I must lie down and die.

What did she give you then?
Poison, poison
What colour was the poison
Red, black, yellow, red, black, yellow.

The ballad is very common still in the United States and
Bronson prints for it 103 versions, of which five are called 'Wee
croodin doo' with which may be compared Lucy Broadwood's
lullaby (chapter 5, Example 51).

As a link between the subject of selecting and editing on the
one hand and arranging with accompaniment, about to be
considered, on the other the citation of the title and preface of
George Thomson's famous publication of Scottish songs neatly
pin-points the issues involved. Thomson was an Edinburgh
publisher (1757–1851) who wished to rescue Scottish folk-song
from oblivion and give it currency among the higher classes of
society as well as the peasantry. To this end he sought the co-
operation of the chief poets and composers of his time, Burns
and Haydn among them. His enthusiasm led him to make
further collections of Irish and Welsh songs over a period of
fifty years, that have bequeathed bibliographical problems to
librarians and biographers of Haydn and Beethoven. His first
publication was in 1793; its second edition of 1803 has the
following title:

A Select Collection of Original Scottish Airs for the Voice with Introductory and Concluding Symphonies and Accompaniments for the Piano Forte, Violin and Violoncello By Pleyel, Kozeluch and Haydn. With Select and Characteristic Verses both Scottish and English adapted to the Airs, including Upwards of One Hundred New Songs by Burns.

His preface, in which incidentally he claims copyright, and threatens anyone who infringes it, runs:

The first object was to procure the Airs in their best form. What their precise *original* form may have been cannot now be ascertained. Although we go back to the earliest printed Collection, it is far from certain that the Airs are there presented to us as they came from the Composers; for they had been preserved, we know not how long, by oral tradition, and thus were liable to change before being collected. Nor is it at all certain that the earliest Collectors had the industry to seek, opportunity to find, the musical taste to select and hand on the Airs in their most approved form. It is certain, however, that in the progress of the Airs to modern times, they have in some part been delicately moulded by judicious Singers, into a more simple and pleasing form than that given to them by the early Publishers. If anyone doubts it, let him compare the Airs in Orpheus Caledonius with the same Airs in this work. . . . [Thomson] chose that set or copy of every Air, whether printed or manuscript, which seemed the most simple and beautiful, freed, he trusts, from vulgar errors on the one hand, and redundant graces on the other.

The first duty of the editor is thus to select the songs and then to select the best versions. Here he touches on the question of origin and, so early, mentions oral tradition. He assumes that for his purpose of spreading acquaintance with them they must be fitted with accompaniments, just as his English successors did a century later. For this, and no doubt good commercial reasons, he hires the best composers. The arrangements they provided are in fact complete without the optional obbligati of violin and cello and will stand for piano alone. But the dressing-up goes a stage further with the provision of new verses by

Burns, adapted to the airs which in most cases Burns had in mind. He claims that the versions so obtained and arranged are nearer the originals than those in the earlier publications, freed, as he says, from vulgar errors and redundant graces.

Incidentally the first copyright act was passed in 1709. Burns gave Thomson exclusive rights. Judged by the aesthetics and ethics of modern times, the tunes are not suitably harmonized by continental composers unfamiliar with their idiom, and the rewriting of the words, though gloriously done, was unnecessary and so outrageous. Yet Thomson's heart was in the right place, and though he never made money out of his enterprise he continued in it till 1849, two years before he died at the age of ninety-four. He certainly made history. His decision to secure the services of the most eminent composers to write arrangements for him raises the aesthetic question of what is a 'suitable' setting whether for instrumental accompaniment or for polyphonic singing.

This problem is not nearly so pressing now as it was half a century ago. Indeed it has been settled in practice – by the guitar. But the issue was important in the early days of the revival – was it proper that an essentially melodic art should be fitted out with harmony? The answer was 'No! it is not proper. See how satisfactory is melody unadorned and unaccompanied.' But no one paid any attention to this purist ruling, the collectors and the scholars least of all. Folk music was accepted as a self-sufficient art but was also regarded as the raw material for further elaboration into art-songs, part-songs and even symphonies. The purist case was best stated by Ernest Walker in his *History of Music in England* (1907) to which reference was made at the beginning of chapter 2 (see pp. 18–19).

But even if the extreme purist position was not successfully defended then and is untenable now, when we have in fact become more familiar with unaccompanied monody, it is nevertheless true that some arrangements are recognized as good, in the sense that they fit the character of the tune, and that others are not so good in that they take too many liberties with the basic character of the melody. Nor is it just a question of simplicity, for some arrangers' harmony is almost as academic as Macfarren's (in Chappell) or Moffatt's, yet somehow makes a suitable setting for the jewel. A musician like T. F. Dunhill or Arthur Somervell of an older generation, Arnold Foster, Imogen Holst and Elizabeth Poston of a later could write acceptable piano accompaniments or arrangements for voices that seemed as apt if not quite so distinguished as those by Gustav Holst or Vaughan Williams. Nor on the other hand is it a matter of avoiding acute dissonances and other modern idioms, since Moeran used the idiom of Delius and Britten follows no laws but his own.

The case of Sharp is instructive. He had not the strong personal idiom of Vaughan Williams or Moeran, only a decent academic technique, because he was not a composer, but it became more personal as he went on. He began cautiously with the negative principle that notes outside the mode of the tune should be avoided, then Vaughan Williams told him to 'take any chord you want'. By the time he had been writing song accompaniments for a few years he did not often go wrong. Lucy Broadwood's are personal only in their delicacy: she did not often go beyond simple chords in neat blocks or very simple figuration. Vaughan Williams and Moeran were composers first and foremost and are likely therefore to express themselves more markedly in anything they handled. It only goes wrong if their personalities intrude upon the song. Vaughan Williams once quoted Kurt Schindler as saying that the true criterion should be whether the adaptation is made 'with love'. Now those who love folk-song are those who know most about it and live with it longest. It is not a question of what is or is not harmonically appropriate. It is that a composer does not know what is appropriate until he has lived with and loved the tunes he wants to set and others like them. His personal idiosyncrasies do not matter because they will march together with those of the tune. Vaughan Williams says:[7]

[7] *Journal of the English Folk Dance and Song Society* (1934), Vol. I, p. 173.

'It is not because the arrangements of Cyril Scott, Eugene Goossens and Howard Brockway (an American who covered some of the same ground as Cecil Sharp in the Appalachian Mountains of America) are harmonically extreme that they seem to me to be all wrong, but because they appear not to grow out of the love of a tune but from a mistaken idea that it is necessary "to make something of it." They obtrude their personality instead of discovering by accident that their personality and that of the tune are running on parallel lines.'

There is no doubt that the settings made by Brahms near the end of his life were made with love. And in spite of Cecil Sharp's strictures,[8] registered at a time when the character of modal music was only just beginning to be rediscovered and ways of treating it were being discussed (as for instance by Stanford), they are splendid – his use of the lower octaves of the piano is only one of the felicities noticeable in his endlessly resourceful keyboard writing. Sometimes in order to accommodate a difference of inflection (sharp and natural on the same degree of the scale) he will harmonize in the minor a tune that appears in another collection as major, and there are several tunes that end on what may be a tonic or a third – hence his use of two tonics, of which Sharp complained. He does not often indulge in chromatics: nos. 34 and 43 are examples. No. 49, the last of the seventh set, which was arranged for solo and chorus, 'Verstohlen geht der Mond auf', he had used as the theme for variations in his first piano sonata, opus 1, and so rounded off his life's work with its beginning. 'The snake bites its own tail', as he said of it. But, though for his versions he consulted various authorities including Erk-Böhme, his scholarship was more dubious than his musical judgment. Thus he himself rejected Erk-Böhme as 'inartistic though historically correct', and some of the songs which he took from Kretchmer and Zuccalmaglio were not genuine but imitations. The second half of 'In stiller Nacht' he composed

[8] Cf. Chapter 2, pp. 32–3 and *Some Conclusions*, chapter 5.

himself. So that though his attitude was not as scrupulous as Bartók's and Kodály's his intention in making settings was much the same as theirs.

Thus Kodály explained the purpose of making arrangements in a preface to his first publication he made in conjunction with Bartók: 'The purpose of the arrangements is to enable the general public to get to know and enjoy folk-song. . . . To this end we have made a selection of the best of them and provided them with a musical arrangement that would make them accessible to public taste. In transferring them from the countryside to the town some such "dressing-up", so to speak, was necessary. But since simply to put them into town clothes would make them awkward and ill at ease, we have had to design a costume which would enable them to breathe freely. In short, whether we were working for chorus or piano, we have attempted, through the accompaniment, to make up for the fields and villages that are missing.' Compare this statement with George Thomson's on page 274.

The country coming to town seems the right approach. An even more apt metaphor might be that of the wild flower being brought indoors to decorate the house. You must have a vase of some sort to hold it; you can't just leave it lying about. So the solution is to find a suitable vase, and on the whole proper composers seem to be better vase makers than good academic musicians. Kodály published fifty-seven ballads and songs in ten booklets between 1924 and 1932. At first he simplified the rich ornamentation as an incrustation possibly acquired from gypsies but he came to realize that 'ornamentation is an organic part of folk singing and can no more be omitted here than it can from the work of Couperin'. He tended to be more sparing with his harmonies as he went on, but figuration derived from the tune or prompted by the words is with him, as with Britten, a frequent source of his accompaniments. Bartók writes – in *Eight Hungarian Folk Songs* (1907–17) – more freely, though he suggests the sound of the cimbalon and pentatonism in the flourishes of the first and second of them. Nos. 4 and 6 are simple chord progressions, though the harmony is chromatic. No. 5 is the most elaborate, employing clashing arpeggio chords and arabesques at the top of the keyboard. In their early publications both Bartók and Kodály incorporated the vocal line in the piano part so as to give the songs a double currency. Experience taught them, as it did their English contemporaries, what would go and what remained alien. It has even been said that each succeeding generation likes to write new settings for itself. Sharp's accompaniments, however, though less idiosyncratic, stand the test of time and provide what one might call standard settings. Vaughan Williams's on examination prove to be not at all elaborate and to owe their character to his harmony, which is triadic, modal, unchromatic though allowing false relation, the harmony in fact which he evolved for himself largely out of his contact with folk-song. There is far less picturesque piano writing than in Bartók, Falla or Britten. It is idiosyncratic but strictly functional.

Britten's settings are unfailingly ingenious; occasionally perhaps one has a slight suspicion that they are too ingenious; but since he is unfailingly sensitive to words he produces a supremely beautiful song like 'Down in the sally gardens' (which in spite of Yeats's words is an authentic Irish folk-song). Falla is concerned to create the Spanish atmosphere by the use of Spanish rhythms in his accompaniments with the suggestion of castanet and guitar in the open air, which he does with intoxicating effect.

Fewer settings of this highly artistic type are being written, since the simple chords of the guitar have won favour as on the whole the most satisfactory accompaniment to the folk-song, satisfactory in that it cannot go far wrong, recalls an old idea of minstrelsy and is simple enough for the singer to play himself. But those of us who grew up with the piano settings value them for the vividness they gave to the experience of folk-song. There seem to be no rules that can be prescribed for a 'good' setting. Each is to be judged on its own merits, rather as orchestral transcriptions of non-orchestral music have to be judged; they can be bad, but when they are good, they seem to yield a double amount of pleasure. They need to be made with love, no doubt, and with unerring good taste.

Choral arrangements permit of a certain amount of freedom. Vaughan Williams scrupulously designated his part-song settings, like 'The dark Eyed Sailor' and 'Wassail Song', as 'freely arranged'. Kodály arranges a group of Hungarian folk-songs into a cantata for unaccompanied voices in his *Matra Pictures*. He will also, e.g. in his Transylvanian folk-ballad 'Annie Miller' do what Holst does in his choral settings of some Welsh songs (and indeed Vaughan Williams on occasion), distribute the melody to single parts or a solo voice and let the other parts hum a harmonic support for it. Kodály used arrangements of this sort as a basis for his reform of Hungarian musical education. Whatever the purists say – and they certainly have a case – they have no hope of winning it, for all the most dedicated, most sympathetic, most understanding musicians, who are eminent as creators in their own right, practice this delightful form of philistinism and have enriched the world by it.

The Study of Ballads
Even the study of ballads has by no means come to an end. Dr Wilgus's history of the ballad war of the nineteenth century, which ended with the publication of Child's great book in 1898, observes that those who, instead of regarding the account as closed and henceforth a matter of history, went out into the field, found the tradition still alive. Sharp and his fellow collectors, who paid attention to the tunes as well as the texts, opened a new period of study, in which the question of diffusion is reopened and the comparative method appropriate to anthropology has been applied in the international field. Studies like W. J. Entwistle's *European Balladry* (1939) is just what its title states it to be, a study of ballads in almost every language spoken in Europe – Hungarian is the principal exception but is central to the work of Lajos Vargyas. By the middle of the

present century the ballads had been scrutinized for their mythological, historical, symbolical, psychoanalytical and sociological (including Marxian) content. If their artistic content was obscured by all these learned enquiries – which need not happen, though some recent writers like Mr A. L. Lloyd, who carries his learning lightly, think it has – this at least is to be said for it, that any discipline that helps a student of folk-art, literary or musical or social, to master the sheer bulk of his material is valuable. True, the comparative method which seeks to trace the spread of the ballad adds to that bulk by bringing in more examples from an ever-widening field, but it does at least map the field. Similarly the other method, of history, in so far as it can be applied to so fluid and, being oral, undocumented a subject, may differentiate the mass by a time scale.

The main effort in this direction has been towards separating the ballad from the epic, which is regarded as its predecessor, and the big or heroic ballad of struggle from its descendant, the more lyrical, shorter and more earthy, more realistic, folk-song. The Hungarian scholar just mentioned, Lajos Vargyas, basing himself on Hungary, which Janus-like faces Asia and Europe, has interested himself in both the geographical and the historical spread of ballads. In the Balkans he finds heroic lays and ballads, as he conceives them, existing side by side, whereas in Western Europe the ballad was later than the epic, consisting perhaps of an episode from the epic treated more psychologically. He is not of course the first to try, in seeking a definition of the ballad, to distinguish the ballad from the epic. In fact there is no getting away from the three eternal ballad problems, origin, definition and diffusion.

It is a good plan to begin with the *Iliad* and the *Odyssey*, which are and always have been everyman's, the ancient Greek's, the modern scholar's and the literary critic's idea of what an epic is, and the question of their authorship has constituted *the* Homeric question for centuries. It is now generally accepted that Homer, or another man of the same name or, as was held by some scholars, two or more poets, put together a series of orally current poems about the Trojan War (epics) and a series about the misadventures of Odysseus on his way home from the Trojan War, a rather different kind of story, in about 850 BC, and that the events described had historical foundation, the Trojan War being assigned to about the twelfth century BC. There is a modern parallel to this theory of composition, that of the Finnish *Kalevala*, which was compiled in AD 1835 by the poet Lönnrot. A further exploration into the composition of oral poetry into epics was made by the American scholar, Milman Parry of Harvard, in 1934-5, when he went to Yugoslavia to see if the heroic and legendary poems still current in an oral and sung tradition in Serbo-Croatia, previously explored by Ferencz Kuhač (of the Haydn controversy fame described in chapter 3), would throw any light on the composition and preservation of the Homeric poems. He was able to take recordings of 350 heroic poems from 90 different singers in 23 villages on 2,200 double-sided disks. Their contents were submitted to the musically expert scrutiny of Bela Bartók after he arrived in the United States in 1940, who before his death was able to publish transcriptions, so that both texts and tunes are available.[9] The texts threw up a complication that supported Vargyas's theory – the heroic lays were men's songs, but there was also another class of song mainly sung by women, shorter and more lyrical. The men's songs are defined as 'narrative poems of ten-syllable lines sung or chanted to the accompaniment of the gusle or tambura by men for the entertainment of men', whereas the women's songs are 'lyric or narrative poems, having lines of various lengths sung with or without (usually without) accompaniment by women or young men for their own amusement'. Seeking confirmation of his views about Homer (e.g. his use of stock formulae), Parry and his coadjutor, Albert Lord, found their interest engaged in oral poetry as such. To show what it is like here is a short extract from Bartók's transcription of the ballad of 'The Captivity of Dulic Ibrahim', which shows not only the highly ornamented

[9] Columbia University Press, 1951. Harvard University Press, 1933-4.

Example 127

type of arioso used but the phenomenon of heterophony provided by the gusle accompaniment [Example 127].

The women's songs are not markedly different – the tunes are similarly short and decorated. They may be compared and contrasted with the tunes collected up by Professor Bronson for the ballads of Child's English and Scottish collection, which have also been orally transmitted, though possibly in a less pure state owing to broadsides and different, i.e. more urban, conditions. But in Yugoslavia in the twentieth century we find both epic and more romantic ballad material existing side by side, though differentiated by the sex of the singers.

In our own English and Scottish ballads we find the same thing without even the differentiation; the ballads deal with heroic fights like 'Chevy Chase', magic as in 'Tam Lin', romance as in 'Young Beichan' (Lord Bateman), family quarrels as in 'Edward' and so on and on to such an extent of mixture that it is difficult to accept Margyas's sharp division – though he is careful to label his analysis the *'mediaevel* history of the folk ballad'. An epic is a long poem, it is national rather than local – in Homer the Greeks recognized themselves as one people, if not a nation, as contrasted with the barbarians – and it tends to be concerned with fighting, so that one cannot deny the propriety of seeking to differentiate it from the more romantic and shorter ballad. Yet it would seem as though the one shades off into the other – even the *Odyssey* is less about fighting than about constant love – and the differences as we feel them are more satisfactorily accounted for by referring each ballad to its environment, as Mr A. L. Lloyd emphasizes in his class-conscious study of ballads, and as Mrs Muir does to some extent in her observation of the consequences of the Reformation upon Scottish ballads.

Mrs Muir's approach to balladry is personal: she describes how she came to it and lived with it and in so doing discovered its essence. Her starting point was the child's singing games, as described in chapter 8, in which the girls formed a closed community such as in the adult world was responsible for the tradition of ballad singing. A year or two later she encountered a ballad in just such conditions when at a farm, where she was spending a holiday, she heard what has since become known as a bothy ballad. A ploughman who lived in the bothy of a neighbouring farm, i.e. slept in the bothy but 'lived in' for their meals at the farm, said to her one evening as they were sitting on a fence out of doors watching others of the party dancing at a cross-road 'Wad ye like to hear an auld sang?' and he plunged into 'Captain Wedderburn's Courtship' (Child no. 46) to a tune which Mrs Muir thinks was current in Aberdeenshire in the first decade of the century and is quoted as no. 10 in Bronson. He sang it with a light head voice in a totally impersonal manner – so much so that the young girl's slight embarrassment soon wore off: 'there was only a voice rhythmically telling a story'. How is that for defining a ballad? And this is the twentieth century!

Sources of Musical Illustrations

It is not so simple a matter to give the sources of some of these tunes as it might seem. Even in the case of Cecil Sharp's tunes, with which I have been familiar for half a century in various editions, I have thought it probably better for ease of access to give the reference to the Centenary Edition which Novello brought out in 1959 rather than the original edition, though I have not been able to be consistent about that. Then there are obscure publications that have come my way over the years from varied and improbable sources such as national publicity bodies and in, to me, unintelligible languages. Thus one such, the little book of Czech songs, *Malý Spaliček* was given to me by a pupil at the Royal College of Music, who was a member of the Czech colony in exile in London during the war which dissolved and disappeared at the time of the Communist revolution. This book was edited and printed in London but the printers could tell me nothing about it. Eventually the Czechoslovakian Embassy in London procured for me a different anthology (containing the relevant songs) from Prague. In a few cases I have forgotten where I got a particular tune or version, having perhaps had it among lecture notes for years. In some cases the book in which I have found the illustration I wanted is itself quoting from a previous book – which source should I give? Legal and moral principles alike require me to make acknowledgment of other men's work on which I have drawn, but scholarship requires me to state for the benefit of other scholars where a particular tune is most easily to be found for reference. I have had to deal with these problems as they arise *ad hoc*.

Index of Tunes and Sources

The Peacock (two examples)	*Zoltan Kodály: His Life and Work*, L. Eosze, pp. 120 and 125.
Rumanian dance	*Rumanian Folk Music*, I, 114, Bartók. Nijhoff, The Hague.
Pygmy dance	*Music in Primitive Culture*, B. Nettl, Ethnic Folkways Library.
Babinga (African)	Ethnic Folkways Library.
Canon from Flores	*Metre, Rhythm and Multi-part Music*, Jaap Kunst. Also quoted in *The Rise of Music in the Ancient World*. Curt Sachs.
3 Czech-Slovak Song: two variants	Grove's *Dictionary*. Stkadu.
Sedlák	*Malý Spaliček*. Also in *Volkslieder aus der Tschechoslowakei*.
Tancuj	*Malý Spaliček*. Ditto.
Dvořák Symphony	Theme from Symphony in G.
Umrem	*Malý Spaliček*.
Haydn symphony – Oj Jelena	Symphony no. 104 in D. *Južnoslovjenske Narodne Popievke no. 905*, Kuhač.
Haydn cello concerto	Theme from Cello Concerto in D.
Norwegian – Spring pols	*Dances of Norway*, Violet Alford.
Finnish – Mieleni	Taken from Kalevala I, *Finland* 1952. Westerlund, Helsinki.
Finnish – Summer Evening	*Finland 1952*. Ditto.
4 Hungarian – Conscripts Song	*Hungarian Folk Music*, Bartók, no. 58. Oxford.

Sheep Shearing Song – It's a rosebud in June	*Folk-Song Journal* no. 5. Also *Sharp Centenary edition II*, no .19.
The Wee Little Croodin' Doo	*Folk-Song Journal* no. 19, Lucy Broadwood.
Sussex Mummers' Carol	*English Traditional Songs and Carols*, Lucy Broadwood.
6 If all the world were paper	*The English Dancing Master*, John Playford
Cante-fable – Bollan Bane	*Folk-Song Journal*, No 28.
Lord Willoughby	*Oxford Song Book II*, Thomas Wood's version.
Rowland	*Fitzwilliam Virginal Book*, no. 160.
Keinem hatt Gott verlassen	*C. P. E. Bach's Collection of his father's Chorales*, Johann Cruger.
Kempe's Jig	*The English Dancing Master*, John Playford.
Barbara Allen	*Sharp Centenary Edition I*, no. 7.
7 Robin Hood and the Pedlar	*Folk-Song Journal*, No. 8, 10.
Keys of Canterbury	*Sharp Centenary Edition II*, no. 43.
The Cuckoo (Kentucky)	*English Folk Songs from the Appalachians*. Sharp & Karpeles.
The Cuckoo (Somerset)	*Sharp Centenary Edition I*, no. 13.
The Brisk Young Widow	*Sharp, Cyril Winn Selection*, no. 2.
Come all ye worthy gentlemen	Ditto.
Elsie Marley	*North Countrie Ballads, Songs and Pipe Tunes*, W. G. Whittaker.
Zörög	*Hungarian Folk Music*, no. 243, Bartók.

Index

Abbots Bromley Horn Dance, 87, 204
Abingdon, morris dance of, 202
Academic discipline, the need for folk-song as, 262
accompaniment, *See* arranging
Adam de la Hale, 126
Adderbury, morris dance of, 202
Adler, Larry, 87
African folk music, 39–41, 48, 87, 262; part-singing and drumming, 151
Aisling, 247
Alfen, H., 66
Alford, Violet, 203 n. 11
All this for a Song, Bronson, 268
alleluias, and folk-song, 33
Allen, Sir Hugh, 181
Altdeutsches Liederbuch, 7 n. 6
Ancient and Modern Scottish Songs, Heroic Ballads, and, Herd, 147
Ancient Ballads and Songs of the North of Scotland, Buchan, 230
Ancient Irish Music, Joyce, 94, 241, 250
Ancient Music of Ireland, Petrie, 248
Andersson, O., 236 n. 9, 238
Ane compendious Booke of Godlie and Spiritualle Songs, the Wedderburn brothers, 91 n. 2
Anglo-American Folksong Scholarship, Wilgus, 141 n. 2
anonymous authorship, 2
anti-Romanism, 192
Appalachian Mountains, the, and songs collected there by Cecil Sharp, 14, 111, 135, 174, 264; and Maud Karpeles, 119
Argo, A., 147 n. 5, 148, 232 n. 7
Aristotle, 10, 42
arranging folk-songs, 273–80
Asian Music Society, The, 49, 87
Athenaeum, The, 3 n. 1
Atterburg, K., 66
Aufsätze über Musik, Meyer, 33 n. 6

Babinga, the, 40
Bach, Carl Philipp Emanuel, 132
Bach, Johann Sebastian, Dorian Toccata and Fugue, 30; setting of *In dulci jubilo*, 188; 'Keinem hat Gott verlassen', 265
Bacup, morris dance of, 173
Baines, A., 82–3, 86
Bake, A., 48, 49
Balakirev, M. I., 52, 53
Balfour Gardiner, H., 118
Balkans, the, ballads in, 281
ballad, the, 90, 121–49; definition and nomenclature, 121–7, and dance-songs, 122–4; distinction between b. and carol, 124; and the Romantic poets, 130; b. collections in libraries, 138; and broadsides, 138–9; and *Percy's Reliques*, 139–42; origins, 140–5; and parodies, 146–7; and classification, 267–8; and editing, 270–1; and scholarship, 280–6; Homer and Yugoslav heroic b., 281–4; and Wilma Muir, 284–5
ballad opera, 6
ballade, the, 124–5
Ballads and Sea Songs of Newfoundland, Greenleaf and Mansfield, 15 n. 11
Bampton, morris dance of, 202
Bantock, Granville, 76
Baring-Gould, Rev. S., 9, 30, 100–2, 272
Barratt, W. H., 102–4
Barry, Phillipps, xv, 17
Bartók, Bela, xv, 19, 37, 48, 53, 59–61; and *tempo giusto*, 35, 67, 69, 72; and Kuhač, 56; and Serbo-Croatian folk-song, 237; and classification, 264–9; and arrangement, 278–9; and Yugoslav heroic ballads, 282
Bayard, S., 268–9
Beethoven, L. van, folk-song quoted in op. 132, 30; and folk-song settings, 252, 273

w   295

Sair fyel'd, hinnie	Ditto.
8 The moon shines bright	*Folk-Song Journal*, No. 8, 132
Joseph was an old man	*Christmas Carols*, William Sandys (in R. R. Terry's reprint and *Two Hundred Folk Carols*).
Lully lullay (Coventry Carol)	
Joseph est bien marié	*Les noels et la tradition populaire* J. R. H. de Smidt.
When righteous Joseph wedded was	*Some Ancient Christmas Carols*, Davies Gilbert. Also in Terry *op. cit.*
Joseph and Mary (Cornish)	*Folk-Song Journal*, No. 33.
O the rising of the sun	*Old Christmas Carols of the Southern Counties*, Alice Gillington.
Puer nobis nascitur	*Piae Cantiones.* Plainsong and Medieval Music Society reprint, 1910.
In Dessexshire	*Old Christmas Carols of the Southern Counties*, Alice E. Gillington.
Our jolly wassail	*English County Songs.* Yorkshire.
Apple wassail	*Folk Songs from Somerset*, no. 128. C. Sharp.
The Rose (dance)	*Morris Dance Tunes*, C. Sharp.
Calling-on song (Earsdon)	*Sword Dances of Northern England*, C. Sharp.
Abbots Bromley Horn Dance	Ditto.
Morpeth Rant	*Twelve Traditional Country Dances*, M. Karpeles.
The Triumph	*English Country Dances*, C. Sharp.

Manx Goodnight	*Twelve Manx Folk Songs*, Set
Snieu, queeyl, snieu (Manx spinning song)	Mona Douglas and Arno Foster.
Dirk Dance	*Folk-Song Journal*, No. 16, I 5, Tolmie.
10 Burgundian basse danse	*Anthology of European F Song*, No. 69. W. Wiora
As I rode over Salisbury Plain	*Folk-Song Journal*, No. Butterworth.
The Captivity of Dulic Ibrahim	*Serbo-Croatian Heroic Songs* Bartók, Parry and Lo No. 4. Harvard.